CEOE Field 27

OSAT
Middle Level Social Studies
Teacher Certification Exam

By: Sharon Wynne, M.S
Southern Connecticut State University

XAMonline, INC.
Boston

Copyright © 2007 XAMonline, Inc.

All rights reserved. No part of the material protected by this copyright notice may be reproduced or utilized in any form or by any means, electronic or mechanical, including photocopying, recording or by any information storage and retrievable system, without written permission from the copyright holder.

To obtain permission(s) to use the material from this work for any purpose including workshops or seminars, please submit a written request to:

XAMonline, Inc.
21 Orient Ave.
Melrose, MA 02176
Toll Free 1-800-509-4128
Email: info@xamonline.com
Web www.xamonline.com
Fax: 1-781-662-9268

Library of Congress Cataloging-in-Publication Data

Wynne, Sharon A.
OSAT Middle Level Social Studies Field 27: Teacher Certification / Sharon A. Wynne. -2nd ed.
ISBN 978-1-58197-790-5
 1. OSAT Middle Level Social Studies Field 27.   2. Study Guides.   3. CEOE
 4. Teachers' Certification & Licensure.   5. Careers

Disclaimer:

The opinions expressed in this publication are the sole works of XAMonline and were created independently from the National Education Association, Educational Testing Service, or any State Department of Education, National Evaluation Systems or other testing affiliates.

Between the time of publication and printing, state specific standards as well as testing formats and website information may change that is not included in part or in whole within this product. Sample test questions are developed by XAMonline and reflect similar content as on real tests; however, they are not former tests. XAMonline assembles content that aligns with state standards but makes no claims nor guarantees teacher candidates a passing score. Numerical scores are determined by testing companies such as NES or ETS and then are compared with individual state standards. A passing score varies from state to state.

Printed in the United States of America œ-1

CEOE: OSAT Middle Level Social Studies Field 27
ISBN: 978-1-58197-790-5

TEACHER CERTIFICATION STUDY GUIDE

About the Subject Assessments

CEOE™: Subject Assessment in the Middle School Social Studies examination

Purpose: The assessments are designed to test the knowledge and competencies of prospective secondary level teachers. The question bank from which the assessment is drawn is undergoing constant revision. As a result, your test may include questions that will not count towards your score.

Test: There are two subject area tests for social science tests in Oklahoma. The versions of the tests emphasize conceptual comprehension, synthesis, and analysis of the principles of the social studies, the major difference between versions lays in the *degree* to which the examinee's knowledge is tested.

> **Version 1: US History/Oklahoma History/Government/Economics Field 17:** This version requires a greater depth of comprehension in US history, world history, economics, political science, and social studies skills. The social studies guide is based on a typical knowledge level of persons who have completed a <u>*bachelor's degree program*</u> in social science.

> **Version 2: Social Studies Middle School Field 27:** This version tests the examinee's knowledge level in less detail than the first version of the subject assessments. The degree of knowledge required is typically based on completion of <u>*introductory-level course work*</u> in the same areas mentioned above.

Taking the Correct Version of the Subject Assessment: While some states other than Oklahoma offer just one test called a social science secondary test, Oklahoma breaks out those topics into more than two tests. The Middle School Field 27 is basically what you would take to become a middle school teacher and US History/Oklahoma History Field 17 if you plan on teaching at the high school level. For initial licenses acquired after 1999, you will also need to take the Oklahoma General Education Test (OGET) and the Oklahoma Professional Teaching Examination (OPTE). However, as Oklahoma's licensure requirements change, it's highly recommended that you consult your educational institution's teaching preparation counselor or your state board of education's teacher licensure division, to verify which version of the assessment you should take. XAMonline.com website can inform you what you need to do to become certified in any particular state.

MIDDLE LEVEL SOCIAL STUDIES

TEACHER CERTIFICATION STUDY GUIDE

Time Allowance, Format, and Length: The time allowance and format for both versions are identical; you will have 4 hours to complete the subject area test and the questions are presented in a multiple-choice question format. Oklahoma does test using a construct essay or other essay formats. On the actual test, competencies, skills, answer key and rationale will not be given.

Content Areas: Both versions of the subject assessments share a degree of commonality in that the test content categories are divided into broad areas that roughly overlap between test versions. However, the US History version has a narrower focus on specific disciplines than does version Middle School.

Test Taxonomy: Both versions of the subject assessments are constructed on the comprehension, synthesis and analysis levels of Bloom's Taxonomy. In many questions, the candidate must apply knowledge of more than one discipline in order to correctly answer the questions.

Additional Information about the CEOE Assessments: The CEOE™ series subject assessments are developed by the *Oklahoma State Department of Education* of Oklahoma City, Oklahoma. They provide additional information on the CEOE, OSAT and other series assessments, including registration, preparation and testing procedures, study materials such as topical guides that are about 25 pages of information including approximately 10 additional sample questions.

TEACHER CERTIFICATION STUDY GUIDE

Table of Contents

DOMAIN I.   **WORLD, U.S., AND OKLAHOMA HISTORY**

COMPETENCY 1.0   UNDERSTAND MAJOR POLITICAL, SOCIAL, ECONOMIC, CULTURAL, AND RELIGIOUS DEVELOPMENTS THAT SHAPED THE COURSE OF WORLD HISTORY THROUGH THE THIRTEENTH CENTURY 1

Skill 1.1   Analyze economic, political, geographic, and cultural relationships within and among ancient Mediterranean civilizations 1

Skill 1.2   Demonstrate knowledge of major characteristics and cultural values of the ancient civilizations of Africa, Asia, and the Americas 5

Skill 1.3   Recognize the characteristics of Byzantine culture and the achievements of Islamic civilization 7

Skill 1.4   Analyze the structure and development of feudal societies in Europe and Asia 9

COMPETENCY 2.0   UNDERSTAND MAJOR POLITICAL, SOCIAL, ECONOMIC, CULTURAL, AND RELIGIOUS DEVELOPMENTS THAT SHAPED THE COURSE OF WORLD HISTORY FROM THE FOURTEENTH CENTURY THROUGH THE EIGHTEENTH CENTURY 11

Skill 2.1   Examine the causes and accomplishments of the Italian Renaissance and its spread to other parts of Europe 11

Skill 2.2   Recognize leading religious reformers of the sixteenth century, and analyze the influence of the Reformation on later religious, artistic, and scientific beliefs and practices 12

Skill 2.3   Analyze major causes and consequences of European expansion during the Age of Discovery 13

Skill 2.4   Demonstrate knowledge of the political, economic, and social environments in which the English, American, and French Revolutions took place 15

MIDDLE LEVEL SOCIAL STUDIES   iii

TEACHER CERTIFICATION STUDY GUIDE

COMPETENCY 3.0 UNDERSTAND MAJOR POLITICAL, SOCIAL, ECONOMIC, CULTURAL, AND RELIGIOUS DEVELOPMENTS THAT SHAPED THE COURSE OF WORLD HISTORY FROM THE NINETEENTH CENTURY TO THE PRESENT 17

Skill 3.1 Analyze major causes of the Industrial Revolution and its impact on the politics, societies, and cultures of the modern world 17

Skill 3.2 Analyze the origins and development of imperialism and its consequences for both colonizers and colonized 20

Skill 3.3 Describe the causes and evaluate the consequences of regional and global warfare in the nineteenth and twentieth centuries 21

Skill 3.4 Examine major political developments, economic trends, and social movements of the twentieth century 30

COMPETENCY 4.0 UNDERSTAND THE IDEAS AND VALUES THAT HAVE SHAPED THE CULTURE OF THE UNITED STATES 33

Skill 4.1 Define the democratic concepts that form the basis of the U.S. political and legal systems 33

Skill 4.2 Recognize the ideas and values contained in historical documents that influenced the development of the United States 44

COMPETENCY 5.0 UNDERSTAND THE CAUSES AND COURSE OF EUROPEAN EXPLORATION AND SETTLEMENT OF NORTH AMERICA, AND EXAMINE POLITICAL AND ECONOMIC RELATIONSHIPS WITHIN AND AMONG THE COLONIES 49

Skill 5.1 Recognize major events related to the exploration and settlement of North America 49

Skill 5.2 Analyze the sources of coexistence and conflict between Europeans and American Indians 56

Skill 5.3 Examine political and economic relations between the colonies and Europe 56

Skill 5.4 Analyze geographic, ethnic, religious, political, and economic differences within and among England's North American colonies ... 59

COMPETENCY 6.0 UNDERSTAND THE PRINCIPAL CAUSES AND EVENTS OF THE REVOLUTIONARY WAR AND THE MAJOR POLITICAL, CONSTITUTIONAL, AND ECONOMIC DEVELOPMENTS RELATED TO THE CREATION OF THE FEDERAL GOVERNMENT AND THE ESTABLISHMENT OF U.S. SOCIETY 62

Skill 6.1 Examine the social, political, and economic origins of the movement for American independence 62

Skill 6.2 Recognize the influence of Revolutionary era ideas on later social and political developments in the United States 64

Skill 6.3 Assess the strengths and weaknesses of the Articles of Confederation, and analyze the debates surrounding the creation and ratification of the Constitution 65

Skill 6.4 Recognize major accomplishments of the early presidential administrations, and examine the development of political parties..71

COMPETENCY 7.0 UNDERSTAND THE SIGNIFICANCE OF WESTWARD MOVEMENT IN U.S. HISTORY AND THE POLITICAL, ECONOMIC, SOCIAL, AND CULTURAL CONSEQUENCES OF TERRITORIAL EXPANSION........74

Skill 7.1 Describe basic characteristics of American Indian life and culture 74

Skill 7.2 Recognize the role of geography, relations between settlers and indigenous populations, and government land policies in the settlement of the trans-Appalachian West 75

Skill 7.3 Identify western land areas acquired by the United States during the nineteenth century 77

Skill 7.4 Analyze the concept of Manifest Destiny, and examine the war with Mexico 78

Skill 7.5 Recognize general patterns of frontier life, and analyze the impact of the frontier on U.S. society 79

TEACHER CERTIFICATION STUDY GUIDE

COMPETENCY 8.0 UNDERSTAND THE CAUSES, COURSE, AND CONSEQUENCES OF THE CIVIL WAR AND THE CONTINUING INFLUENCE OF THE CIVIL WAR AND RECONSTRUCTION PERIOD ON U.S. SOCIETY 80

Skill 8.1 Analyze the impact of slavery on U.S. society, and understand the role of sectionalism in American life 80

Skill 8.2 Recognize major political developments and military campaigns of the war years 81

Skill 8.3 Examine the political and social conflicts of the Reconstruction era 87

Skill 8.4 Analyze the effect of war and Reconstruction on U.S. economic growth, political structures, and social relations 91

COMPETENCY 9.0 UNDERSTAND MAJOR POLITICAL, MILITARY, SOCIAL, ECONOMIC, AND CULTURAL DEVELOPMENTS IN THE UNITED STATES FROM 1877 TO 1919 94

Skill 9.1 Analyze factors related to the industrialization of the U.S. economy, and examine the effect of industrialization on U.S. social and political life 94

Skill 9.2 Identify major causes and effects of immigration to the United States, and evaluate the importance of cultural diversity in the continuing development of U.S. society 95

Skill 9.3 Describe the U.S. rise to world power and the effects of this development on the economy, culture, and foreign policy of the United States 97

Skill 9.4 Compare the participants, goals, and accomplishments of the Populist and Progressive movements 98

MIDDLE LEVEL SOCIAL STUDIES

TEACHER CERTIFICATION STUDY GUIDE

COMPETENCY 10.0 UNDERSTAND MAJOR POLITICAL, MILITARY, SOCIAL, ECONOMIC, AND CULTURAL DEVELOPMENTS IN THE UNITED STATES FROM 1920 TO THE PRESENT 100

Skill 10.1 Examine major political developments, economic trends, and social movements in the United States since World War I........................... 100

Skill 10.2 Identify the causes of the Great Depression, and evaluate the effects of the New Deal on U.S. society 103

Skill 10.3 Describe the causes, course, and consequences of World War II, and analyze the impact of the Cold War on U.S. politics and foreign relations 112

Skill 10.4 Assess the impact of the Vietnam War on U.S. government and society 120

COMPETENCY 11.0 UNDERSTAND MAJOR POLITICAL, SOCIAL, CULTURAL, AND ECONOMIC DEVELOPMENTS, GEOGRAPHIC FEATURES, AND KEY ERAS AND EVENTS IN THE HISTORY OF THE STATE OF OKLAHOMA 123

Skill 11.1 Recognize the role played by American Indian peoples in the development of Oklahoma... 123

Skill 11.2 Identify important individuals and groups in Oklahoma history, and analyze major events that shaped Oklahoma's political, economic, and cultural development 125

Skill 11.3 Describe the structure, functions, and operation of Oklahoma government at the state and local levels 127

Skill 11.4 Recognize major geographic features of Oklahoma, and use this knowledge to examine relationships between the physical environment and the historical development of Oklahoma 128

MIDDLE LEVEL SOCIAL STUDIES

TEACHER CERTIFICATION STUDY GUIDE

DOMAIN II.	GOVERNMENT AND ECONOMICS

COMPETENCY 12.0   UNDERSTAND DEMOCRATIC PRINCIPLES AND THE STRUCTURE, ORGANIZATION, AND OPERATION OF DIFFERENT LEVELS OF GOVERNMENT IN THE UNITED STATES 130

Skill 12.1   Relate democratic principles to the structure and function of government in the United States 130

Skill 12.2   Examine the structure and operation of the federal government 132

Skill 12.3   Compare the structures and functions of federal, state, and local government 132

Skill 12.4   Analyze ways in which democracy has evolved to meet the needs of diverse groups in the United States 134

COMPETENCY 13.0   UNDERSTAND THE U.S. ELECTION PROCESS AND THE ROLES OF POLITICAL PARTIES AND INTEREST GROUPS IN THE U.S. POLITICAL SYSTEM 140

Skill 13.1   Identify and describe the components of the U.S. electoral process 140

Skill 13.2   Examine the organization and functions of political parties in the United States 143

Skill 13.3   Recognize the role of lobbyists in the modern legislative process 145

Skill 13.4   Analyze factors that influence political processes at the local, state, and national levels 146

MIDDLE LEVEL SOCIAL STUDIES

TEACHER CERTIFICATION STUDY GUIDE

COMPETENCY 14.0 UNDERSTAND THE RIGHTS AND RESPONSIBILITIES OF INDIVIDUAL CITIZENS IN A DEMOCRATIC SOCIETY AND THE SKILLS, KNOWLEDGE, AND VALUES NECESSARY FOR SUCCESSFUL PARTICIPATION IN DEMOCRATIC SELF-GOVERNMENT 149

Skill 14.1   Analyze the political, legal, and personal rights guaranteed by the U.S. Constitution 149

Skill 14.2   Describe ways citizens participate in and influence the political process in the United States 151

Skill 14.3   Demonstrate the ability to identify central questions in public policy debates, and to distinguish between fact, opinion, and interpretation 152

Skill 14.4   Analyze factors that have expanded or limited the role of individuals in U.S. political life during the twentieth century 153

COMPETENCY 15.0 UNDERSTAND THE COMPONENTS, ORGANIZATION, AND OPERATION OF THE U.S. ECONOMY AND THE BASIC PRINCIPLES OF CONSUMER ECONOMICS 156

Skill 15.1   Recognize the basic principles and processes of capitalism 156

Skill 15.2   Identify the functions of and describe relationships among basic components of the U.S. economic system 158

Skill 15.3   Analyze domestic and global factors affecting the formulation of U.S. economic policy 161

Skill 15.4   Examine principles of consumer economics and factors affecting economic choices in everyday contexts 163

MIDDLE LEVEL SOCIAL STUDIES   ix

DOMAIN III. GEOGRAPHY AND CULTURE

COMPETENCY 16.0 UNDERSTAND MAJOR PHYSICAL FEATURES OF THE EARTH AND THE NATURAL PROCESSES THAT SHAPE THE EARTH AND INFLUENCE LIVING ORGANISMS 164

Skill 16.1 Demonstrate knowledge of the shape and location of major landmasses, their significant landforms, and the relationship of these landmasses to bodies of water 164

Skill 16.2 Analyze geological and hydrological processes that alter the earth's surface 167

Skill 16.3 Describe the main elements of climate and recognize characteristics of major climate zones 168

Skill 16.4 Analyze ways in which climate and other geographic factors affect plant and animal life and human societies 171

COMPETENCY 17.0 UNDERSTAND GLOBAL AND REGIONAL PATTERNS OF CULTURE AND RELATIONSHIPS BETWEEN GEOGRAPHY AND HISTORY 173

Skill 17.1 Recognize major cultural groups associated with particular regions, including the United States, and significant cultural variations within and among regions 173

Skill 17.2 Analyze the interactions of human societies with one another and with their physical environments 175

Skill 17.3 Recognize relationships between the environment and the development of particular societies, including U.S. society 177

Skill 17.4 Analyze the effects of human activity on the environment in the United States and other world regions 178

TEACHER CERTIFICATION STUDY GUIDE

COMPETENCY 18.0 UNDERSTAND GLOBAL AND REGIONAL PATTERNS OF POPULATION MOVEMENT, RURAL/URBAN SETTLEMENT, RESOURCE DISTRIBUTION, AND LAND USE AND DEVELOPMENT 180

Skill 18.1 Recognize historical and contemporary patterns of human migration and population distribution in the United States and other world regions 180

Skill 18.2 Analyze the effect of different patterns of urban/rural settlement on the physical environment 182

Skill 18.3 Locate major concentrations of important natural resources in the United States and other world regions, and examine the connection between resource distribution and regional development 184

Skill 18.4 Analyze factors that influence patterns of land use in the United States and other world regions 186

Skill 18.5 Examine the environmental, cultural, and economic consequences of different types of land use and development 188

COMPETENCY 19.0 UNDERSTAND CONCEPTS RELATED TO THE STRUCTURE AND ORGANIZATION OF HUMAN SOCIETY AND THE PROCESSES OF SOCIALIZATION AND SOCIAL INTERACTION 191

Skill 19.1 Recognize basic sociological and anthropological concepts and use that knowledge to examine general social phenomena 191

Skill 19.2 Analyze the relationship between language and culture 192

Skill 19.3 Compare the social and economic organization of pre-industrial and postindustrial societies 193

Skill 19.4 Assess the development and significance of social customs, cultural values, and norms 195

TEACHER CERTIFICATION STUDY GUIDE

DOMAIN IV.   **RESEARCH SKILLS**

COMPETENCY 20.0   UNDERSTAND HOW TO LOCATE, GATHER, AND ORGANIZE PRIMARY AND SECONDARY INFORMATION USING STANDARD HISTORICAL AND SOCIAL SCIENCE RESOURCES AND RESEARCH METHODOLOGIES 196

Skill 20.1   Compare the characteristics of materials used in historical and social science research 196

Skill 20.2   Apply research procedures used in history and the social sciences 197

Skill 20.3   Understand how to use maps and globes to answer social science questions 198

Skill 20.4   Identify the uses of traditional information sources and current technologies for historical and social science research 200

COMPETENCY 21.0   UNDERSTAND AND APPLY METHODS FOR EVALUATING SOURCES OF SOCIAL SCIENCE INFORMATION 201

Skill 21.1   Recognize primary and secondary sources and their advantages and limitations 201

Skill 21.2   Analyze factors affecting the reliability of source materials 203

Skill 21.3   Evaluate the appropriateness of evidence used to substantiate a historical or social science argument 204

COMPETENCY 22.0   UNDERSTAND HOW TO FORMULATE ISSUES OR FRAME QUESTIONS 205

Skill 22.1   Evaluate alternative formulations of a research problem 205

Skill 22.2   Summarize the main points and supporting evidence of a historical, economic, sociological, political, or geographic point of view 206

Skill 22.3   Determine whether specific conclusions or generalizations are supported by verifiable evidence 208

Skill 22.4   Interpret social science information presented in various formats 209

MIDDLE LEVEL SOCIAL STUDIES

Bibliography 213

Sample Test 215

Sample Essay 242

Answer Key 245

Rationales with Sample Questions 246

TEACHER CERTIFICATION STUDY GUIDE

Great Study and Testing Tips!

What to study in order to prepare for the subject assessments are the focus of this study guide but equally important is *how* you study.

You can increase your chances of truly mastering the information by taking some simple, but effective steps.

Study Tips:

1. <u>**Some foods aid the learning process.**</u> Foods such as milk, nuts, seeds, rice, and oats help your study efforts by releasing natural memory enhancers called CCKs (*cholecystokinin*) composed of *tryptophan*, *choline*, and *phenylalanine*. All of these chemicals enhance the neurotransmitters associated with memory. Before studying, try a light, protein-rich meal of eggs, turkey, and fish. All of these foods release the memory enhancing chemicals. The better the connections, the more you comprehend.

Likewise, before you take a test, stick to a light snack of energy boosting and relaxing foods. A glass of milk, a piece of fruit, or some peanuts all release various memory-boosting chemicals and help you to relax and focus on the subject at hand.

2. <u>**Learn to take great notes.**</u> A by-product of our modern culture is that we have grown accustomed to getting our information in short doses (i.e. TV news sound bites or USA Today style newspaper articles.)

Consequently, we've subconsciously trained ourselves to assimilate information better in <u>neat little packages</u>. If your notes are scrawled all over the paper, it fragments the flow of the information. Strive for clarity. Newspapers use a standard format to achieve clarity. Your notes can be much clearer through use of proper formatting. A very effective format is called the <u>*"Cornell Method."*</u>

Take a sheet of loose-leaf lined notebook paper and draw a line all the way down the paper about 1-2" from the left-hand edge.

Draw another line across the width of the paper about 1-2" up from the bottom. Repeat this process on the reverse side of the page.

Look at the highly effective result. You have ample room for notes, a left hand margin for special emphasis items or inserting supplementary data from the textbook, a large area at the bottom for a brief summary, and a little rectangular space for just about anything you want.

MIDDLE LEVEL SOCIAL STUDIES   xiv

3. **Get the concept then the details.** Too often we focus on the details and don't gather an understanding of the concept. However, if you simply memorize only dates, places, or names, you may well miss the whole point of the subject.

A key way to understand things is to put them in your own words. If you are working from a textbook, automatically summarize each paragraph in your mind. If you are outlining text, don't simply copy the author's words.

Rephrase them in your own words. You remember your own thoughts and words much better than someone else's, and subconsciously tend to associate the important details to the core concepts.

4. **Ask Why?** Pull apart written material paragraph by paragraph and don't forget the captions under the illustrations.

Example: If the heading is "Stream Erosion", flip it around to read "Why do streams erode?" Then answer the questions.

If you train your mind to think in a series of questions and answers, not only will you learn more, but it also helps to lessen the test anxiety because you are used to answering questions.

5. **Read for reinforcement and future needs.** Even if you only have 10 minutes, put your notes or a book in your hand. Your mind is similar to a computer; you have to input data in order to have it processed. *By reading, you are creating the neural connections for future retrieval.* The more times you read something, the more you reinforce the learning of ideas.

Even if you don't fully understand something on the first pass, *your mind stores much of the material for later recall.*

6. **Relax to learn so go into exile.** Our bodies respond to an inner clock called biorhythms. Burning the midnight oil works well for some people, but not everyone.

If possible, set aside a particular place to study that is free of distractions. Shut off the television, cell phone, pager and exile your friends and family during your study period.

If you really are bothered by silence, try background music. Light classical music at a low volume has been shown to aid in concentration over other types.

Music that evokes pleasant emotions without lyrics are highly suggested. Try just about anything by Mozart. It relaxes you.

7. **Use arrows not highlighters.** At best, it's difficult to read a page full of yellow, pink, blue, and green streaks.

Try staring at a neon sign for a while and you'll soon see my point, the horde of colors obscure the message.

A quick note, a brief dash of color, an underline, and an arrow pointing to a particular passage is much clearer than a horde of highlighted words.

8. **Budget your study time.** Although you shouldn't ignore any of the material, *allocate your available study time in the same ratio that topics may appear on the test.*

TEACHER CERTIFICATION STUDY GUIDE

Testing Tips:

1.   Get smart, play dumb. **Don't read anything into the question.** Don't make an assumption that the test writer is looking for something else than what is asked. Stick to the question as written and don't read extra things into it.

2.   Read the question and all the choices *twice* before answering the question. You may miss something by not carefully reading, and then re-reading both the question and the answers.

If you really don't have a clue as to the right answer, leave it blank on the first time through. Go on to the other questions, as they may provide a clue as to how to answer the skipped questions.

If later on, you still can't answer the skipped ones . . . ***Guess.***
The only penalty for guessing is that you *might* get it wrong. Only one thing is certain; if you don't put anything down, you will get it wrong!

3.   Turn the question into a statement. Look at the way the questions are worded. The syntax of the question usually provides a clue. Does it seem more familiar as a statement rather than as a question? Does it sound strange?

By turning a question into a statement, you may be able to spot if an answer sounds right, and it may also trigger memories of material you have read.

4.   Look for hidden clues. It's actually very difficult to compose multiple-foil (choice) questions without giving away part of the answer in the options presented.

In most multiple-choice questions you can often readily eliminate one or two of the potential answers. This leaves you with only two real possibilities and automatically your odds go to Fifty-Fifty for very little work.

5.   Trust your instincts. For every fact that you have read, you subconsciously retain something of that knowledge. On questions that you aren't really certain about, go with your basic instincts. **Your first impression on how to answer a question is usually correct.**

6.   Mark your answers directly on the test booklet. Don't bother trying to fill in the optical scan sheet on the first pass through the test.

7.   Watch the clock! You have a set amount of time to answer the questions. Don't get bogged down trying to answer a single question at the expense of 10 questions you can more readily answer.

MIDDLE LEVEL SOCIAL STUDIES

THIS PAGE BLANK

TEACHER CERTIFICATION STUDY GUIDE

DOMAIN I. **WORLD, U.S., AND OKLAHOMA HISTORY**

COMPETENCY 1.0 UNDERSTAND MAJOR POLITICAL, SOCIAL, ECONOMIC, CULTURAL, AND RELIGIOUS DEVELOPMENTS THAT SHAPED THE COURSE OF WORLD HISTORY THROUGH THE THIRTEENTH CENTURY

Skill 1.1 Analyze economic, political, geographic, and cultural relationships within and among ancient Mediterranean civilizations.

The culture of Mesopotamia was autocratic in nature, with a single ruler at the head of the government and, in many cases, also the head of the religion. The people followed his strict instructions or faced the consequences, which were often life-threatening.

The civilizations of the Sumerians, Amorites, Hittites, Assyrians, Chaldeans, and Persians controlled various areas of Mesopotamia. With few exceptions, tyrants and military leaders controlled the vast majority of aspects of society, including trade, religions, and the laws. Each Sumerian city-state (and there were a few) had its own god, with the city-state's leader doubling as the high priest of worship of that local god. Subsequent cultures had a handful of gods as well, although they had more of a national worship structure, with high priests centered in the capital city as advisors to the tyrant.

Trade was vastly important to these civilizations since they had access to some but not all of the things that they needed to survive. Some trading agreements led to occupation, as was the case with the Sumerians, who didn't bother to build walls to protect their wealth of knowledge. Egypt and the Phoenician cities were powerful and regular trading partners of the various Mesopotamian cultures.

Legacies handed down to us from these civilizations include:

- The first use of writing, the wheel, and banking (Sumeria);
- The first written set of laws (Code of Hammurabi);
- The first epic story (*Gilgamesh*);
- The first library dedicated to preserving knowledge (instituted by the Assyrian leader Ashurbanipal);
- The Hanging Gardens of Babylon (built by the Chaldean Nebuchadnezzar)

The ancient civilization of the **Sumerians** invented the wheel; developed irrigation through use of canals, dikes, and devices for raising water; devised the system of cuneiform writing; learned to divide time; and built large boats for trade. The Babylonians devised the famous **Code of Hammurabi**, a code of laws.

Egypt made significant contributions including construction of the great pyramids; development of hieroglyphic writing; preservation of bodies after death; making paper from papyrus; contributing to developments in arithmetic and geometry; the invention of the method of counting in groups of 1-10 (the decimal system); completion of a solar calendar; and laying the foundation for science and astronomy.

The earliest historical record of **Kush** is in Egyptian sources. They describe a region upstream from the first cataract of the Nile as "wretched." This civilization was characterized by a settled way of life in fortified mud-brick villages. They subsisted on hunting and fishing, herding cattle, and gathering grain. Skeletal remains suggest that the people were a blend of Negroid and Mediterranean peoples. This civilization appears to be the second-oldest in Africa (after Egypt).

Either the people were Egyptian or heavily influenced by Egyptians at a very early period in the development of the society. They appear to have spoken Nilo-Saharan languages. The area in which they lived is called Nubia. The capital city was Kerma, a major trading center between the northern and southern parts of Africa.

During the period of Egypt's Old Kingdom (ca. 2700-2180 BCE), this civilization was essentially a diffused version of Egyptian culture and religion. When Egypt came under the domination of the Hyksos, Kush reached its greatest power and cultural energy (1700-1500 BCE). When the Hyksos were eventually expelled from Egypt, the New Kingdom brought Kush back under Egyptian colonial control.

The collapse of the New Kingdom in Egypt (ca. 1000 BCE), provided the second opportunity for Kush to develop independently of Egyptian control and to conquer the Nubian region. The capital was then moved to Napata.

For the most part, the Kushites apparently considered themselves Egyptian and inheritors of the pharaonic tradition. Their society was organized on the Egyptian model, adopting Egyptian royal titles, etc. Even their art and architecture was based on Egyptian models. But their pyramids were smaller and steeper.

In what has been called "a magnificent irony of history" the Kushites conquered Egypt in the eighth century, creating the twenty-fifth dynasty. The dynasty ended in the seventh century when Egypt was defeated by the Assyrians.

TEACHER CERTIFICATION STUDY GUIDE

The Kushites were gradually pushed farther south by the Assyrians and later by the Persians. This essentially cut off contact with Egypt, the Middle East and Europe. They moved their capital to Meroe in about 591 BC, when Napata was conquered. Their attention then turned to sub-Saharan Africa. Free of Egyptian dominance, they developed innovations in government and other areas.

In government, the king ruled through a law of custom that was interpreted by priests. The king was elected from the royal family. Descent was determined through the mother's line (as in Egypt). But in an unparalleled innovation, the Kushites were ruled by a series of female monarchs.

The Kushite religion was polytheistic, including all of the primary Egyptian gods. There were, however, regional gods which were the principal gods in their regions. Derived from other African cultures, there was also a lion warrior god.

This civilization was vital through the last half of the first millennium BC, but it suffered about 300 years of gradual decline until it was eventually conquered by the Nuba people.

The ancient **Assyrians** were warlike and aggressive due to a highly organized military and used horse drawn chariots.

The **Hebrews**, also known as the ancient Israelites instituted "monotheism," which is the worship of one God, Yahweh, and combined the 66 books of the Hebrew and Christian Greek scriptures into the Bible we have today.

The **Minoans** had a system of writing using symbols to represent syllables in words. They built palaces with multiple levels containing many rooms, water and sewage systems with flush toilets, bathtubs, hot and cold running water, and bright paintings on the walls.

The **Mycenaeans** changed the Minoan writing system to aid their own language and used symbols to represent syllables.

The **Phoenicians** were sea traders well known for their manufacturing skills in glass and metals and the development of their famous purple dye. They became so very proficient in the skill of navigation that they were able to sail by the stars at night. Further, they devised an alphabet using symbols to represent single sounds, which was an improved extension of the Egyptian principle and writing system.

The classical civilization of **Greece** reached the highest levels in man's achievements based on the foundations already laid by such ancient groups as the Egyptians, Phoenicians, Minoans, and Mycenaeans.

MIDDLE LEVEL SOCIAL STUDIES

Among the more important contributions of Greece were the Greek alphabet derived from the Phoenician letters which formed the basis for the Roman alphabet and our present-day alphabet. Extensive trading and colonization resulted in the spread of the Greek civilization. The love of sports, with emphasis on a sound body, led to the tradition of the Olympic Games. Greece was responsible for the rise of independent, strong city-states. Note the complete contrast between independent, freedom-loving Athens with its practice of pure democracy i.e. direct, personal, active participation in government by qualified citizens and the rigid, totalitarian, militaristic Sparta. Other important areas that the Greeks are credited with influencing include drama, epic and lyric poetry, fables, myths centered on the many gods and goddesses, science, astronomy, medicine, mathematics, philosophy, art, architecture, and recording historical events.

The conquests of Alexander the Great spread Greek ideas to the areas he conquered and brought to the Greek world many ideas from Asia. In summary, the major objectives of the conquests were: valuable new ideas, wisdom, and the curiosity and desire to learn as much about the world as possible.

The ancient civilization of **Rome** lasted approximately 1,000 years including the periods of Republic and Empire, although its lasting influence on Europe and its history was for a much longer period. There was a very sharp contrast between the curious, imaginative, inquisitive Greeks and the practical, simple, down-to-earth, no-nonsense Romans, who spread and preserved the ideas of ancient Greece and other culture groups. The contributions and accomplishments of the Romans are numerous but their greatest included language, engineering, building, law, government, roads, trade, and the "**Pax Romana**". Pax Romana was the long period of peace enabling free travel and trade, spreading people, cultures, goods, and ideas all over a vast area of the known world.

A most interesting and significant characteristic of the Greek, Hellenic, and Roman civilizations was "**secularism**" where emphasis shifted away from religion to the state. Men were not absorbed in or dominated by religion as had been the case in Egypt and the nations located in Mesopotamia. Religion and its leaders did not dominate the state and its authority was greatly diminished.

Skill 1.2 **Demonstrate knowledge of major characteristics and cultural values of the ancient civilizations of Africa, Asia, and the Americas.**

The Ottoman Empire is noted for its ability to unite a highly varied population growing through conquest and treaty arrangement. This ability is attributed to military strength, a policy of strict control of recently invaded territories, and an Islamic-inspired philosophy that stated that all Muslims, Christians and Jews were related because they were all "People of the Book." The major religious groups were permitted to construct their own semi-autonomous communities.

Conquering armies immediately repaired buildings, roads, bridges, and aqueducts or built them where needed. They also built modern sanitary facilities and linked the city to a supply structure that was able to provide for the needs of the people. This religious and ethnic tolerance was the basis upon which a heterogeneous culture was built. It quickly transformed a Turkish empire into the Ottoman Empire.

The attitude of tolerant blending and respect for diverse ethnic and cultural groups, in time produced a rich mix of people that was reflected in multi-cultural and multi-religious policies that were based on recognition and respect for different perspectives. Ottoman architecture, although influenced by Seljuk, Byzantine and Arab styles, developed a unique style of its own. Music was important to the elites of the empire. Two primary styles of music that developed were Ottoman classical music and folk music. Again, both styles reflect a basis in the diversity of influences that came together in the unified empire.

The Mongol Empire, founded by Genghis Khan, included the majority of the territory from Southeast Asia to central Europe during the height of the empire. One of the primary military tactics of conquest was to annihilate any cities that refused to surrender.

Government was by decree on the basis on a code of laws developed by Genghis Khan. It is interesting that one of the tenets of this code was that the nobility and the commoners shared the same hardship. The society, and the opportunity to advance within the society, was based on a system of meritocracy. The carefully structured and controlled society was efficient and safe for the people. Religious tolerance was guaranteed. Theft and vandalism were strictly forbidden. Trade routes and an extensive postal system were created linking the various parts of the empire. Taxes were quite onerous, but teachers, artists and lawyers were exempted from the taxes. Mongol rule, however, was absolute. The response to all resistance was collective punishment in the form of destruction of cities and slaughter of the inhabitants.

The lasting achievements of the Mongol Empire include:

- Reunification of China and expansions of its borders,
- Unification of the Central Asian Republics that later formed part of the USSR,
- Expansion of Europe's knowledge of the world.

The Ming Dynasty in China followed the Mongol-led Yuan Dynasty. In addition to its expansion of trade and exploration of surrounding regions, the period is well known for its highly talented artists and craftsmen. The Hongwu emperor rose from peasant origins. He distributed land to small farmers in an effort to help them support their families.

To further protect family farms, he proclaimed title of the land non-transferable. He also issued an edict by which anyone who cultivated wasteland could keep the land as their property and would never be taxed. One of the major developments of the time was the development of systems of irrigation for farms throughout the empire. Hongwu maintained a strong army by creating military settlements. During peacetime, each soldier was given land to farm and, if he could not afford to purchase equipment, it was provided by the government.

The legal code created during the period is generally considered one of the greatest achievements of the dynasty. The laws were written in understandable language and in enough detail to prevent misinterpretation. The law reversed previous policy toward slaves, and promised them the same protection as free citizens. Great emphasis was placed on family relations. It was clearly based on Confucian ideas. The other major accomplishment of this dynasty was the decision to begin building the Great Wall of China to provide protection from northern horsemen.

The Mogul Empire reached its height during the reign of Akbar. In the administration of the empire, Akbar initiated two approaches that are notable. First, he studied local revenue statistics for the various provinces within the empire. He then developed a revenue plan that matched the revenue needs of the empire with the ability of the people to pay the taxes. Although the taxes were heavy (one third to one half of the crop), it was possible to collect the taxes and meet the financial needs of the empire. Second, he created a rank and pay structure for the warrior aristocracy that was based on number of troops and obligations.

He introduced a policy of acceptance and assimilation of Hindus, allowed temples to be built, and abolished the poll tax on non-Muslims. He devised a theory of "rulership as a divine illumination" and accepted all religions and sects. He encouraged widows to remarry, discouraged marriage of children, outlawed the practice of sati, and persuaded the merchants in Delhi to recognize special market days for women who were otherwise required to remain secluded at home. The empire supported a strong cultural and intellectual life. He sponsored regular debates among religious and scholarly individuals with different points of view.

The unique style of architecture of the Mogul Empire was its primary contribution to South Asia. The Taj Mahal was one of many monuments built during this period. The cultural was a blend of Indian, Iranian and Central Asian traditions. Other major accomplishments were:

- Centralized government,
- Blending of traditions in art and culture,
- Development of new trade routs to Arab and Turkish lands,
- A unique style of architecture,
- Landscape gardening,
- A unique cuisine,
- The creation of to languages (Urdu and Hindi) for the common people.

Skill 1.3   Recognize the characteristics of Byzantine culture and the achievements of Islamic civilization.

The **Byzantine Empire**, which the Eastern Empire became, was closer to the Middle East and so inherited the traditions of Mesopotamia and Persia. This was in stark contrast to the Western Empire, which inherited the traditions of Greece and Carthage. Byzantium was known for its exquisite artwork including the famous church Hagia Sophia. Perhaps the most wide-ranging success of the Byzantine Empire was in the area of trade. Uniquely situated at the gateway to both West and East, Byzantium could control trade going in both directions. Indeed, the Eastern Empire was much more centralized and rigid in its enforcement of its policies than the feudal West.

The **Byzantine** and **Saracenic** (or Islamic) civilizations were both dominated by religion. The major contributions of the Saracens were in the areas of science and philosophy including accomplishments in astronomy, mathematics, physics, chemistry, medicine, literature, art, trade and manufacturing, agriculture, and a marked influence on the Renaissance Period of history.

The **Byzantines** (Christians) made important contributions in art and the preservation of Greek and Roman achievements including architecture (especially in eastern Europe and Russia), the Code of Justinian and Roman law.

During the 14th and 15th centuries, the Muslim Empire experienced great expansion. The conquest of Ghana by Muslim Berbers in 1076 permitted rule to devolve to a series of lesser successor states. By the 13th century, the successor state of Kangaba established the Kingdom of Mali. This vast trading state extended from the Atlantic coast of Africa to beyond Gao on the Niger River in the east.

Much of the history of Mali was preserved by Islamic scholars because the Mali rulers converted to Islam and were responsible for the spread of Islam throughout Africa. The expansion of the Mali kingdom began from the city of Timbuktu and gradually moved downstream along the Niger River. This provided increasing control of the river and the cities along its banks, which were critical for both travel and trade. The Niger River was a central link in trade for both west and north African trade routes. The government of the Mali kingdom was held together by military power and trade.

The kingdom was organized into a series of feudal states that were ruled by a king. Most of the kings used the surname "Mansa" (meaning, "sultan"). The most powerful and effective of the kings was Mansa Musa.

The religion and culture of the kingdom of Mali was a blend of Islamic faith and traditional African belief. The influence of the Islamic empire provided the basis of a large and very structured government which allowed the king to expand both territory and influence. The people, however, did not follow strict Islamic law. The king was thought of in traditional African fashion as a divine ruler removed from the people. A strong military and control of the Niger River and the trade that flourished along the river enabled Mali to build a strong feudal empire.

Farther to the east, the king of the Songhai people had earlier converted to Islam in the 11th century. Songhai was at one time a province of Mali. By the 15th century, Songhai was stronger than Mali and it emerged as the next great power in western Africa. Songhai was situated on the great bend of the Niger River. From the early 15th to the late 16th centuries, the Songhai Empire stood, one of the largest empires in the history of Africa. The first king Sonni Ali conquered many neighboring states, including the Mali Empire. This gave him control of the trade routes and cities like Timbuktu. He was succeeded by Askia Mohammad who initiated political reform and revitalization. He also created religious schools, built mosques, and opened his court to scholars and poets from all parts of the Muslim world.

During the same period, the Zimbabwe kingdom was built. "Great Zimbabwe" was the largest of about 300 stone structures in the area. This capital city and trading center of the Kingdom of Makaranga was built between the 12th and 15th centuries. It was believed to have housed as many as 20,000 people. The structures are built entirely of stone, without mortar. The scanty evidence that is available suggests that the kingdom was a trading center that was believed to be part of a trading network that reached as far as China.

The area known today as the Republic of Benin was the site of an early African kingdom known as Dahomey. By the 17th century, the kingdom included a large part of West Africa. The kingdom was economically prosperous because of slave trading relations with Europeans, primarily the Dutch and Portuguese, who arrived in the 15th century. The coastal part of the kingdom was known as "the Slave Coast." This kingdom was known for a very distinct culture and some very unusual traditions. In 1729 the kingdom started a female army system. A law was passed stating that females would be inspected at the age of 15. Those thought beautiful were sent to the Palace to become wives of the king. Those who were sick or were considered unattractive were executed. The rest were trained as soldiers for two years. Human sacrifice was practiced on holidays and special occasions. Slaves and prisoners of war were sacrificed to gods and ancestors.

The slave trade provided economic stability for the kingdom for almost three hundred years. The continuing need for human sacrifices caused a decrease in the number of slaves available for export. As many colonial countries declared the trade of slaves illegal, demand for slaves subsided steadily until 1885 when the last Portuguese slave ship left the coast. With the decline of the slave trade, the kingdom began a slow disintegration. The French took over in 1892.

Skill 1.4 Analyze the structure and development of feudal societies in Europe and Asia.

The system of **feudalism** became a dominant feature of the economic and social system in Europe. It was a system of loyalty and protection. The strong protected the weak that returned the service with farm labor, military service, and loyalty. Life was lived out on a vast estate, owned by a nobleman and his family, called a "manor." It was a complete village supporting a few hundred people, mostly peasants. Improved tools and farming methods made life more bearable although most never left the manor or traveled from their village during their lifetime.

Feudalism was the organization of people based on the ownership of land by a **Lord** or other **Noble** who allowed individuals known as *peasants* or **serfs** to farm the land and to keep a portion of it. The lord or noble, in return for the serfs' loyalty, offered them his protection. In practical effect, the serf is considered property owned by his lord with little or no rights at all. The lord's sole obligation to the serfs is to protect them so they could continue to work for him (in most cases, though not all lords were men). This system would last for many centuries. In Russia it would last until the 1860s.

The end of the feudal manorial system was sealed by the outbreak and spread of the infamous **Black Death**, which killed over one-third of the total population of Europe. Those who survived and were skilled in any job or occupation were in demand and many serfs or peasants found freedom and, for that time, a decidedly improved standard of living. Strong nation-states became powerful and people developed a renewed interest in life and learning.

From its beginnings, Japan morphed into an imperial form of government, with the divine emperor being able to do no wrong and, therefore, serving for life. **Kyoto**, the capital, became one of the largest and most powerful cities in the world. Slowly, though, as in Europe, the nobility - rich and powerful landowners - grew powerful. Eventually, they had more power than the emperor.

The nobles were lords of great lands and were called **Daimyos**. They were of the highest social class and had working for them people of lower social classes, including the lowly peasants, who had few privileges other than being allowed to work for the great men that the Daimyos told everyone they were.

The Daimyos had warriors serving them known as **Shogun**, who were answerable only to the Daimyo. The Shogun code of honor was an exemplification of the overall Japanese belief that every man was a soldier and a gentleman. The contradiction that the emerging social classes identified didn't seem to get noticed much, nor did the needs of women.

The main economic difference between imperial and feudal Japan was that the money that continued to flow into the country from trade with China, Korea, and other Asian countries and from good, old-fashioned plundering on the high seas made its way no longer into the emperor's coffers but rather the pockets of the Daimyos.

Feudalism developed in Japan later than it did in Europe and lasted longer as well. Japan dodged one huge historical bullet when a huge Mongol invasion was driven away by the famed **kamikaze**, or "divine wind," in the twelfth century. Japan was thus free to continue to develop itself as it saw fit and to refrain from interacting with the West, especially. This isolation lasted until the nineteenth century.

TEACHER CERTIFICATION STUDY GUIDE

COMPETENCY 2.0   **UNDERSTAND MAJOR POLITICAL, SOCIAL, ECONOMIC, CULTURAL, AND RELIGIOUS DEVELOPMENTS THAT SHAPED THE COURSE OF WORLD HISTORY FROM THE FOURTEENTH CENTURY THROUGH THE EIGHTEENTH CENTURY'**

Skill 2.1   **Examine the causes and accomplishments of the Italian Renaissance and its spread to other parts of Europe.**

The word "**Renaissance**" literally means "rebirth", and signaled the rekindling of interest in the glory of ancient classical Greek and Roman civilizations. It was the period in human history marking the start of many ideas and innovations leading to our modern age. The Renaissance began in Italy with many of its ideas starting in Florence, controlled by the infamous Medici family. Education, especially for some of the merchants, required reading, writing, math, the study of law, and the writings of classical Greek and Roman writers.

Most famous are the Renaissance artists, first and foremost Leonardo Da Vinci, Michelangelo, and Raphael but also Titian, Donatello, and Rembrandt. All of these men pioneered a new method of painting and sculpture—that of portraying real events and real people as they really looked, not as the artists imagined them to be.
Literature was a focus as well during the Renaissance. Humanists Petrarch, Boccaccio, Erasmus, and Sir Thomas More advanced the idea of being interested in life here on earth and the opportunities it can bring, rather than constantly focusing on heaven and its rewards. The monumental works of Shakespeare, Dante, and Cervantes found their origins in these ideas as well as the ones that drove the painters and sculptors. All of these works, of course, owe much of their existence to the invention of the printing press, which occurred during the Renaissance.

The Renaissance changed music as well. No longer just a religious experience, music could be fun and composed for its own sake, to be enjoyed in fuller and more humanistic ways than in the Middle Ages. Musicians worked for themselves, rather than for the churches, as before, and so could command good money for their work, increasing their prestige. Science advanced considerably during the Renaissance, especially in the area of physics and astronomy. Copernicus, Kepler, and Galileo led a Scientific Revolution in proving that the earth was round and certainly not perfect, an earth-shattering revelation to those who clung to medieval ideals of a geocentric, church-centered existence.

MIDDLE LEVEL SOCIAL STUDIES   11

Skill 2.2 **Recognize leading religious reformers of the sixteenth century, and analyze the influence of the Reformation on later religious, artistic, and scientific beliefs and practices.**

The Reformation period consisted of two phases: the **Protestant Revolution** and the **Catholic Reformation**. The Protestant Revolution came about because of religious, political, and economic reasons. The religious reasons stemmed from abuses in the Catholic Church including fraudulent clergy with their scandalous immoral lifestyles; the sale of religious offices, indulgences, and dispensations; different theologies within the Church; and frauds involving sacred relics.

The political reasons for the Protestant Revolution involved the increase in the power of rulers who were considered "absolute monarchs", who desired all power and control, especially over the Church. The growth of "nationalism" or patriotic pride in one's own country was another contributing factor.

Economic reasons included the greed of ruling monarchs to possess and control all lands and wealth of the Church, the deep animosity against the burdensome papal taxation, the rise of the affluent middle class and its clash with medieval Church ideals, and the increase of an active system of "intense" capitalism.

The Protestant Revolution began in Germany with the revolt of Martin Luther against Church abuses. It spread to Switzerland where it was led by Calvin. It began in England with the efforts of King Henry VIII to have his marriage to Catherine of Aragon annulled so he could wed another and have a male heir. The results were the increasing support given not only by the people but also by nobles and some rulers, and of course, the attempts of the Church to stop it.

The Catholic Reformation was undertaken by the Church to "clean up its act" and to slow or stop the Protestant Revolution. The major efforts to this end were supplied by the Council of Trent and the Jesuits. Six major results of the Reformation included:

- Religious freedom,
- Religious tolerance,
- More opportunities for education,
- Power and control of rulers limited,
- Increase in religious wars, and
- An increase in fanaticism and persecution.

Skill 2.3　Analyze major causes and consequences of European expansion during the Age of Discovery.

The Age of Exploration actually had its beginnings centuries before exploration actually took place. The rise and spread of Islam in the seventh century and its subsequent control over the holy city of Jerusalem led to the European so-called holy wars, the Crusades, to free Jerusalem and the Holy Land from this control. Even though the Crusades were not a success, those who survived and returned to their homes and countries in Western Europe brought back with them new products such as silks, spices, perfumes, new and different foods.
New ideas, inventions, and methods also went to Western Europe with the returning Crusaders and from these new influences was the intellectual stimulation which led to the period known as the Renaissance. The revival of interest in classical Greek art, architecture, literature, science, astronomy, medicine and increased trade between Europe and Asia and the invention of the printing press helped to push the spread of knowledge and start exploring.

For many centuries, mapmakers produced maps and charts, which in turn stimulated curiosity and the seeking more knowledge. At the same time, the Chinese were using the magnetic compass in their ships. Pacific Islanders were going from island to island, covering thousands of miles in open canoes navigating by sun and stars. Arab traders were sailing all over the Indian Ocean in their **dhows**. The trade routes between Europe and Asia were slow, difficult, dangerous, and very expensive. Between sea voyages on the Indian Ocean and Mediterranean Sea and the camel caravans in central Asia and the Arabian Desert, the trade was still controlled by the Italian merchants in Genoa and Venice. It would take months and even years for the exotic luxuries of Asia to reach the markets of Western Europe. A faster, cheaper way was needed.

Prince Henry of Portugal (also called the Navigator) encouraged and supported the Portuguese seamen who led in the search for an all-water route to Asia. A shipyard was built along with a school teaching navigation. New types of sailing ships were built which would carry the seamen safely through the ocean waters. Experiments were conducted with newer maps, navigational methods, and instruments. These included the astrolabe and the compass enabling sailors to determine direction as well as latitude and longitude for exact location.

Although Prince Henry died in 1460, the Portuguese continue to sail and explore Africa's west coastline. In 1488, Bartholomew Diaz and his men sailed around Africa's southern tip and headed toward Asia. Diaz wanted to push on but turned back because his men were discouraged and weary from the long months at sea, extremely fearful of the unknown, and refused to travel any further.

The Portuguese were finally successful ten years later in 1498 when **Vasco da Gama** and his men, continuing the route of Diaz, rounded Africa's Cape of Good Hope, sailing across the Indian Ocean, reaching India's port of Calicut (Calcutta). Although, six years earlier, Columbus had reached the New World and an entire hemisphere, da Gama had proved Asia could be reached from Europe by sea.

Christopher Columbus' first transatlantic voyage was to prove his theory that Asia could be reached by sailing west. It could be done but only after figuring how to go around or across or through the landmass in between. Long after Spain dispatched explorers and her famed conquistadors to gather the wealth for the Spanish monarchs and their coffers, the British were searching valiantly for the "Northwest Passage," a land-sea route across North America and open sea to the wealth of Asia. It wasn't until after the Lewis and Clark Expedition when Captains Meriwether Lewis and William Clark proved conclusively that there simply was no Northwest Passage..

However, this did not deter exploration and settlement. Spain, France, and England with some participation by the Dutch led the way with expanding Western European civilization to the New World. The three nations (Spain, France, England) had strong monarchial governments and were struggling for dominance and power in Europe. With the defeat of Spain's mighty Armada in 1588, England became undisputed mistress of the seas. Spain lost its power and influence in Europe and it was left to France and England to carry on the rivalry, leading to eventual British control in Asia as well.

The importance of the Age of Exploration was not just the discovery and colonization of the New World, but a) better maps and charts, b) newer, more accurate navigational instruments, c) increased knowledge, d) great wealth, e) new and different foods and items unknown in Europe and, f) a new hemisphere as a refuge from poverty, persecution, and a place to start a new and better life.

With the increase in trade and travel, cities germinated and began to grow. Craft workers in the cities developed their skills to a high degree, eventually organizing guilds to protect the quality of the work and regulate the buying and selling of their products.

City government developed and flourished centered on strong town councils. Active in city government and the town councils were the wealthy businessmen who made up the growing middle class.

In addition, there were a number of individuals and events during the time of exploration and discoveries. The Vivaldo brothers and Marco Polo wrote of their travels and experiences, which signaled the early beginnings. From the Crusades, the survivors made their way home to different places in Europe bringing with them fascinating, new information about exotic lands, people, customs, and desired foods and goods such as spices and silks.

For France, claims to various parts of North America were the result of the efforts of such men as Verrazano, Champlain, Cartier, LaSalle, Father Marquette and Joliet. Dutch claims were based on the work of Henry Hudson. John Cabot gave England its stake in North America along with John Hawkins, Sir Francis Drake, and the half-brothers Sir Walter Raleigh and Sir Humphrey Gilbert.

Actually the first Europeans in the New World were Norsemen led by Eric the Red and later, his son Leif the Lucky. However, before any of these, the ancestors of today's Native Americans and Latin American Indians crossed the Bering Strait from Asia to Alaska, eventually settling in all parts of the Americas.

Skill 2.4 Demonstrate knowledge of the political, economic, and social environments in which the English, American, and French

Revolutions took place.

The period from the 1700s to the 1800s was characterized in Western countries by opposing political ideas of democracy and nationalism. This resulted in strong nationalistic feelings and people of common cultures asserting their belief in the right to have a part in their government.

The **American Revolution** resulted in the successful efforts of the English colonists in America to win their freedom from Great Britain. After more than one hundred years of mostly self-government, the colonists resented the increased British meddling and control, they declared their freedom, won the Revolutionary War with aid from France, and formed a new independent nation.

The **French Revolution** was a revolt of the middle and lower classes against the gross political and economic excesses of the rulers and the supporting nobility. It ended with the establishment of the first in a series of French Republics. Conditions leading to revolt included extreme taxation, inflation, lack of food, and the total disregard for the degrading, and unacceptable condition of the people by the rulers, nobility, and the Church.

TEACHER CERTIFICATION STUDY GUIDE

The American Revolution and the French Revolution were similar yet different, liberating their people from unwanted government interference and leading to the creation of a different model of government. They were both fought for the liberty of the common people, and they both were built on writings and ideas that embraced such an outcome; yet that is where the similarities end. Several important differences need to be emphasized:

- The British colonists were striking back against unwanted taxation and other sorts of "government interference." The French people were starving and, in many cases, destitute and were striking back against an autocratic regime that cared more for high fashion and courtly love.
- The American Revolution involved a long campaign, of often bloody battles, skirmishes, and stalemates. The French Revolution was bloody to a degree but mainly an overthrow of society and its outdated traditions.
- The American Revolution resulted in a representative government, which marketed itself as a beacon of democracy for the rest of the world. The French Revolution resulted in a consulship, a generalship, and then an emperor—probably not what the perpetrators of the Revolution had in mind when they first struck back at the king and queen.

Still, both Revolutions are looked back on as turning points in history, as times when the governed stood up to the governors and said, "Enough."

TEACHER CERTIFICATION STUDY GUIDE

COMPETENCY 3.0   **UNDERSTAND MAJOR POLITICAL, SOCIAL, ECONOMIC, CULTURAL, AND RELIGIOUS DEVELOPMENTS THAT SHAPED THE COURSE OF WORLD HISTORY FROM THE NINETEENTH CENTURY TO THE PRESENT**

Skill 3.1   **Analyze major causes of the Industrial Revolution and its impact on the politics, societies, and cultures of the modern world.**

The **Industrial Revolution**, which began in Great Britain and spread elsewhere, saw the development of power-driven machinery (fueled by coal and steam) leading to the accelerated growth of industry with large factories replacing homes and small workshops as work centers. The lives of people changed drastically and a largely agricultural society changed to an industrial one. In Western Europe, the period of empire and colonialism began. The industrialized nations seized and claimed parts of Africa and Asia in an effort to control and provide the raw materials needed to feed the industries and machines in the "mother country". Later developments included power based on electricity and internal combustion, replacing coal and steam.

There was a marked degree of industrialization before and during the Civil War, but at war's end, industry in America was small. After the war, dramatic changes took place. Machines replaced hand labor, extensive nationwide railroad service made possible the wider distribution of goods, invention of new products made available in large quantities, and large amounts of money from bankers and investors for expansion of business operations. American life was definitely affected by this phenomenal industrial growth. Cities became the centers of this new business activity resulting in mass population movements there and tremendous growth. This new boom in business resulted in huge fortunes for some Americans and extreme poverty for many others. The discontent this caused resulted in a number of new reform movements from which came measures controlling the power and size of big business and helping the poor.

The use of machines in industry enabled workers to produce a large quantity of goods much faster than by hand. With the increase in business, hundreds of workers were hired, assigned to perform a certain job in the production process. This was a method of organization called "**division of labor**" and by its increasing the rate of production, businesses lowered prices for their products making the products affordable for more people. As a result, sales and businesses were increasingly successful and profitable.

A great variety of new products or inventions became available such as: the typewriter, the telephone, barbed wire, the electric light, the phonograph, and the gasoline automobile. From this list, the one that had the greatest effect on America's economy was the automobile.

MIDDLE LEVEL SOCIAL STUDIES   17

The increase in business and industry was greatly affected by the many rich natural resources that were found throughout the nation. The industrial machines were powered by the abundant water supply. The construction industry as well as products made from wood depended heavily on lumber from the forests. Coal and iron ore in abundance were needed for the steel industry, which profited and increased from the use of steel in such things as skyscrapers, automobiles, bridges, railroad tracks, and machines. Other minerals such as silver, copper, and petroleum played a large role in industrial growth, especially petroleum, from which gasoline was refined as fuel for the increasingly popular automobile.

Between 1870 and 1916, more than 25 million immigrants came into the United States adding to the phenomenal population growth taking place. This tremendous growth aided business and industry in two ways: (1) The number of consumers increased creating a greater demand for products thus enlarging the markets for the products, and (2) with increased production and expanding business, more workers were available for newly created jobs. The completion of the nation's transcontinental railroad in 1869 contributed greatly to the nation's economic and industrial growth. Some examples of the benefits of using the railroads include raw materials were shipped quickly by the mining companies and finished products were sent to all parts of the country. Many wealthy industrialists and railroad owners saw tremendous profits steadily increasing due to this improved method of transportation.

As business grew, new methods of sales and promotion were developed. Salespersons went to all parts of the country promoting the various products, opening large department stores in the growing cities, offering the varied products at reasonable affordable prices. People who lived too far from the cities, making it impossible to shop there, had the advantage of using a mail order service, buying what they needed from catalogs furnished by the companies. The developments in communication, such as the telephone and telegraph, increased the efficiency and prosperity of big business.

Investments in corporate stocks and bonds resulted from business prosperity. Individuals began investing heavily with an eager desire to share in the profits and their investments provided the needed capital for companies to expand operations. Banks increased in number throughout the country, making loans to businesses and significant contributions to economic growth. During the 1880s, government made little effort to regulate businesses. This gave rise to monopolies where larger businesses were rid of their smaller competitors and assumed complete control of their industries.

Some owners in the same business would join or merge to form one company. Others formed what were called "trusts," a type of monopoly in which rival businesses were controlled but not formally owned. Monopolies had some good effects on the economy. Out of them grew the large, efficient corporations, which made important contributions to the growth of the nation's economy. Also, the monopolies enabled businesses to keep their sales steady and avoid sharp fluctuations in price and production. At the same time, the downside of monopolies was the unfair business practices of the business leaders. Some acquired so much power that they took unfair advantage of others. Those who had little or no competition would require their suppliers to supply goods at a low cost, sell the finished products at high prices, and reduce the quality of the product to save money.

The late 1800s and early 1900s were a period of the efforts of many to make significant reforms and changes in the areas of politics, society, and the economy. There was a need to reduce the levels of poverty and to improve the living conditions of those affected by it. Regulations of big business, eliminating governmental corruption and making it more responsive to the needs of the people were also on the list of reforms to be accomplished. Until 1890, there was very little success, but from 1890 on the reformers gained increased public support and were able to achieve some influence in government. Since some of these individuals referred to themselves as "**progressives**," the period of 1890 to 1917 is referred to by historians as the Progressive Era.

Skilled laborers were organized into a labor union called the American Federation of Labor in an effort to gain better working conditions and wages for its members. Farmers joined organizations such as the National Grange and Farmers Alliances. Farmers were producing more food than people could afford to buy. This was the result of (1) new farmlands rapidly sprouting on the plains and prairies, and (2) development and availability of new farm machinery and newer and better methods of farming. They tried selling their surplus abroad but faced stiff competition from other nations selling the same farm products. Other problems contributed significantly to their situation. Items they needed for daily life were priced exorbitantly high. Having to borrow money to carry on farming activities kept them constantly in debt. Higher interest rates, shortage of money, falling farm prices, dealing with the so-called middlemen, and the increasingly high charges by the railroads to haul farm products to large markets all contributed to the desperate need for reform to relieve the plight of American farmers.

Skill 3.2 Analyze the origins and development of imperialism and its consequences for both colonizers and colonized.

In Europe, Italy and Germany each were totally united into one nation from many smaller states. There were revolutions in Austria and Hungary, the Franco-Prussian War, the dividing of Africa among the strong European nations, interference and intervention of Western nations in Asia, and the breakup of Turkish dominance in the Balkans.

In Africa, France, Great Britain, Italy, Portugal, Spain, Germany, and Belgium controlled the entire continent except Liberia and Ethiopia. In Asia and the Pacific Islands, only China, Japan, and present-day Thailand (Siam) kept their independence. The others were controlled by the stronger European nations.

An additional reason for **European imperialism** was the harsh, urgent demand for the raw materials needed to fuel and feed the great Industrial Revolution. These resources were not available in the huge quantity so desperately needed which necessitated (and rationalized) the partitioning of the continent of Africa and parts of Asia. In turn, these colonial areas would purchase the finished manufactured goods. Europe in the nineteenth century was a crowded place. Populations were growing but resources were not. The peoples of many European countries were also agitating for rights as never before. To address these concerns, European powers began to look elsewhere for relief.

One of the main places for European imperialist expansion was Africa. Britain, France, Germany, and Belgium took over countries in Africa and claimed them as their own. The resources (including people) were then shipped back to the mainland and claimed as colonial gains. The Europeans made a big deal about "civilizing the savages," reasoning that their technological superiority gave them the right to rule and "educate" the peoples of Africa.

Southeast Asia was another area of European expansion at this time, mainly by France. So, too, was India, colonized by Great Britain. These two nations combined with Spain to occupy countries in Latin America. Spain also seized the rich lands of the Philippines.

As a result of all this activity, a whole new flood of goods, people, and ideas began to come back to Europe and a whole group of people began to travel to these colonies, to oversee the colonization and to "help bring the people up" to the European level. European leaders could also assert their authority in these colonies as they could not back home.

In the United States, **territorial expansion** occurred in the expansion westward under the banner of **"Manifest Destiny."** In addition, the U.S. was involved in the War with Mexico, the Spanish-American War, and support of the Latin American colonies of Spain in their revolt for independence. In Latin America, the Spanish colonies were successful in their fight for independence and self-government.

The time from 1830 to 1914 is characterized by the extraordinary growth and spread of patriotic pride in a nation along with intense, widespread imperialism. Loyalty to one's nation included national pride; extension and maintenance of sovereign political boundaries; unification of smaller states with common language, history, and culture into a more powerful nation; or smaller national groups who, as part of a larger multi-cultural empire, wished to separate into smaller, political, cultural nations.

Skill 3.3   Describe the causes and evaluate the consequences of regional and global warfare in the nineteenth and twentieth centuries.

For example:

Napoleon was a dominating figure on the European landscape, shaping and reshaping the fabric of the Continent in ways that are still being explained. He rose from the ranks of a common soldier to become a powerful politician and then, eventually, ruler of an empire. He was totally the product of his age, but he ushered in a new one as well.

First and foremost, he changed the geography of Europe. The borders of France swelled under his reign, as did the Grand Armee and its reputation. Napoleon brought to the battlefield brilliant tactics and sound military mind, in addition to a great daring to attempt the seemingly impossible and make it work. As with Alexander before him, Napoleon could snatch the grandest victory from the jaws of defeat. One need look no further than **Jena**, perhaps Napoleon's most stunning victory.

With a numerically inferior force, he crushed the Prussian army, inflicting on it a number of casualties five times as much as his own army suffered. On the same day, the Grand Armee inflicted an ever greater defeat on the Prussian Army, crushing it completely with a much wider disparity in troop numbers. The result was a capitulation, effectively ending Prussia's influence in Europe for years to come.

His ability to move his troops with lightning speed, before and during battles, earned Napoleon a reputation for being an expert in mobile warfare, and indeed he was that, even when heavy cannons were involved. He was also a master at the use of cavalry on the battlefield, sending many a numerically superior force scurrying from the battlefield in flying defeat. This translated into new strategies and technologies on the battlefield, not only for France but also for the rest of Europe. Napoleon's tactics, successes, and failures continue to be studied for their effectiveness and their innovation.

His ambition eventually outstripped his fortune, however, and he effected a humiliating retreat from Russia, effectively ending his reign. Other battles followed, but the twin defeats of Russia and Trafalgar ended his hopes and dreams of being Master of Europe.

Napoleon was certainly a unifier, of his own people and of the rest of Europe against him. In the early days of the Continental System, he ruled Europe (Russia excluded) and dreamed of a huge political state with himself at the head and the peoples of Europe under his banner, albeit reluctantly. As they began to chip away at this authority, however, they began to follow Britain's and Russia's leads and became more bold in their opposition. This eventually resulted in the kind of united force that opposed the French at **Waterloo**. Such union continued throughout the Congress of Vienna, the political end of the **Napoleonic Wars**, and lasted for a time until nationalism gripped Europe fully and fomented the Revolutions of 1848.

The transformation of Napoleon from a hero of the egalitarian French Revolution idealist into an overarching monarch was a cautionary tale for both French people and the rest of Europe. The ideals that fired the revolution against the monarchy in France took root in other European countries, and Napoleon's assumption of absolute power proved a perfect example of how the common people should be given more of a check on governmental power. The emperor's ultimate defeat (twice, actually) was a victory for nationalists everywhere as well as being the end of an era.

The major turning point for Latin America, already unhappy with Spanish restrictions on trade, agriculture, and the manufacture of goods, was Napoleon's move into Spain and Portugal. Napoleon's imprisonment of King Ferdinand VII, made the local agents of the Spanish authorities feel that they were in fact agents of the French. Conservative and liberal locals joined forces, declared their loyalty to King Ferdinand, and formed committees (*juntas*). Between May of 1810 and July of 1811, the *juntas* in Argentina, Chile, Paraguay, Venezuela, Bolivia and Colombia all declared independence. Fighting erupted between Spanish authorities in Latin America and the members and followers of the *juntas*. In Mexico City another *junta* declared loyalty to Ferdinand and independence.

The United States' unintentional and accidental involvement in what was known as the **War of 1812** came about due to the political and economic struggles between France and Great Britain. Napoleon's goal was complete conquest and control of Europe, including and especially Great Britain. Although British troops were temporarily driven off the mainland of Europe, the navy still controlled the seas, the seas across which France had to bring the products needed. America traded with both nations, especially with France and its colonies. The British decided to destroy the American trade with France, mainly for two reasons: (a) Products and goods from the U.S. gave Napoleon what he needed to keep up his struggle with Britain. He and France was the enemy and it was felt that the Americans were aiding the Mother Country's enemy. (b) Britain felt threatened by the increasing strength and success of the U.S. merchant fleet. They were becoming major competitors with the ship owners and merchants in Britain.

The British issued the **Orders in Council** which was a series of measures prohibiting American ships from entering any French ports, not only in Europe but also in India and the West Indies. At the same time, Napoleon began efforts for a coastal blockade of the British Isles. He issued a series of Orders prohibiting all nations, including the United States, from trading with the British. He threatened seizure of every ship entering French ports after they stopped at any British port or colony, even threatening to seize every ship inspected by British cruisers or that paid any duties to their government. British were stopping American ships and impressing American seamen to service on British ships. Americans were outraged.

The period of European peace after the defeat of Napoleon and the reliance upon the gold standard in that time is often referred to as "The First Era of Globalization." This period began to disintegrate with the crisis of the gold standard in the late 1920s and early 1930s.

*   *   *

Karl Marx (1818-1883) was perhaps the most influential theorist of the nineteenth century and his influence has continued in various forms until this day. He was not the first to believe in socialist ideas, many of which had been around for some time and in various forms. Nevertheless, he was the first to call his system truly "scientific" or **Scientific Socialism**. (Also called Marxian Socialism or as it is more widely known Marxism). It was opposed to other forms of socialism that had been called, (with some derision), **Utopian Socialism**. It is this very idea of Marxism being "scientific" that has been appealing to so many thinkers in modern history. Marx expounded his ideas in two major theoretical works, *The Communist Manifesto* (1848) and *Das Capital*, (Volume 1 1867).

Until the early years of the twentieth century **Russia** was ruled by a succession of Tsars. The Tsars ruled as autocrats or, sometimes, despots. Society was essentially feudalistic and was structured in three levels. The top level was held by the Tsar. The second level was composed of the rich nobles who held government positions and owned vast tracts of land. The third level of the society was composed of the remaining people who lived in poverty as peasants or serfs. There was discontent among the peasants. There were several unsuccessful attempts to revolt during the nineteenth century, but they were quickly suppressed. The revolutions of 1905 and 1917, however, were quite different.

Until the early years of the twentieth century Russia was ruled by a succession of Czars. The Czars ruled as autocrats or, sometimes, despots. Society was essentially feudalistic and was structured in three levels. The top level was held by the Czar. The second level was composed of the rich nobles who held government positions and owned vast tracts of land. The third level of the society was composed of the remaining people who lived in poverty as peasants or serfs.

There was discontent among the peasants. There were several unsuccessful attempts to revolt during the nineteenth century, but they were quickly suppressed. The revolutions of 1905 and 1917, however, were quite different.

The causes of the 1905 Revolution were:

- Discontent with the social structure.
- Discontent with the living conditions of the peasants.
- Discontent with working conditions despite industrialization.
- The general discontent was aggravated by the Russo-Japanese War (1904-1905) with inflation, rising prices, etc. Peasants who had been able to eke out a living began to starve.
- Many of the fighting troops were killed in battles Russia lost to Japan because of poor leadership, lack of training, and inferior weaponry.
- Czar Nicholas II refused to end the war despite setbacks.
- In January 1905 Port Arthur fell.

A trade union leader, Father Gapon, organized a protest to demand an end to the war, industrial reform, more civil liberties, and a constituent assembly. Over 150,000 peasants joined a demonstration outside the Czar's Winter Palace. Before the demonstrators even spoke, the palace guard opened fire on the crowd. This destroyed the people's trust in the Czar. Illegal trade unions and political parties formed and organized strikes to gain power.

The strikes eventually brought the Russian economy to a halt. This led Czar Nicholas II to sign the October Manifesto which created a constitutional monarchy, extended some civil rights, and gave the parliament limited legislative power. In a very short period of time, the Czar disbanded the parliament and violated the promised civil liberties.

The causes of the 1917 Revolution were:

- The violation of the October Manifesto.
- Defeats on the battlefields during WWI caused discontent, loss of life, and a popular desire to withdraw from the war.
- The Czar continued to appoint unqualified people to government posts and handle the situation with general incompetence.
- The Czar also listened to his wife's (Alexandra) advice. She was strongly influenced by Rasputin. This caused increased discontent among all level of the social structure.
- WWI had caused another surge in prices and scarcity of many items. Most of the peasants could not afford to buy bread.

Workers in Petrograd went on strike in 1917 over the need for food. The Czar again ordered troops to suppress the strike. This time, however, the troops sided with the workers. The revolution then took a unique direction. The parliament created a provisional government to rule the country. The military and the workers also created their own governments called soviets (popularly elected local councils). The parliament was composed of nobles who soon lost control of the country when they failed to comply with the wishes of the populace. The result was chaos.

The political leaders who had previously been driven into exile returned. Lenin, Stalin and Trotsky won the support of the peasants with the promise of "Peace, Land, and Bread". The parliament, on the other hand, continued the country's involvement in the war. Lenin and the Bolshevik Party gained the support of the Red Guard and together overthrew the provisional government. In short order they had complete control of Russia and established a new communist state.

The most significant differences between the 1905 and 1917 revolutions were the formation of political parties and their use of propaganda and the support of the military and some of the nobles in 1917.

World War I ■ 1914 to 1918

Causes were the surge of nationalism, the increasing strength of military capabilities, massive colonization for raw materials needed for industrialization and manufacturing, and military and diplomatic alliances.

In Europe, Italy and Germany were each totally united into one nation from many smaller states. There were revolutions in Austria and Hungary, the Franco-Prussian War, the dividing of Africa among the strong European nations, interference and intervention of Western nations in Asia, and the breakup of Turkish dominance in the Balkans.

In Africa, France, Great Britain, Italy, Portugal, Spain, Germany, and Belgium controlled the entire continent except Liberia and Ethiopia. In Asia and the Pacific Islands, only China, Japan, and present-day Thailand (Siam) kept their independence. The others were controlled by the strong European nations.

This success enlarged and expanded the U.S. role in foreign affairs. Under the administration of Theodore Roosevelt, the U.S. armed forces were built up, greatly increasing its strength. Roosevelt's foreign policy was summed up in the slogan of "Speak softly and carry a big stick," backing up the efforts in diplomacy with a strong military. During the years before the outbreak of World War I, evidence of U.S. emergence as a world power could be seen in a number of actions. Using the Monroe Doctrine of non-involvement of Europe in affairs of the Western Hemisphere, President Roosevelt forced Italy, Germany, and Great Britain to remove their blockade of Venezuela. He gained the rights to construct the Panama Canal by threatening force; assumed the finances of the Dominican Republic to stabilize it and prevent any intervention by Europeans; and in 1916 under President Woodrow Wilson, U.S. troops were sent to the Dominican Republic to keep order.

Emotions ran high and minor disputes magnified into major ones and sometimes quickly led to threats of war. Especially sensitive to these conditions was the area of the states on the Balkan Peninsula. Along with the imperialistic colonization for industrial raw materials, military build-up (especially by Germany), and diplomatic and military alliances, the conditions for one tiny spark to set off the explosion were in place. In July 1914, a Serbian national assassinated the Austrian heir to the throne and his wife and war began a few weeks later. There were a few attempts to keep war from starting, but these efforts were futile.

In Europe, war broke out in 1914, eventually involving nearly 30 nations and ended in 1918. One of the major causes of the war was the tremendous surge of nationalism during the 1800s and early 1900s. People of the same nationality or ethnic group sharing a common history, language or culture began uniting or demanding the right of unification, especially in the empires of Eastern Europe, such as the Russian Ottoman and Austrian-Hungarian Empires.

Getting stronger and more intense were the beliefs of these peoples in loyalty to common political, social, and economic goals considered to be before any loyalty to the controlling nation or empire.

World War I saw the introduction of such warfare as use of tanks, airplanes, machine guns, submarines, poison gas, and flame throwers. Fighting on the Western front was characterized by a series of trenches that were used throughout the war until 1918. U.S. involvement in the war did not occur until 1916. When war began in 1914, President Woodrow Wilson declared that the U.S. was neutral and most Americans were opposed to any involvement anyway. In 1916, Wilson was reelected to a second term based on the slogan proclaiming his efforts at keeping America out of the war. For a few months after, he put forth most of his efforts to stopping the war but German submarines began unlimited warfare against American merchant shipping.

At the same time, Great Britain intercepted and decoded a secret message from Germany to Mexico urging Mexico to go to war against the U.S. The publication of this information, along with continued German destruction of American ships resulted in the eventual entry of the U.S. into the conflict; the first time the country prepared to fight in a conflict not on American soil. Though unprepared for war, government efforts and activities resulted in massive defense mobilization with America's economy directed to the war effort. Though America made important contributions of war materials, its greatest contribution to the war was manpower, soldiers desperately needed by the Allies.

Some ten months before the war ended, President Wilson had proposed a program called the Fourteen Points as a method of bringing the war to an end with an equitable peace settlement. In these Points he had five points setting out general ideals; there were eight pertaining to immediately working to resolve territorial and political problems; and the fourteenth point counseled establishing an organization of nations to help keep world peace.

When Germany agreed in 1918 to an armistice, it assumed that the peace settlement would be drawn up on the basis of these Fourteen Points. However, the peace conference in Paris ignored these points and Wilson had to be content with efforts at establishing the League of Nations. Italy, France, and Great Britain, having suffered and sacrificed far more in the war than America, wanted retribution. The treaties punished severely the Central Powers, taking away arms and territories and requiring payment of reparations. Germany was punished more than the others and, according to one clause in the treaty, was forced to assume the responsibility for causing the war.

World War II 1939 – 1942
Pre-war empires lost tremendous amounts of territories as well as the wealth of natural resources in them. New, independent nations were formed and some predominately ethnic areas came under control of nations of different cultural backgrounds. Some national boundary changes overlapped and created tensions and hard feelings as well as political and economic confusion. The wishes and desires of every national or cultural group could not possibly be realized and satisfied, resulting in disappointments for both; those who were victorious and those who were defeated. Germany received harsher terms than expected from the treaty which weakened its post-war government and, along with the world-wide depression of the 1930s, set the stage for the rise of Adolf Hitler and his Nationalist Socialist Party and World War II.

The world after World War II was a complicated place. The Axis powers, Nazi German, Fascist Italy and the Empire of Japan were defeated, but the Cold War had sprung up in its place. Many countries struggled to get out of the debt and devastation that their Nazi occupiers had wrought. The American Marshall Plan helped the nations of Western Europe get back on their feet. The Soviet Union helped the Eastern European nations return to greatness, with Communist governments at the helm. The nations of Asia were rebuilt as well, with Communism taking over China and Americanization taking over Japan and Taiwan. East and West struggled for control in this arena, especially in Korea and Southeast Asia. When Communism fell in the USSR and Eastern Europe, it remained in China, North Korea, and Vietnam. Vietnam's neighbors, however set their own path to government.

The United Nations, a more successful successor to the League of Nations (which couldn't prevent World War II), began in the waning days of the war. It brought the nations of the world together to discuss their problems, rather than fight about them. Another successful method of keeping the peace since the war has been the atomic bomb. On a more specific note, UNICEF, a worldwide children's fund, has been able to achieve great things in just a few decades of existence. Other peace-based organizations like the Red Cross and Doctors Without Borders have seen their membership and their efficacy rise during this time as well.

In America, President Wilson lost in his efforts to get the U.S. Senate to approve the peace treaty. The Senate at the time was a reflection of American public opinion and its rejection of the treaty was a rejection of Wilson. The approval of the treaty would have made the U.S. a member of the League of Nations but Americans had just come off a bloody war to ensure that democracy would exist throughout the world. Americans just did not want to accept any responsibility that resulted from its new position of power and were afraid that membership in the League of Nations would embroil the U.S. in future disputes in Europe.

The kind of nationalism that Europe saw in the nineteenth century spilled over into the mid-twentieth century, with former colonies of European powers declaring themselves independent all the time, especially in Africa. India, a longtime British protectorate, also achieved independence at this time. With independence, these countries continued to grow. Some of these nations now experience severe overcrowding and dearth of precious resources. Some who can escape do; others have no way to escape.

The Middle East has been an especially violent part of the world since the war and the inception of the State of Israel. The struggle for supremacy in the Persian Gulf area has brought about a handful of wars as well. Oil, needed to power the world's devastatingly large transportation and manufacturing engines, is king of all resources.

There were 28 nations involved in the war, not including colonies and territories. It began July 28, 1914 and ended November 11, 1918 with the signing of the Treaty of Versailles. Economically, the war cost a total of $337 billion; increased inflation and huge war debts; and caused a loss of markets, goods, jobs, and factories. Politically, old empires collapsed; many monarchies disappeared; smaller countries gained temporary independence; Communists seized power in Russia; and, in some cases, nationalism increased. Socially, total populations decreased because of war casualties and low birth rates. There were millions of displaced persons and villages and farms were destroyed. Cities grew while women made significant gains in the work force and the ballot box. There was less social distinction and classes. Attitudes completely changed and old beliefs and values were questioned. The peace settlement established the League of Nations to ensure peace, but it failed to do so.

Skill 3.4 **Examine major political developments, economic trends, and social movements of the twentieth century.**

Decolonization refers to the period after World War II when many African and Asian colonies and protectorates gained independence from the powers that had colonized them. The independence of India and Pakistan from Britain in 1945 marked the beginning of an especially important period of decolonization that lasted through 1960. Several British colonies in eastern Africa and French colonies in western Africa and Asia also formed as independent countries during this period.

Colonial powers had found it efficient to draw political boundaries across traditional ethnic and national lines, thereby dividing local populations and making them easier to control. With the yoke of colonialism removed, many new nations found themselves trying to reorganize into politically stable and economically viable units. The role of nationalism was important in this reorganization, as formerly divided peoples had opportunity to reunite. **Nationalism** is most simply defined as the belief that the nation is the basic unit of human association, and that a nation is a well-defined group of people sharing a common identity. This process of organizing new nations out of the remains of former colonies was called nation building.

Nation building in this fashion did not always result in the desired stability. Pakistan, for example, eventually split into Bangladesh and Pakistan along geographic and religious lines. Ethnic conflicts in newly formed African nations arose, and are still flaring in some areas. As the United States and the Soviet Union emerged as the dominant world powers, these countries encouraged dissent in post-colonial nations such as Cuba, Vietnam and Korea, which became arenas for Cold War conflict.

With the emergence of so many new independent nations, the role of **international organizations** such as the newly formed United Nations grew in importance. The United Nations was formed after World War II to establish peaceful ties between countries. Dismayed by the failure of the former League of Nations to prevent war, the organizers of the United Nations provided for the ability to deploy peacekeeping troops and to impose sanctions and restrictions on member states. Other international organizations arose to take the place of former colonial connections. The British Commonwealth and the French Union, for example, maintained connections between Britain and France and their former colonies.

Global migration saw an increase in the years during and following World War II. During the war years, many Jews left the hostile climate under Nazi Germany for the United States and Palestine. Following the war, the Allied countries agreed to force German people living in Eastern Europe to return to Germany, affecting over 16 million people. In other parts of the world, instability in post-colonial areas often led to migration.

Colonial settlers who had enjoyed the protection of a colonial power sometimes found themselves in hostile situations as native peoples gained independence and ascended to power, spurring migration to more friendly nations. Economic instability in newly forming countries created incentive for people to seek opportunity in other countries.

The Cold War was, more than anything else, an ideological struggle between proponents of democracy and those of communism. The two major players were the United States and the Soviet Union, but other countries were involved as well. It was a "cold" war because no large-scale fighting took place directly between the two big protagonists.

It wasn't just form of government that was driving this war, either. Economics were a main concern as well. A concern in both countries was that the precious resources (such as oil and food) from other like-minded countries wouldn't be allowed to flow to "the other side." These resources didn't much flow between the U.S. and Soviet Union, either.

The Soviet Union kept much more of a tight leash on its supporting countries, including all of Eastern Europe, which made up a military organization called the **Warsaw Pact**. The Western nations responded with a military organization of their own, **NATO** or North American Treaty Organization. Another prime battleground was Asia, where the Soviet Union had allies in China, North Korea, and North Vietnam and the U.S. had allies in Japan, South Korea, Taiwan, and South Vietnam. The Korean War and Vietnam War were major conflicts in which both protagonists played big roles but didn't directly fight each other. The main symbol of the Cold War was the **arms race**, a continual buildup of missiles, tanks, and other weapons that became ever more technologically advanced and increasingly more deadly. The ultimate weapon, which both sides had in abundance, was the nuclear bomb. Spending on weapons and defensive systems eventually occupied great percentages of the budgets of the U.S. and the USSR, and some historians argue that this high level of spending played a large part in the end of the latter.

The war was a cultural struggle as well. Adults brought up their children to hate "the Americans" or "the Communists." Cold War tensions spilled over into many parts of life in countries around the world. The ways of life in countries on either side of the divide were so different that they seemed entirely foreign to outside observers.

The Cold War continued to varying degrees from 1947 to 1991, when the Soviet Union collapsed. Other Eastern European countries had seen their communist governments overthrown by this time as well, marking the shredding of the "Iron Curtain." The "**Iron Curtain**" referred to the ideological, symbolic and physical separation of Europe between East and West.

The major thrust of U.S. foreign policy from the end of World War II to 1990 was the post-war struggle between non-Communist nations, led by the United States, and the Soviet Union and the Communist nations who were its allies. It was referred to as a "Cold War" because its conflicts did not lead to a major war of fighting, or a "hot war." Both the Soviet Union and the United States embarked on an arsenal buildup of atomic and hydrogen bombs as well as other nuclear weapons. Both nations had the capability of destroying each other but because of the continuous threat of nuclear war and accidents, extreme caution was practiced on both sides. The efforts of both sides to serve and protect their political philosophies and to support and assist their allies resulted in a number of events during this 45-year period.

TEACHER CERTIFICATION STUDY GUIDE

COMPETENCY 4.0 UNDERSTAND THE IDEAS AND VALUES THAT HAVE SHAPED THE CULTURE OF THE UNITED STATES

Skill 4.1 Define the democratic concepts that form the basis of the U.S. political and legal systems.

The Political System

In the United States, the three branches of the federal government mentioned earlier, the **Executive**, the **Legislative**, and the **Judicial**, divide up their powers thus:

Legislative – Article 1 of the Constitution established the legislative, or law-making branch of the government called the Congress. It is made up of two houses, the House of Representatives and the Senate. Voters in all states elect the members who serve in each respective House of Congress. The legislative branch is responsible for making laws, raising and printing money, regulating trade, establishing the postal service and federal courts, approving the President's appointments, declaring war and supporting the armed forces. The Congress also has the power to change the Constitution itself, and to *impeach* (bring charges against) the President. Charges for impeachment are brought by the House of Representatives, and are then tried in the Senate.

Executive – Article 2 of the Constitution created the executive branch of the government, headed by the President, who leads the country, recommends new laws, and can veto bills passed by the legislative branch. As the chief of state, the President is responsible for carrying out the laws of the country and the treaties and declarations of war passed by the legislative branch. The President also appoints federal judges and is commander-in-chief of the military when it is called into service. Other members of the executive branch include the Vice-President, also elected, and various cabinet members as he might appoint: ambassadors, presidential advisors, members of the armed forces, and other appointed and civil servants of government agencies, departments and bureaus. Though the President appoints them, they must be approved by the legislative branch.

Judicial – Article 3 of the Constitution established the judicial branch of government headed by the Supreme Court. The Supreme Court has the power to rule that a law passed by the legislature, or an act of the executive branch is illegal and unconstitutional. Citizens, businesses, and government officials can also, in an appeal capacity, ask the Supreme Court to review a decision made in a lower court if someone believes that the ruling by a judge is unconstitutional. The judicial branch also includes lower federal courts known as federal district courts that have been established by the Congress. These courts try law breakers and review cases referred from other courts.

MIDDLE LEVEL SOCIAL STUDIES 33

TEACHER CERTIFICATION STUDY GUIDE

Powers delegated to the federal government:

1. To tax.
2. To borrow and coin money.
3. To establish postal service.
4. To grant patents and copyrights.
5. To regulate interstate and foreign commerce.
6. To establish courts.
7. To declare war.
8. To raise and support the armed forces.
9. To govern territories.
10. To define and punish felonies and piracy on the high seas.
11. To fix standards of weights and measures.
12. To conduct foreign affairs.

Powers reserved to the states:

1. To regulate intrastate trade.
2. To establish local governments.
3. To protect general welfare.
4. To protect life and property.
5. To ratify amendments.
6. To conduct elections.
7. To make state and local laws.

Concurrent powers of the federal government and states.

1. Both Congress and the states may tax.
2. Both may borrow money.
3. Both may charter banks and corporations.
4. Both may establish courts.
5. Both may make and enforce laws.
6. Both may take property for public purposes.
7. Both may spend money to provide for the public welfare.

Implied powers of the federal government.

1. To establish banks or other corporations, implied from delegated powers to tax, borrow, and to regulate commerce.
2. To spend money for roads, schools, health, insurance, etc. implied from powers to establish post roads, to tax to provide for general welfare and defense, and to regulate commerce.
3. To create military academies, implied from powers to raise and support an armed force.
4. To locate and generate sources of power and sell surplus, implied from powers to dispose of government property, commerce, and war powers.
5. To assist and regulate agriculture, implied from power to tax and spend for general welfare and regulate commerce.

The Legal System

The Federal Court System - is provided for in the Constitution of the United States on the theory that the judicial power of the federal government could not be entrusted to the individual states, many of which had opposed the idea of a strong federal government in the first place. Thus Article III, Section 1, of the Constitution says: *"the judicial power of the United States shall be vested in one Supreme Court, and in such inferior courts as the Congress may from time to time ordain and establish"*. In accordance with these provisions, Congress passed the ***Judiciary Act*** in 1789, organizing the Supreme Court of the United States and establishing a system of federal courts of inferior jurisdiction. The states were left to establish their own judicial systems subject to the exclusive overall jurisdiction of the federal courts and to Article VI of the Constitution declaring the judges of the state courts to be bound to the Constitution and to the laws and treaties of the United States. Thus, developed in the United States a dual system of judicial power and authority.

The jurisdiction of the federal courts is further defined in Article III, Section 2 of the Constitution as extending in law and in equity to all cases arising under the Constitution and through federal legislation to controversies in which the United States is a party, including those arising from treaties with other governments, to maritime cases on the high seas in areas under American control, to disagreements between the states, between a citizen and a state, between citizens in different states and between a citizen and a foreign nation. The federal courts were also originally empowered with jurisdiction over problems airing between citizens of one state and the government of another state. The 11th amendment to the Constitution (ratified 1795) however removed from federal jurisdiction those cases in which citizens of one state were the plaintiffs and the government of another state was the defendant. The amendment, though, did not disturb the jurisdiction of the federal courts in cases in which a state government is a plaintiff and a citizen of another state the defendant. The federal courts also have exclusive jurisdiction in all patent and copyright cases and by congressional law in 1898, the federal courts were empowered with original jurisdiction in all bankruptcy cases.

The courts established under the powers granted by Article III Section 1 & 2 of the Constitution are known as Constitutional Courts. Judges of the Constitutional courts are appointed for life by the President with the approval of the Senate. These courts are the ***district courts, lower courts of original jurisdiction,*** **the *courts of appeals*** (before 1948, known as the circuit court of appeals), exercising appellate jurisdiction over the district courts and the ***Supreme Court***. A district court functions in each of the more than ninety federal judicial districts and in the District of Columbia.

A court of appeals functions in each of the ten federal judicial circuits and also in the District of Columbia, (The federal district court and the circuit court of appeals of the District of Columbia performs all of the same functions discharged in the states by the state courts). All of the lower federal courts operate under the uniform rules of procedure promulgated by the Supreme Court.

The Supreme Court of the United States is the highest appellate court in the country and is a court of original jurisdiction according to the Constitution *"in all cases affecting ambassadors, other public ministers and consuls, and those in which a state shall be a party".* By virtue of its' power to declare legislation unconstitutional (see Section 1.2 Marbury vs. Madison), the Supreme Court is also the final arbitrator of all Constitutional questions.

Other federal courts, established by Congress under powers to be implied in other articles of the Constitution, are called legislative courts. These courts are the **Court of Claims, the Court of Customs and Patent Appeals, the Customs Court,** and the territorial courts established in the federally administered territories of the United States.

The special jurisdictions of these courts are defined by the Congress of the United States. (Except in the case of the territorial courts, which are courts of general jurisdiction), the specialized functions of these courts are suggested by their titles.

The State Courts - Each State has an independent system of courts operating under the laws and constitution of that particular individual state. Broadly speaking, the state courts are based on the English judicial system as it existed in colonial times, but as modified by succeeding statues. The character and names of the various courts differ from state to state, but the state courts as a whole have general jurisdiction, except in cases in which exclusive jurisdiction has by law been vested in the federal courts. In cases involving the United States Constitution or federal laws or treaties and the such, the state courts are governed by the decisions of the Supreme Court of the United States and their decisions are subject to review by it.

Cases involving the federal Constitution, federal laws, or treaties and the like, may be brought to either the state courts, or the federal courts. Ordinary **civil suits** not involving any of the aforementioned elements, can be brought only to the state courts, except in cases of different state citizenship between the parties, in which case the suit may be brought to a federal court. By an act of Congress, however, suits involving different federal questions, or different state citizenship may be brought to a federal court only when it is a civil suit that involves $3,000 or more. All such cases that involve a smaller amount must be brought to a state court only. In accordance with a congressional law, a suit brought before a state court may be removed to a federal court at the option of the defendant.

Bearing in mind that any statements about state courts that is trying to give a typical explanation of all of them is subject to many exceptions. The following may be taken as a general comprehensive statement of their respective jurisdictions, functions, and organization.

County courts of general original jurisdiction exercise both criminal and civil jurisdictions in most states. A few states maintain separate courts of criminal and civil law inherited from the English judicial system. Between the lower courts and the supreme appellate courts of each state in a number of states, are intermediate appellate courts which, like the federal courts of appeals, provide faster justice for individuals by disposing of a large number of cases which would otherwise be added to the overcrowded calendars of the higher courts. Courts of last resort, the highest appellate courts for the states in criminal and civil cases are usually called **State Supreme Courts**.

The state court system also includes a number of minor, local courts with limited jurisdictions; these courts dispose of minor offenses and relatively small civil actions. Included in this classification are police and municipal courts in various cities and towns, and the courts presided over by justices of the peace in rural areas. Specifically, in regards to the state of Florida, they are **16 circuit courts**, Florida is also part of the **United States Fifth Judicial Circuit of the Federal Court system** and Florida also has two federal court districts at a lower level. The State Supreme Court is comprised of seven justices that are elected for six-year terms.

Vocabulary for American government.

Amendment - An amendment is a change or addition to the United States Constitution. Two-thirds of both houses of Congress must propose and then pass one. Or two-thirds of the state legislatures must call a convention to propose one and then it must be ratified by three-fourths of the state legislatures. To date there are only 26 amendments to the Constitution that have passed. An amendment may be used to cancel out a previous one such as the 18th Amendment (1919) known as Prohibition, being canceled by the 21st Amendment (1933).

Articles of Confederation - The first American document that attempted to unite the newly independent colonies after the Revolution. It proved to be unworkable. It was superseded by the Constitution in 1787.

Australian Ballot - A device originated in Australia for choosing candidates for public office. Distinct features include that it is prepared and handled by public officials, paid for with public funds, is secret, and uniform in color and composition. It was used in the United States before the introduction of voting machines in 1892.

Bill Of Rights - The first ten amendments to the United States Constitution dealing with civil liberties and civil rights. They were written mostly by James Madison. They are:

1. **Freedom of Religion.**
2. **Right To Bear Arms.**
3. **Security from the quartering of troops in homes.**
4. **Right against unreasonable search and seizures.**
5. **Right against self-incrimination.**
6. **Right to trial by jury, right to legal council.**
7. **Right to jury trial for civil actions.**
8. **No cruel or unusual punishment allowed.**
9. **These rights shall not deny other rights the people enjoy.**
10. **Powers not mentioned in the Constitution shall be retained by the states or the people.**

Checks and Balances - System set up by the Constitution in which each branch of the federal government has the power to check, or limit the actions of other branches.

Confederate States of America - The nation formed by the states that seceded from the federal Union around 1860 and 1861. It ceased to exist after its loss in the American Civil War in 1865.

Congress - In the United States it is the supreme legislative assembly. It is a bicameral body, (one that consists of two parts), the **House of Representatives** and the **Senate**.

Constitution - The written document that describes and defines the system and structure of the United States government. Ratification of the Constitution by the required number of states, (nine of the original thirteen), was completed on June 21, *1788,* and thus the Constitution officially became the law of the land.

Constitutional Convention - Meeting of delegates from 12 states who wrote a new constitution for the United States in 1787.

County - A unit of local government formerly known in Great Britain as "shire." All states now have county governments except for Louisiana, (which prefers the term "parish"), Alaska, and Connecticut.

Declaration Of Independence - The document that stated that the British colonies in America had become a free and independent nation, adopted July 4, 1776.

Democracy - A form of government in which the people rule. The word "democrat" comes from the ancient Greek "demo"-people and "kratia"-to rule.

Democracy (Direct) - A form of government in which the people assemble at a specific period and times to perform the functions usually delegated to a representative legislature. Sometimes the term "pure" democracy is used. It was prevalent in ancient Greece.

Democracy (Indirect) - A form of government in which the people rule through elected representatives in a legislature. Sometimes called a "**republican**" form of government, or "**democracy in republic**," the United States is this form of government.

Executive - A branch of the federal government. It consists of two office-holders, a President and a Vice-President, elected by indirect election for a period of four years. The President is responsible for carrying out the laws of Congress. The President may also propose new laws for Congressional consideration. (See: President and Vice-President)

Federal - It is the organization of the government of the United States. It consists of two parts that are the national government based in Washington DC and the various individual state governments.

House of Representatives - It is part of the bicameral legislature of the United States chosen by direct election based on population for a period of two years. An individual must be twenty-five years old and a citizen of the United States for seven years in order to be eligible to be elected.

Legislative - The law making branch of the government. In the United States, it is bicameral, consisting of the House of Representatives and the Senate.

Magna Carta - The document that guaranteed rights to English nobles, forced on the British King John in 1215. It is considered an important forerunner to the idea of government having a written limitation of its power.

Manifest Destiny - Belief of many Americans in the 1840s that the United States should own all the land between the Atlantic and Pacific oceans.

Monroe Doctrine - Policy statement made by President James Monroe in 1823 that warned the European powers that the United States considered the American continent and the western hemisphere as its special sphere of influence and that others should stay out of it.

Pocket Veto - When a President neither signs or "officially" has vetoed a bill. If within ten days, (not including Sundays), Congress adjourns the bill is killed. If Congress is in session, the bill will automatically become a law. (See: Veto)

Popular Sovereignty - In American history in the 19th century, right of territorial inhabitants applying for statehood to determine whether or not their state would or would not permit slavery.

President - The Chief Executive of the United States, responsible for carrying out the laws passed by Congress, Commander In Chief of the armed forces, elected by indirect election for a period of four years. One must have been born a citizen and thirty-five years old in order to be eligible to be elected. (See: Executive)

Primary Election - Election in which candidates from a particular political party are chosen to run for office. As a rule, usually, only registered party members are allowed to vote in such elections.

Representative Government - Type of government in which voters elect representatives to make laws for them. (See: indirect democracy)

Senate - Part of the bicameral legislature of the United States government, consisting of two members from each state (one hundred members at present) chosen by direct election for a period of six years. An individual must be thirty years old and a citizen of the United States for nine years in order to be eligible to be elected.

Separation of Powers - System of American government in which each branch of government has its own specifically designated powers and can not interfere with the powers of another.

States' Rights - Idea that the individual states had the right to limit the power of the federal government, that the states' authority should be supreme within it, as opposed to guidance from the federal government. An important contributing factor in the American Civil War.

Supreme Court - It is the highest court in the land and the court of final appeal. Only court of law specifically established by the Constitution.

Unitary Government - A form of government in which power is held by the central government which may or may not choose to delegate power to lesser governmental units. Examples are Great Britain, France and Israel. As opposed to *"Federal Government",* in which power is shared by national and state governments. (See: Federal)

Veto - To oppose a motion or enactment of a law from taking effect.

Vice-President - Assistant to the President, his immediate successor in case of disability or death. He also functions as the President of the Senate when it is in session. (See: Executive)

TEACHER CERTIFICATION STUDY GUIDE

Vocabulary for law studies.

Bail - Money left with the court in order for an individual to be released from jail pending trial. When an individual returns for trial the money is returned. If one flees the money is forfeited.

Civil - A lawsuit brought before a court usually to recover monetary funds as opposed to a criminal action brought for a penal offense.

Criminal - A penal crime, one that normally results in an imposition of a term of imprisonment, or of a monetary fine by the state or both.

Double Jeopardy - Subjecting an accused person to repeated trials for the same criminal offense. Forbidden by the Fifth Amendment to the Constitution.

Due Process - The right of a defendant to go through the established legal system before imprisonment i.e. trial, have legal counsel, verdict rendered in a court of law.

Equity - A branch of civil law that provides remedial justice when there is no remedy in common or prescribed law.

Grand Jury - As specified in the Constitution, it is a body of persons called to hear complaints of the commission of criminal offenses and to determine if enough evidence is available for a criminal indictment. It is normally composed of twelve to twenty-four individuals who hear the evidence and deliberate in private.

Habeas Corpus - The right to appear in court in order to determine if an imprisonment is lawful. Also known as a *"Writ of Habeas Corpus."*

Exclusionary Rule - As defined from the Fourth and Fifth Amendments, it is the inability of evidence seized unlawfully or statements gathered wrongly, to be brought into a court of law.

Ex Post Facto Law - A law created to punish an act after it has been committed. Prohibited by the Constitution, i.e. you can not prosecute someone for an act, if it was legal at the time, although a law was subsequently enacted against it.

Impeach - To bring charges against an official in the government such as the President. In the case of the President, the House of Representatives is the only branch of government empowered to bring such charges. They are then tried in the Senate.

Judicial Review - The right of the court to review laws and acts of the legislature and executive branches and to declare them unconstitutional. (Established in *"Marbury* vs. *Madison"* 1803).

MIDDLE LEVEL SOCIAL STUDIES

Judiciary - The legal system, including but not limited to, courts of law and appeal.

Judiciary Act - Law that organized the federal court system into Federal and Circuit Courts in 1789.

Jurisprudence - Of relating to, or pertaining to, the law or the legal system and its practice or exercise thereof.

Miranda Warning - As defined from the Fifth and Sixth Amendments. The right to remain silent so one does not incriminate oneself and the right to legal counsel during questioning.

Penal - Having to do with punishment, most often in regards to imprisonment and incarceration by the state.

Tort - A private or civil action brought before a court of law i.e. a civil lawsuit.

Vocabulary for international relations.

Balance of Trade - The difference between the value of goods a given nation exports and the value of goods it imports.

Boycott - The refusal to buy certain goods or services of one party from another based on a specific grievance.

Embargo - The ban on trade between one country and another based on a conflict that exists between them.

European Union - An economic and political organization of European countries that allows free trade among the member countries.

General Agreement On Tariffs and Trade (GATT) - The periodic international conference that meets to reduce trade barriers among member countries.

Group of Seven - Group of nations that meet to promote negotiations and coordinate economic relations and agreements among the member countries. The seven are: The *United States, Japan, Germany, Great Britain, France, Canada, and Italy*. (The "Group of Five" excludes Canada and Italy).

International - Having to do with more than one nation, relationships between nations.

International Law - System of legal statutes set up and agreed upon by several individual nations regulating conduct between them. The International Court of Law as established in the United Nations charter is located in The Hague, in The Netherlands.

International Monetary Fund - A multinational institution concerned mostly with world financial issues.

Nation - The modern establishment of a political community covering a set geographic area, population, and laws. Evolved from the primitive city-state of ancient times.

Nationalism - Strong pride in one's own country, sometimes taken to an extreme and in believing that one's own country is superior to all others, can be an important cause of war.

Parliamentary System - A system of government with a legislature, usually involving a multiplicity of political parties and often coalition politics. There is division between the head of state and head of government. Head of government is usually known as a Prime Minister who is also usually the head of the largest party. The head of government and cabinet usually both sit and vote in the parliament. Head of state is most often an elected president, (though in the case of a constitutional monarchy, like Great Britain, the sovereign may take the place of a president as head of state). A government may fall when a majority in parliament votes "no confidence" in the government.

Presidential System - A system of government with a legislature, can involve few or many political parties, no division between head of state and head of government. The President serves in both capacities. The President is elected either by direct or indirect election. A President and cabinet usually do not sit or vote in the legislature and The President may or may not be the head of the largest political party. A President can thus rule even without a majority in the legislature. He can only be removed from office before an election for major infractions of the law.

State - A political community covering a set geographic area, population and laws. Can be another name for nation.

Tariff - The tax that a government places on internationally traded goods, most often imported goods.

Treaty - A document between individual nation-states covering specific areas of agreement.

United Nations - International organization established in 1945 at the close of the Second World War. It replaced the defunct League of Nations. World headquarters is located in **New York City,** though various agencies are located in several different world cities, such as the World Court in The Hague, in The Netherlands.

World Bank - International institution set up to assist developing nations by helping them to secure low interest loans.

World Court - International body based in The Netherlands city of **The Hague** that was established by the original United Nations Charter. Set up to peacefully mediate disputes among the member nations and to investigate violations of agreed international law.

Skill 4.2 **Recognize the ideas and values contained in historical documents that influenced the development of the United States.**

The Magna Carta - This document is considered the basis of English constitution liberties. It was granted to a representative group of English barons and nobles on **June 15, 1215** by the British King John. The English barons and nobles sought to limit what they perceived as the overwhelming power of the Monarchy in public affairs. The Magna Carta is considered to be the first modern document which limited the powers of the state authority. It guaranteed feudal rights, regulated the justice system, and abolished many abuses of the King's power to tax and regulate trade The king could not raise new taxes without first consulting a Great Council, made up of nobles, barons, and the Church. Significantly the Magna Carta only dealt with the rights of the noble upper class and all of its provisions excluded rights of the common people. However, gradually the rights won by the nobles were given to other English citizens. The Great Council grew into a representative assembly called the Parliament. By the 1600s, Parliament was divided into the House of Lords, made up of nobles and the House of Commons. Members of the House of Commons were elected to office. In the beginning, only wealthy men could vote. Still English people firmly believed that the ruler must obey the law and consult Parliament on money matters. Thus, it did set a precedent that there was a limit to the allowed power of the state.

The Petition of Right - In English history, it was the title of a petition that was addressed to the King of England **Charles I,** by the British parliament in **1628**. The Parliament demanded that the king stop proclaiming new taxes without its' consent. Parliament demanded that Charles cease housing soldiers and sailors in the homes of private citizens, proclaiming martial law in times of peace, and that no subject should be imprisoned without a good cause being shown.

After some attempts to circumvent these demands, Charles finally agreed to them. They later had an important effect on the demands of the revolutionary colonists, as these were some of the rights that as Englishmen, they felt were being denied to colonists. The Petition of Right was also the basis of specific protections that the designers of the Constitution made a point of inserting in the document.

British Bill of Rights - Also known as the *Declaration of Rights*, it spelled out the rights that were considered to belong to Englishmen. It was granted by *King William III* in 1869. It had previously been passed by a convention of the Parliament and resulted from a struggle for power that took place in Great Britain, *The Glorious Revolution*. It was a revolution that was accomplished with virtually no bloodshed and led to King William III and Queen Mary II becoming joint sovereigns.

The Declaration itself was very similar in style to the later American Bill of Rights. It protected the rights of individuals and gave anyone accused of a crime the right to trial by jury. It outlawed cruel punishments; also, it stated that a ruler could not raise taxes or an army without the consent of Parliament. The colonists as Englishmen were protected by these provisions. The colonists considered abridgments of these rights that helped to contribute to the revolutionary spirit of the times.

These events and the principles are importance in understanding the process that eventually led to the ideals that are inherent in the Constitution of the United States. In addition, the fact is that f these ideals are universal in nature and have become the basis for human freedoms throughout the world.

Declaration of Independence - The Declaration of Independence was the founding document of the United States of America. The Declaration was intended to demonstrate the reasons that the colonies were seeking separation from Great Britain. Conceived by and written for the most part by Thomas Jefferson, it is not only important for what it says, but also for how it says it. The Declaration is in many respects a poetic document. Instead of a simple recitation of the colonists' grievances, it set out clearly the reasons why the colonists were seeking their freedom from Great Britain. They had tried all means to resolve the dispute peacefully. It was the right of a people, when all other methods of addressing their grievances have been tried and failed, to separate themselves from that power that was keeping them from fully expressing their rights to "**life, liberty, and the pursuit of happiness**".

The Declaration of independence is an outgrowth of both ancient Greek ideas of democracy and individual rights and the ideas of the European Enlightenment and the Renaissance, especially the ideology of the political thinker *John Locke*. Thomas Jefferson (1743-1826) the principle author of the Declaration borrowed much from Locke's theories and writings,

Essentially, Jefferson applied Locke's principles to the contemporary American situation. Jefferson argued that the currently reigning King George III had repeatedly violated the rights of the colonists as subjects of the British Crown.

Disdaining the colonial petition for redress of grievances (a right guaranteed by the Declaration of Rights of 1689), the King seemed bent upon establishing an "absolute tyranny" over the colonies. Such disgraceful behavior itself violated the reasons for which government had been instituted. The American colonists were left with no choice, *"it is their right, it is their duty, to throw off such a government, and to provide new guards for their future security"* so wrote Thomas Jefferson.

Yet, though his fundamental principles were derived from Locke's, Jefferson was bolder than his intellectual mentor was. He went farther in that his view of natural rights was much broader than Locke's and less tied to the idea of property rights.

For instance, though both Jefferson and Locke believed very strongly in property rights, especially as a guard for individual liberty, the famous line in the Declaration about people being endowed with the inalienable right to "life, liberty and the pursuit of happiness", was originally Locke's idea. It was "life, liberty, and *private property*". Jefferson didn't want to tie the idea of rights to any one particular circumstance however, thus, he changed Locke's original specific reliance on property and substituted the more general idea of human happiness as being a fundamental right that is the duty of a government to protect.
Locke and Jefferson both stressed that the individual citizen's rights are prior to and more important than any obligation to the state. Government is the servant of the people. The officials of government hold their positions at the sufferance of the people. Their job is to ensure that the rights of the people are preserved and protected by that government. The citizen come first, the government comes second. The Declaration thus produced turned out to be one of the most important and historic documents that expounded the inherent rights of all peoples; a document still looked up to as an ideal and an example.

Articles of Confederation - This was the first political system under which the newly independent colonies organized. It was drafted after the Declaration of Independence, in 1776, was passed by the Continental Congress on November 15, 1777, ratified by the thirteen states, and took effect on March 1, 1781.

The newly independent states were unwilling to give too much power to a national government. They were already fighting Great Britain. They did not want to replace one harsh ruler with another. After many debates, the form of the Articles was accepted. Each state agreed to send delegates to the Congress. Each state had one vote in the Congress. The Articles gave Congress the power to declare war, appoint military officers, and coin money. The Congress was also responsible for foreign affairs. The Articles of Confederation limited the powers of Congress by giving the states final authority. Although Congress could pass laws, at least nine of the thirteen states had to approve a law before it went into effect. Congress could not pass any laws regarding taxes. To get money, Congress had to ask each state for it, no state could be forced to pay.
Thus, the Articles created a loose alliance among the thirteen states. The national government was weak, in part, because it didn't have a strong chief executive to carry out laws passed by the legislature. This weak national government might have worked if the states were able to get along with each other. However, many different disputes arose and there was no way of settling them..

Within a few months from the adoption of the Articles of Confederation, it became apparent that there were serious defects in the system of government established for the new republic. There was a need for change that would create a national government with adequate powers to replace the Confederation, which was actually only a league of sovereign states. In 1786, an effort to regulate interstate commerce ended in what is known as the **Annapolis Convention**. Because only five states were represented, this Convention was not able to accomplish definitive results. The debates, however, made it clear that a government with as little authority could not regulate foreign and interstate commerce as the government established by the Confederation. Congress was, therefore, asked to call a convention to provide a constitution that would address the emerging needs of the new nation.

The convention met under the presidency of George Washington, with fifty-five of the sixty-five appointed members present. A constitution was written in four months. The Constitution of the United States is the fundamental law of the republic. It is a precise, formal, written document of the *extraordinary*, or *supreme*, type of constitution. The founders of the Union established it as the highest governmental authority. There is no national power superior to it. The foundations were so broadly laid as to provide for the expansion of national life and to make it an instrument which would last for all time. To maintain its stability, the framers created a difficult process for making any changes to it. No amendment can become valid until it is ratified by three fourths of all of the states. The British system of government was part of the basis of the final document. But significant changes were necessary to meet the needs of a partnership of states that were tied together as a single federation, yet sovereign in their own local affairs. This constitution established a system of government that was unique and advanced far beyond other systems of its day.

There were, to be sure, differences of opinion. The compromises that resolved these conflicts are reflected in the final document. The first point of disagreement and compromise was related to the Presidency. Some wanted a strong, centralized, individual authority. Others feared autocracy or the growth of monarchy. The compromise was to give the President broad powers but to limit the amount of time, through term of office, that any individual could exercise that power. The power to make appointments and to conclude treaties was controlled by the requirement of the consent of the Senate.

The second conflict was between large and small states. The large states wanted power proportionate to their voting strength; the small states opposed this plan. The compromise was that all states should have equal voting power in the Senate, but to make the membership of the House of Representatives determined in proportion to population.

The third conflict was about slavery. The compromise was that (a) fugitive slaves should be returned by states to which they might flee for refuge, and (b) that no law would be passed for 20 years prohibiting the importation of slaves.

The fourth major area of conflict was how the President would be chosen. One side of the disagreement argued for election by direct vote of the people. The other side thought Congress should choose the President. One group feared the ignorance of the people; the other feared the power of a small group of people. The Compromise was the **Electoral College**.

The constitution binds the states in a governmental unity in everything that affects the welfare of all. At the same time, it recognizes the right of the people of each state to independence of action in matters that relate only to them. Since the Federal Constitution is the law of the land, all other laws must conform to it.

The debates conducted during the Constitutional Congress represent the issues and the arguments that led to the compromises in the final document. The debates also reflect the concerns of the Founding Fathers that the rights of the people be protected from abrogation by the government itself and the determination that no branch of government should have enough power to continually dominate the others. There is, therefore, a system of checks and balances.

COMPETENCY 5.0 **UNDERSTAND THE CAUSES AND COURSE OF EUROPEAN EXPLORATION AND SETTLEMENT OF NORTH AMERICA, AND EXAMINE POLITICAL AND ECONOMIC RELATIONSHIPS WITHIN AND AMONG THE COLONIES**

Skill 5.1 Recognize major events related to the exploration and settlement of North America.

Columbus' first trans-Atlantic voyage was to prove his theory that Asia could be reached by sailing west.. Long after Spain dispatched explorers and her famed conquistadors to gather the wealth for the Spanish monarchs and their coffers, the British were searching valiantly for the "Northwest Passage," a land-sea route across North America and the eventual open sea to the wealth of Asia. It wasn't until after the Lewis and Clark Expedition when Captains Meriwether Lewis and William Clark proved conclusively that there simply was no Northwest Passage.

However, this did not deter exploration and settlement. **Spain, France, and England** along with some participation by the **Dutch** led the way with expanding Western European civilization in the New World. These three nations had strong monarchial governments and were struggling for dominance and power in Europe. With the defeat of Spain's mighty Armada in 1588, England became undisputed mistress of the seas. Spain lost its power and influence in Europe and it was left to France and England to carry on the rivalry, leading to eventual British control in Asia as well.

Spain's influence was in Florida, the Gulf Coast from Texas all the way west to California and south to the tip of South America and some of the islands of the West Indies. French control centered from New Orleans north to what is now northern Canada including the entire Mississippi Valley, the St. Lawrence Valley, the Great Lakes, and the land that was part of the Louisiana Territory. A few West Indies islands were also part of France's empire. England settled the eastern seaboard of North America, including parts of Canada and from Maine to Georgia. Some West Indies islands also came under British control. The Dutch had New Amsterdam for a period but later ceded it into British hands. One interesting aspect of this was each of these three nations, especially England, the land claims extended partly or all the way across the continent, regardless of the fact that the others claimed the same land. The wars for dominance and control of power and influence in Europe would undoubtedly and eventually extend to the Americas, especially North America.

The part of North America claimed by **France** was called New France and consisted of the land west of the Appalachian Mountains. This area of claims and settlement included the St. Lawrence Valley, the Great Lakes, the Mississippi Valley, and the entire region of land westward to the Rocky Mountains. They established the permanent settlements of Montreal and New Orleans, thus giving them control of the two major gateways into the heart of North America, the vast, rich interior. The St. Lawrence River, the Great Lakes, and the Mississippi River along with its tributaries made it possible for the French explorers and traders to roam at will, virtually unhindered in exploring, trapping, trading, and furthering the interests of France.

Most of the French settlements were in Canada along the St. Lawrence River. Only scattered forts and trading posts were found in the upper Mississippi Valley and Great Lakes region. The French rulers originally intended New France to have vast estates owned by nobles and worked by peasants who would live on the estates in compact farming villages--the New World version of the Old World's medieval system of feudalism. However, it didn't work out that way. Each of the nobles wanted his estate to be on the river for ease of transportation. The peasants working the estates wanted the prime waterfront location. The result of all this real estate squabbling was that New France's settled areas wound up mostly as a string of farmhouses stretching from Quebec to Montreal along the St. Lawrence and Richelieu Rivers.

In the non-settled areas in the interior were the French fur traders. They made friends with the friendly tribes of Indians, spending the winters with them getting the furs needed for trade. In the spring, they would return to Montreal in time to take advantage of trading their furs for the products brought by the cargo ships from France, which usually arrived at about the same time. Most of the wealth for New France and its "Mother Country" was from the fur trade, which provided a livelihood for many, many people. Manufacturers and workmen back in France, ship-owners and merchants, as well as the fur traders and their Indian allies all benefited. However, the freedom of roaming and trapping in the interior was a strong enticement for the younger, stronger men and resulted in the French not strengthening the areas settled along the St. Lawrence.

Into the 18th century, the rivalry with the British was growing more intense. New France was united under a single government and enjoyed the support of many Indian allies. The French traders were very diligent in not destroying the forests and driving away game upon which the Indians depended for life. It was difficult for the French to defend all of their settlements as they were scattered over half of the continent. However, by the early 1750s, in Western Europe, France was the most powerful nation. Its armies were superior to all others and its navy was giving the British stiff competition for control of the seas. The stage was set for confrontation in both Europe and America.

Spanish settlement had its beginnings in the Caribbean with the establishment of colonies on Hispaniola (at Santo Domingo which became the capital of the West Indies), Puerto Rico, and Cuba. There were a number of reasons for Spanish involvement in the Americas, to name just a few:

- the spirit of adventure
- the desire for land
- expansion of Spanish power, influence, and empire
- the desire for great wealth
- expansion of Roman Catholic influence and conversion of native peoples

The first permanent settlement in the United States was in 1565 at St. Augustine, Florida. A later permanent settlement in the southwestern United States was in 1609 at Santa Fe, New Mexico. At the peak of Spanish power, the area in the United States claimed, settled, and controlled by Spain included Florida and all land west of the Mississippi River--quite a piece of choice real estate. France and England also lay claim to the same areas. Nonetheless, ranches and missions were built and the Indians who came in contact with the Spaniards were introduced to animals, plants, and seeds from the Old World that they had never seen before. Animals brought in included: horses, cattle, donkeys, pigs, sheep, goats and poultry.

Spain's control over her New World colonies lasted more than 300 years, longer than England or France. To this day, Spanish influence remains in names of places, art, architecture, music, literature, law, and cuisine. The Spanish settlements in North America were not commercial enterprises but were for protection and defense of the trading and wealth from their colonies in Mexico and South America. The Russians hunting seals came down the Pacific coast, the English moved into Florida and west into and beyond the Appalachians, and the French traders and trappers were making their way from Louisiana and other parts of New France into Spanish territory. The Spanish never realized or understood that self-sustaining economic development and colonial trade was so important. Consequently, the Spanish settlements in the U.S. never really prospered.

Before 1763, when England was rapidly on the way to becoming the most powerful of the three major Western European powers, its thirteen colonies, located between the Atlantic and the Appalachians, physically occupied the least amount of land. Moreover, it is interesting that even before the Spanish Armada was defeated, two Englishmen, Sir Humphrey Gilbert and his half-brother Sir Walter Raleigh were unsuccessful in their attempts to build successful permanent colonies in the New World. Nonetheless, the thirteen English colonies were successful and, by the time they had gained their independence from Britain, were more than able to govern themselves. They had a rich historical heritage of law, tradition, and documents leading the way to constitutional government conducted according to laws and customs.

The settlers in the British colonies highly valued individual freedom, democratic government, and getting ahead through hard work.

The English colonies, with only a few exceptions, were considered commercial ventures to make a profit for the crown or the company or whoever financed its beginnings. One was strictly a philanthropic enterprise and three others were primarily for religious reasons but the other nine were started for economic reasons. Settlers in these unique colonies came for different reasons:

a) religious freedom
b) political freedom
c) economic prosperity
d) land ownership

The colonies were divided generally into the three regions of **New England, Middle Atlantic, and Southern**. The culture of each was distinct and affected attitudes, ideas towards politics, religion, and economic activities. The geography of each region also contributed to its unique characteristics.

The **New England colonies** consisted of Massachusetts, Rhode Island, Connecticut, and New Hampshire. Life in these colonies was centered on the towns. What farming was done was by each family on its own plot of land but a short summer growing season and limited amount of good soil gave rise to other economic activities such as manufacturing, fishing, shipbuilding, and trade. The vast majority of the settlers shared similar origins, coming from England and Scotland. Towns were carefully planned and laid out the same way. The form of government was the town meeting where all adult males met to make the laws. The legislative body, the General Court, consisted of an Upper and Lower House.

The **Middle or Middle Atlantic colonies** included New York, New Jersey, Pennsylvania, Delaware, and Maryland. New York and New Jersey were at one time the Dutch colony of New Netherlands and Delaware at one time was New Sweden. These five colonies, from their beginnings were considered "melting pots" with settlers from many different nations and backgrounds. The main economic activity was farming with the settlers scattered over the countryside cultivating rather large farms. The Indians were not as much of a threat as in New England so they did not have to settle in small farming villages. The soil was very fertile, the land was gently rolling, and a milder climate provided a longer growing season.

These farms produced a large surplus of food, not only for the colonists themselves but also for sale. This colonial region became known as the "breadbasket" of the New World and the New York and Philadelphia seaports were constantly filled with ships being loaded with meat, flour, and other foodstuffs for the West Indies and England.

There were other economic activities such as shipbuilding, iron mines, and factories producing paper, glass, and textiles. The legislative body in Pennsylvania was unicameral or consisted of one house. In the other four colonies, the legislative body had two houses. Also units of local government were in counties and towns.

The **Southern colonies** were Virginia, North and South Carolina, and Georgia. Virginia was the first permanent successful English colony and Georgia was the last. The year 1619 was a very important year in the history of Virginia and the United States with three very significant events. First, sixty women were sent to Virginia to marry and establish families, Second, twenty Africans, the first of thousands, arrived, Third, most importantly, the Virginia colonists were granted the right to self-government and they began by electing their own representatives to the House of Burgesses, their own legislative body.

The major economic activity in this region was farming. Here the soil was very fertile and the climate was very mild with an even longer growing season. The large plantations eventually requiring large numbers of slaves were found in the coastal or tidewater areas. Although the wealthy slave-owning planters set the pattern of life in this region, most of the people lived inland away from coastal areas. They were small farmers and very few, it any, owned slaves.

The settlers in these four colonies came from diverse backgrounds and cultures. Virginia was colonized mostly by people from England while Georgia was started as a haven for debtors from English prisons. Pioneers from Virginia settled in North Carolina while South Carolina welcomed people from England and Scotland, French Protestants, Germans, and emigrants from islands in the West Indies. Products from farms and plantations included rice, tobacco, indigo, cotton, some corn and wheat. Other economic activities included lumber and naval stores (tar, pitch, rosin, and turpentine) from the pine forests and fur trade on the frontier. Cities such as Savannah and Charleston were important seaports and trading centers.

In the colonies, the daily life of the colonists differed greatly between the coastal settlements and the inland or interior. The Southern planters and the people living in the coastal cities and towns had a way of life similar to that in towns in England. The influence was seen and heard in how people dressed and talked. The architectural styles of houses and public buildings, and the social divisions or levels of society mimicked that of England. Both the planters and city dwellers enjoyed an active social life and had strong emotional ties to England.

On the other hand, life inland on the frontier had marked differences. All facets of daily living--clothing, food, housing, economic and social activities--were all connected to what was needed to sustain life and survive in the wilderness. Everything was produced practically themselves. They were self-sufficient and extremely individualistic and independent.

There were little, if any, levels of society or class distinctions as they considered themselves to be the equal to all others, regardless of station in life. The roots of equality, independence, individual rights and freedoms were strong and well developed. People were not judged by their fancy dress, expensive house, eloquent language, or titles following their names.

The colonies had from 1607 to 1763 to develop, refine, practice, experiment, and experience life in a rugged, uncivilized land. The Mother Country had virtually left them on their own to take care of their selves all that time. When in 1763, Britain decided she needed to regulate and "mother" the "little ones," to her surprise she had a losing fight on her hands.

By the 1750s in Europe, Spain was "out of the picture," no longer the most powerful nation and not even a contender. The remaining rivalry was between Britain and France. For nearly 25 years, between 1689 and 1748, a series of "armed conflicts" involving these two powers had been taking place. These conflicts had spilled over into North America. The War of the League of Augsburg in Europe, 1689 to 1697, had been King William's War. The War of the Spanish Succession, 1702 to 1713, had been Queen Anne's War. The War of the Austrian Succession, 1740 to 1748, was called King George's War in the colonies. The two nations fought for possession of colonies, especially in Asia and North America, and for control of the seas, but none of these conflicts was decisive.

The final conflict, which decided once and for all who was the most powerful, began in North America in 1754, in the Ohio River Valley. It was known in America as the **French and Indian War** and in Europe as the Seven Years' War, since it began there in 1756. In America, both sides had advantages and disadvantages. The British colonies were well established and consolidated in a smaller area. British colonists outnumbered French colonists 23 to 1. Except for a small area in Canada, French settlements were scattered over a much larger area (roughly half of the continent) and were smaller. However, the French settlements were united under one government and were quick to act and cooperate when necessary. In addition, the French had many more Indian allies than the British. The British colonies had separate, individual governments and very seldom cooperated, even when needed. In Europe, at that time, France was the more powerful of the two nations.

The French depended on the St. Lawrence River for transporting supplies, soldiers, and messages-the link between New France and the Mother Country. Tied into this waterway system were the connecting links of the Great Lakes, Mississippi River and its tributaries along which were scattered French forts, trading posts, and small settlements.

In 1758, the British captured Louisburg on Cape Breton Island, New France was doomed. Louisburg gave the British navy a base of operations preventing French reinforcements and supplies getting to their troops. Other forts fell to the British: Frontenac, Duquesne, Crown Point, Ticonderoga, Niagara, those in the upper Ohio Valley, and, most importantly, Quebec and finally Montreal. Spain entered the war in 1762 to aid France but it was too late. British victories occurred all around the world: in India, in the Mediterranean, and in Europe.

In 1763 in Paris, Spain, France, and Britain met to draw up the Treaty of Paris. Great Britain got most of India and all of North America east of the Mississippi River, except for New Orleans. Britain received from Spain control of Florida and returned to Spain Cuba and the islands of the Philippines, taken during the war. France lost nearly all of its possessions in America. India and was allowed to keep four islands: Guadeloupe, Martinique, Haiti on Hispaniola, and Miquelon and St. Pierre. France gave Spain New Orleans and the vast territory of Louisiana, west of the Mississippi River. Britain was now the most powerful nation.

Where did all of this leave the British colonies? Their colonial militias had fought with the British and they too benefited. The militias and their officers gained much experience in fighting which was very valuable later. The thirteen colonies began to realize that cooperating with each other was the only way to defend themselves. They didn't really understand that until the war for independence and setting up a national government, but a start had been made. At the start of the war in 1754, Benjamin Franklin proposed to the thirteen colonies that they unite permanently to be able to defend themselves. This was after the French and their Indian allies had defeated Major George Washington and his militia at **Fort Necessity**. This left the entire northern frontier of the British colonies vulnerable and open to attack.

Delegates from seven of the thirteen colonies met at Albany, New York, along with the representatives from the **Iroquois Confederation** and British officials. Franklin's proposal, known as the Albany Plan of Union, was totally rejected by the colonists, along with a similar proposal from the British. They simply did not want each of the colonies to lose its right to act independently. However, the seed was planted.

Skill 5.2   Analyze the sources of coexistence and conflict between Europeans and American Indians.

Colonists from England, France, Holland, Sweden, and Spain all settled in North America, on lands once frequented by Native Americans. Spanish colonies were mainly in the south, French colonies were mainly in the extreme north and in the middle of the continent, and the rest of the European colonies were in the northeast and along the Atlantic coast. These colonists got along with their new neighbors with varying degrees of success.

The French colonists seemed the most willing to work with the Native Americans. Even though their pursuit of animals to fill the growing demand for the fur trade was overpowering, they managed to find a way to keep their new neighbors happy. The French and Native Americans even fought on the same side of the war against England.

The Dutch and Swedish colonists were interested mainly in surviving in their new homes. They didn't last long in their struggles against England, however.

The English and Spanish colonists had the worst relations with the Native Americans, mainly because the Europeans made a habit of taking land, signing and then breaking treaties, massacring, and otherwise abusing their new neighbors. The Native Americans were only too happy to share their agriculture and jewel-making secrets with the Europeans; what they got in return was grief and deceit. The term "Manifest Destiny" meant nothing to the Native Americans, who believed that they lived on land granted access to them by the gods above.

Skill 5.3   Examine political and economic relations between the colonies and Europe.

The New England colonies were primarily settled by English colonists but other nations had a presence in the New World as well and the colonies remained connected to the political and economic developments in Europe.

The Dutch West India Company founded a colony in what is now New York, establishing it as New Holland. It was eventually captured by English settlers and named New York, but many of the Dutch families that had been granted large segments of land by the Dutch government were allowed to keep their estates. As hostility built between England and the colonies over the taxation of tea, colonists turned to the Dutch to supply them with this important import.

To the north of the Anglo-American colonies, the French were establishing a significant presence in what is now eastern Canada. Spain was advancing in its colonization of parts of the Caribbean, where much of the early slave trade originated.

MIDDLE LEVEL SOCIAL STUDIES

The American colonies found themselves swept into international political affairs whenever the homeland, Britain, found itself in conflict with Europe. England and France were historic rivals who found themselves with a new common border in the New World. A dispute over control of the Ohio River between French and British colonies was one of the primary causes leading into the Seven Years' War among many of the European powers.

Anglo-American colonists, still considering themselves British subjects, fought valiantly against the French and their Indian allies. George Washington emerged as an effective military leader during this conflict.

Later, the animosity between the English and French would work to the advantage of the revolutionary colonists, who received aid from France in their struggle against England. Holland, with its long connection to the American colonies, was the second nation after France to recognize their independence. Spain, while not officially recognizing the independence of the colonies, joined the Revolutionary War on the side of the colonists owing to a disagreement with Britain over possession of Gibraltar.

From the earliest times, the fortunes of the colonists were caught up in international affairs, and relied on their political and economic connections with Europe to advance and gain eventual independence.

The war for independence occurred due to a number of changes, the two most important ones being economic and political. By the end of the French and Indian War in 1763, Britain's American colonies were thirteen out of a total of thirty-three scattered around the earth. Like all other countries, Britain desired a strong economy and a favorable balance of trade. To have that delicate balance a nation needs wealth, self-sufficiency, and a powerful army and navy. This is why the overseas colonies developed. The colonies would provide raw materials for the industries in the Mother Country, be a market for finished products by buying them and assist the Mother Country in becoming powerful and strong. Great Britain believed having a strong merchant fleet which provided a school for training for the Royal Navy and bases of operation for the Royal Navy was important.

Between 1607 and 1763, for various reasons, the British Parliament enacted laws to assist the government in achieving a trade balance.

One series of laws required that most of the manufacturing be done only in England, such as: prohibition of exporting any wool or woolen cloth from the colonies, no manufacture of beaver hats or iron products. The colonists weren't concerned as they had no money and no highly skilled labor to set up any industries, anyway.

The **Navigation Acts of 1651** put restrictions on shipping and trade within the British Empire by requiring that it was allowed only on British ships. This increased the strength of the British merchant fleet and greatly benefited the American colonists. Since they were British citizens, they could have their own vessels, building and operating them as well. By the end of the war in 1763, the shipyards in the colonies were building one third of the merchant ships under the British flag. There were quite a number of wealthy, American, colonial merchants.

The **Navigation Act of 1660** restricted the shipment and sale of colonial products to England only. In 1663 another Navigation Act stipulated that the colonies had to buy manufactured products only from England and that any European goods going to the colonies had to go to England first. These acts were a protection from enemy ships and pirates and from competition from European rivals.

The New England and Middle Atlantic colonies at first felt threatened by these laws as they had started producing many of the products already being produced in Britain. But they soon found new markets for their goods and began what was known as a **"triangular trade**." Colonial vessels started the first part of the triangle by sailing for Africa loaded with kegs of rum from colonial distilleries. On Africa's West Coast, the rum was traded for either gold or slaves. The second part of the triangle was from Africa to the West Indies where slaves were traded for molasses, sugar, or money. The third part of the triangle was home, bringing sugar or molasses (to make more rum), gold, and silver.

The major concern of the British government was that the trade violated the 1733 Molasses Act. Planters had wanted the colonists to buy all of their molasses in the British West Indies but these islands could give the traders only about one eighth of the amount of molasses needed for distilling the rum. The colonists were forced to buy the rest of what they needed from the French, Dutch, and Spanish islands, thus evading the law by not paying the high duty on the molasses bought from these islands. If Britain had enforced the Molasses Act, economic and financial chaos and ruin would have occurred. Nevertheless, for this act and all the other mercantile laws, the government followed the policy of "salutary neglect," deliberately failing to enforce the laws.

In 1763, after the war, money was needed to pay the British war debt, for the defense of the empire, and to pay for the governing of 33 colonies scattered around the earth. It was decided to adopt a new colonial policy and pass laws to raise revenue.

The reasoning was that the colonists were subjects of the king and since the king and his ministers had spent a great deal of money defending and protecting them, especially for the American colonists, it was only right and fair that the colonists should help pay the costs of their defense. The earlier laws passed had been for the purposes of regulating production and trade which generally put money into colonial pockets. These new laws would take some of that rather hard-earned money out of their pockets and it would be done, in colonial eyes, unjustly and illegally.

Skill 5.4 **Analyze geographic, ethnic, religious, political, and economic differences within and among England's North American colonies.**

The colonies were divided generally into the three regions of New England, Middle Atlantic, and Southern. The culture of each was distinct and affected attitudes, ideas towards politics, religion, and economic activities. The geography of each region also contributed to its unique characteristics.

The **New England** colonies consisted of Massachusetts, Rhode Island, Connecticut, and New Hampshire. Life in these colonies was centered on the towns. Each family farmed its own plot of land but a short summer growing season and limited amount of good soil gave rise to other economic activities such as manufacturing, fishing, shipbuilding, and trade. The vast majority of the settlers shared similar origins, coming from England and Scotland. Towns were carefully planned and laid out the same way. The form of government was the town meeting where all adult males met to make the laws. The legislative body, the General Court, consisted of an upper and lower house.

The **Middle or Middle Atlantic** colonies included New York, New Jersey, Pennsylvania, Delaware, and Maryland. New York and New Jersey were at one time the Dutch colony of New Netherland and Delaware at one time was New Sweden. These five colonies, from their beginnings were considered "melting pots" with settlers from many different nations and backgrounds. The main economic activity was farming with the settlers scattered over the countryside cultivating rather large farms. The Indians were not as much of a threat as in New England so they did not have to settle in small farming villages. The soil was very fertile, the land was gently rolling, and a milder climate provided a longer growing season. These farms produced a large surplus of food, not only for the colonists themselves but also for sale. This colonial region became known as the "breadbasket" of the New World and the New York and Philadelphia seaports were constantly filled with ships being loaded with meat, flour, and other foodstuffs for the West Indies and England.

There were other economic activities such as shipbuilding, iron mines, and factories producing paper, glass, and textiles. The legislative body in Pennsylvania was unicameral or consisted of one house. In the other four colonies, the legislative body had two houses. Also units of local government were in counties and towns.

The **Southern** colonies were Virginia, North and South Carolina, and Georgia. Virginia was the first permanent successful English colony and Georgia was the last. The year 1619 was a very important year in the history of Virginia and the United States with three very significant events. First, sixty women were sent to Virginia to marry and establish families; second, twenty Africans, the first of thousands, arrived; and third, most importantly, the Virginia colonists were granted the right to self-government and they began by electing their own representatives to the House of Burgesses, their own legislative body.
The major economic activity in this region was farming. Here too the soil was very fertile and the climate was very mild with an even longer growing season. The large plantations eventually requiring large numbers of slaves were found in the coastal or tidewater areas. Although the wealthy slave-owning planters set the pattern of life in this region, most of the people lived inland away from coastal areas. They were small farmers and very few, it any, owned slaves.

The settlers in these four colonies came from diverse backgrounds and cultures. Virginia was colonized mostly by people from England while Georgia was started as a haven for debtors from English prisons. Pioneers from Virginia settled in North Carolina while South Carolina welcomed people from England and Scotland, French Protestants, Germans, and emigrants from islands in the West Indies. Products from farms and plantations included rice, tobacco, indigo, cotton, some corn and wheat. Other economic activities included lumber and naval stores (tar, pitch, rosin, and turpentine) from the pine forests and fur trade on the frontier. Cities such as Savannah and Charleston were important seaports and trading centers.

In the colonies, the daily life of the colonists differed greatly between the coastal settlements and the inland or interior. The Southern planters and the people living in the coastal cities and towns had a way of life similar to that in towns in England. The influence was seen and heard in the way people dressed and talked; the architectural styles of houses and public buildings; and the social divisions or levels of society. Both the planters and city dwellers enjoyed an active social life and had strong emotional ties to England.

On the other hand, life inland on the frontier had marked differences. All facets of daily living--clothing, food, home, economic and social activities--were all connected to what was needed to sustain life and survive in the wilderness. Everything was produced practically themselves. They were self-sufficient and extremely individualistic and independent. There were little, if any, levels of society or class distinctions as they considered themselves to be the equal to all others, regardless of station in life. The roots of equality, independence, individual rights and freedoms were extremely strong and well developed. People were not judged by their fancy dress, expensive house, eloquent language, or titles following their names.

COMPETENCY 6.0   **UNDERSTAND THE PRINCIPAL CAUSES AND EVENTS OF THE REVOLUTIONARY WAR AND THE MAJOR POLITICAL, CONSTITUTIONAL, AND ECONOMIC DEVELOPMENTS RELATED TO THE CREATION OF THE FEDERAL GOVERNMENT AND THE ESTABLISHMENT OF U.S. SOCIETY**

Skill 6.1   **Examine the social, political, and economic origins of the movement for American independence.**

Causes for the War for Independence

- With the end of the French and Indian War (The Seven Years' War), England decided to reassert control over the colonies in America. They particularly needed the revenue from the control of trade to pay for the recent war and to defend the new territory obtained as a result of the war.
- English leaders decided to impose a tax that would pay for the military defense of the American lands. The colonists rejected this idea for two reasons: (1) they were undergoing an economic recession, and (2) they believed it unjust to be taxed unless they had representation in the Parliament.
- England passed a series of laws that provoked fierce opposition:
    - The Proclamation Act prohibited English settlement beyond the Appalachian Mountains to appease the Native Americans.
    - The Sugar Act imposed a tax on foreign molasses, sugar, and other goods imported into the colonies.
    - The Currency Act prohibited colonial governments from issuing paper money.

Opposition melded in Massachusetts. Leaders denounced "taxation without representation" and a boycott was organized against imported English goods. The movement spread to other colonies rapidly.

The Stamp Act placed a tax on newspapers, legal documents, licenses, almanacs and playing cards. This was the first instance of an "internal" tax on the colonies. In response the colonists formed secret groups called "the Sons of Liberty" and staged riots against the agents collecting the taxes and marking items with a special stamp. In October of 1765, representatives of nine colonies met in the Stamp Act Congress. They drafted resolutions stating their reasons for opposing the Act and sent them to England. Merchants throughout the colonies applied pressure with a large boycott of imported English goods. The Stamp Act was repealed three months later.

England then had a dual concern: to generate revenue and to regain control of the colonists. They passed the Townshend Acts in 1767. These acts placed taxes on lead, glass, paint, paper and tea. This led to another very successful boycott of English goods. England responded by limiting the tax to tea. This ended the boycotts of everything except tea.

The situation in the colonies between colonists and British troops was becoming increasingly strained. Despite a skirmish in New York and the "Boston Massacre" in 1770, tensions abated over the next few years.

The Tea Act of 1773 gave the British East India Company a monopoly on sales of tea. The colonists responded with the "Boston Tea Party. England responded with the "Coercive Acts (called the "Intolerable Acts" by the colonists) in 1774. This closed the port of Boston, changed the charter of the Massachusetts colony, and suppressed town meetings. Eleven colonies sent delegates to the first Continental Congress in 1774. The group issued the "Declaration of Rights and Grievances" which vowed allegiance to the king but protested the right of Parliament to tax the colonies. The boycotts resumed at the same time.

Massachusetts mobilized its colonial militia in anticipation of difficulties with England. The British troops attempted to seize their weapons and ammunition. The result was two clashes with "minute men" at Lexington and Concord. The Second Continental Congress met a month later. Many of the delegates recommended a declaration of independence from Britain. The group established an army and commissioned George Washington as its commander.

British forces attacked patriot strongholds at Breed's Hill and Bunker Hill. Although the colonists withdrew, the loss of life for the British was nearly fifty percent of the army. The next month King George III declared the American colonies to be in a state of rebellion. The war quickly began in earnest. On July 3, 1776, British General Howe arrived in New York harbor with 10,000 troops to prepare for an attack on the city. The following day, the Second Continental Congress accepted the final draft of the Declaration of Independence by unanimous vote.

Although the colonial army was quite small in comparison to the British army, and although it was lacking in formal military training, the colonists had learned a new method of warfare from the Indians. To be sure, many battles were fought in the traditional style of two lines of soldiers facing off and firing weapons. But the advantage the patriots had was the understanding of guerilla warfare – fighting from behind trees and other defenses.

When the war began, the colonies began to establish state governments. To a significant extent, the government that was defined for the new nation was intentionally weak. The colonies/states feared centralized government. But the lack of continuity between the individual governments was confusing and economically damaging. The Constitutional Convention in 1787 devised an entirely new form of government and outlined it in the Constitution of the United States. The Constitution was ratified quickly and took effect in 1789. Concerns that had been raised in or by the states regarding civil liberties and states rights led to the immediate adoption of twelve amendments to the Constitution, the first ten known as the Bill of Rights.

Skill 6.2   Recognize the influence of Revolutionary era ideas on later social and political developments in the United States.

The American nation was founded with the idea that the people would have a large degree of **autonomy** and **liberty**. The famous maxim "no taxation without representation" was a rallying cry for the Revolution, not only because the people didn't want to suffer the series of taxes imposed on them by the British Parliament, but also because the people could not in any way influence the lawmakers in Parliament in regard to those taxes. No American colonist had a seat in Parliament, and no American colonist could vote for members of Parliament.

The American people had become used to doing things their own way and solving their own problems, especially during the French and Indian War, during which a large number of soldiers who served and died for the British Army called America home. They had been given the opportunity to choose some of the people who governed them; but the big prizes, the governors of colonies and, of course, the members of Parliament were still out of reach. When the French and Indian War ended, the British Government attempted to levy heavy taxes on the American colonists, since the war had taken place in their own back yard. Not only were these taxes an infringement on the autonomy that the American colonists had become accustomed to, they were also a measure of just how little liberty those people had when it came to things like taxation and representation.

One of the most famous words in the Declaration of Independence is "liberty," which all people should be free to pursue. That idea, that a people should be free to pursue their own course, even to the extent of making their own mistakes, has dominated political thought in the 200-plus years of the American republic. **Representation**, the idea that a people can vote—or even replace—their lawmakers was not a new idea, except in America. Residents of other British colonies did not have these rights, of course, and America was only a colony, according to the conventional wisdom of the British Government at the time. What the Sons of Liberty and other revolutionaries were asking for was to stand on an equal footing with the Mother Country.

Along with the idea of representation comes the idea that key ideas and concepts can be deliberated and discussed, with theoretically everyone having a chance to voice their views. This applied to both lawmakers and the people who elected them. Lawmakers wouldn't just pass bills that became laws; rather, they would debate the particulars and go back and forth on the strengths and weaknesses of proposed laws before voting on them. Members of both houses of Congress had the opportunity to speak out on the issues, as did the people at large, who could contact their lawmakers and express their views. This idea ran very much counter to the experience that the Founding Fathers had before the Revolution—that of taxation without representation.

Another key concept in the American ideal is equality, the idea that every person has the same rights and responsibilities under the law. The Great Britain that the American colonists knew was one of a stratified society, with social classes firmly in place. Not everyone was equal under the law or in the coffers; and it was clear for all to see that the more money and power a person had, the easier it was for that person to avoid things like serving in the army and being charged with a crime. The goal of the Declaration of Independence and the Constitution was to provide equality for all who read those documents. The reality, though, was vastly different for large sectors of society, including women and non-white Americans.

This feeds into the idea of basic opportunity. The "American Dream" is the belief that every individual has an equal change to make his or her fortune and the United States will welcome and encourage that initiative. The history of the country is filled with stories of people who ventured to America and made their fortunes in the Land of Opportunity. Unfortunately for anyone who wasn't a white male, that basic opportunity was sometimes difficult to achieve.

Skill 6.3 Assess the strengths and weaknesses of the Articles of Confederation, and analyze the debates surrounding the creation and ratification of the Constitution.

Articles of Confederation - This was the first political system under which the newly independent colonies tried to organize themselves. It was drafted after the Declaration of Independence in 1776, was passed by the Continental Congress on November 15, 1777, ratified by the thirteen states, and took effect on March 1, 1781.

The newly independent states were unwilling to give too much power to a national government. They were already fighting Great Britain. They did not want to replace one harsh ruler with another. After many debates, the form of the Articles was accepted. Each state agreed to send delegates to the Congress. Each state had one vote in the Congress. The Articles gave Congress the power to declare war, appoint military officers, and coin money.

The Congress was also responsible for foreign affairs. The Articles of Confederation limited the powers of Congress by giving the states final authority. Although Congress could pass laws, at least nine of the thirteen states had to approve a law before it went into effect. Congress could not pass any laws regarding taxes. To get money, Congress had to ask each state for it, no state could be forced to pay.

Thus, the Articles created a loose alliance among the thirteen states. The national government was weak, in part, because it didn't have a strong chief executive to carry out laws passed by the legislature. This weak national government might have worked if the states were able to get along with each other. However, many different disputes arose and there was no way of settling them. Thus, the delegates went to meet again to try to fix the Articles; instead they ended up scrapping them and created a new Constitution that learned from these earlier mistakes.

The central government of the new United States of America consisted of a Congress of two to seven delegates from each state with each state having just one vote. The government under the Articles solved some of the postwar problems but had serious weaknesses. Some of its powers included: borrowing and coining money, directing foreign affairs, declaring war and making peace, building and equipping a navy, regulating weights and measures, asking the states to supply men and money for an army. The delegates to Congress had no real authority as each state carefully and jealously guarded its own interests and limited powers under the Articles. Also, the delegates to Congress were paid by their states and had to vote as directed by their state legislatures. The serious weaknesses were the lack of power: to regulate finances, over interstate trade, over foreign trade, to enforce treaties, and military power. Something better and more efficient was needed.

In May of 1787, delegates from all states except Rhode Island began meeting in Philadelphia. At first, they met to revise the Articles of Confederation as instructed by Congress; but they soon realized that much more was needed. Abandoning the instructions, they set out to write a new Constitution, a new document, the foundation of all government in the United States and a model for representative government throughout the world.

The first order of business was the agreement among all the delegates that the convention would be kept secret. No discussion of the convention outside of the meeting room would be allowed. They wanted to be able to discuss, argue, and agree among themselves before presenting the completed document to the American people.

The delegates were afraid that if the people were aware of what was taking place before it was completed the entire country would be plunged into argument and dissension. It would be extremely difficult, if not impossible, to settle differences and come to an agreement. Between the official notes kept and the complete notes of future President James Madison, an accurate picture of the events of the Convention is part of the historical record.

The delegates went to Philadelphia representing different areas and different interests. They all agreed on a strong central government but not one with unlimited powers. They also agreed that no one part of government could control the rest. It would be a republican form of government (sometimes referred to as representative democracy) in which the supreme power was in the hands of the voters who would elect the men who would govern for them.

One of the first serious controversies involved the small states versus the large states over representation in Congress. Virginia's Governor Edmund Randolph proposed that state population determine the number of representatives sent to Congress, also known as the Virginia Plan. New Jersey delegate William Paterson countered with what is known as the New Jersey Plan, each state having equal representation.

After much argument and debate, the Great Compromise was devised, known also as the Connecticut Compromise, as proposed by Roger Sherman. It was agreed that Congress would have two houses. The Senate would have two Senators, giving equal powers in the Senate. The House of Representatives would have its members elected based on each state's population. Both houses could draft bills to debate and vote on with the exception of bills pertaining to money, which must originate in the House of Representatives.

Another controversy involved economic differences between North and South. One concerned the counting of the African slaves for determining representation in the House of Representatives. The southern delegates wanted this but didn't want it to determine taxes to be paid. The northern delegates argued the opposite: count the slaves for taxes but not for representation. The resulting agreement was known as the "three-fifths" compromise. Three-fifths of the slaves would be counted for both taxes and determining representation in the House.

The last major compromise, also between North and South, was the Commerce Compromise. The economic interests of the northern part of the country were ones of industry and business whereas the south's economic interests were primarily in farming. The Northern merchants wanted the government to regulate and control commerce with foreign nations and with the states. Of course, Southern planters opposed this idea as they felt that any tariff laws passed would be unfavorable to them. The acceptable compromise to this dispute was that Congress was given the power to regulate commerce with other nations and the states, including levying tariffs on imports. However, Congress did not have the power to levy tariffs on any exports. This increased Southern concern about the effect it would have on the slave trade. The delegates finally agreed that the importation of slaves would continue for 20 more years with no interference from Congress. Any import tax could not exceed 10 dollars per person. After 1808, Congress would be able to decide whether to prohibit or regulate any further importation of slaves.

Of course, when work was completed and the document was presented, nine states needed to approve for it to go into effect. There was no little amount of discussion, arguing, debating, and haranguing. The opposition had three major objections:

1) The states seemed as if they were being asked to surrender too much power to the national government.
2) The voters did not have enough control and influence over the men who would be elected by them to run the government.
3) A lack of a "bill of rights" guaranteeing hard-won individual freedoms and liberties.

Eleven states finally ratified the document and the new national government went into effect. It was no small feat that the delegates were able to produce a workable document that satisfied all opinions, feelings, and viewpoints. The separation of powers of the three branches of government and the built-in system of checks and balances to keep power balanced were a stroke of genius. It provided for the individuals and the states as well as an organized central authority to keep a new inexperienced young nation on track. They created a system of government so flexible that it had continued in its basic form to this day. In 1789, the Electoral College unanimously elected George Washington as the first President and the new nation was on its way.

They created a government that as Benjamin Franklin said, *"though it may not be the best there is";* he said that he, *"wasn't sure that it could be possible to create one better".* A fact that might be true considering that the Constitution has lasted, through civil war, foreign wars, depression, and social revolution for over 200 years.

It is truly a living document because of its ability to remain strong while allowing itself to be changed with changing times.

Ratification of the U.S. Constitution was by no means a foregone conclusion. The representative government had powerful enemies, especially those who had seen firsthand the failure of the Articles of Confederation. The strong central government had powerful enemies, including some of the guiding lights of the American Revolution.

Those who wanted to see a strong central government were called Federalists, because they wanted to see a federal government reign supreme. Among the leaders of the Federalists were Alexander Hamilton and John Jay. These two, along with James Madison, wrote a series of letters to New York newspapers, urging that that state ratify the Constitution. These became known as the **Federalist Papers**.

In the Anti-Federalist camp were Thomas Jefferson and Patrick Henry. These men and many others like them were worried that a strong national government would descend into the kind of tyranny that they had just worked so hard to abolish. In the same way that they took their name from their foes, they wrote a series of arguments against the Constitution called the **Anti-Federalist Papers.**

In the end, both sides got most of what they wanted. The Federalists got their strong national government, which was held in place by the famous "checks and balances." The Anti-Federalists got the Bill of Rights, the first ten Amendments to the Constitution and a series of laws that protect some of the most basic of human rights. The states that were in doubt for ratification of the Constitution signed on when the Bill of Rights was promised.

The first amendment guarantees the basic rights of freedom of religion, freedom of speech, freedom of the press, and freedom of assembly.

The next three amendments came out of the colonists' struggle with Great Britain. For example, the third amendment prevents Congress from forcing citizens to keep troops in their homes. Before the Revolution, Great Britain tried to coerce the colonists to house soldiers.

Amendments five through eight protect citizens who are accused of crimes and are brought to trial. Every citizen has the right to due process of law (due process as defined earlier, being that the government must follow the same fair rules for everyone brought to trial.) These rules include the right to a trial by an impartial jury, the right to be defended by a lawyer, and the right to a speedy trial.

The last two amendments limit the powers of the federal government to those that are expressly granted in the Constitution, any rights not expressly mentioned in the Constitution, thus, belong to the states or to the people. In regards to specific guarantees:

Freedom of Religion: Religious freedom has not been seriously threatened in the United States historically. The policy of the government has been guided by the premise that church and state should be separate. When religious practices have been at cross purposes with attitudes prevailing in the nation at particular times, there have been restrictions placed on these practices. Some of these have been restrictions against the practice of polygamy that is supported by certain religious groups. The idea of animal sacrifice that is promoted by some religious beliefs is generally prohibited. The use of mind altering illegal substances that some have used in religious rituals has been restricted. In the United States, all recognized religious institutions are tax-exempt in following the idea of separation of church and state, and therefore, there have been many quasi-religious groups that have in the past tried to take advantage of this fact. All of these issues continue, and most likely will continue to occupy both political and legal considerations for some time to come.

Freedom of Speech, Press, and Assembly: These rights historically have been given wide latitude in their practice though there have been instances when one or the other freedoms have been limited for various reasons. The classic limitation, for instance, in regards to freedom of speech, has been the famous precept that an individual is prohibited from yelling fire! in a crowded theatre. This prohibition is an example of the state saying that freedom of speech does not extend to speech that might endanger other people. There is also a prohibition against slander, or the knowingly stating of a deliberately falsehood against one party by another. Also there are many regulations regarding freedom of the press, the most common example are the various laws against libel, (or the printing of a known falsehood). In times of national emergency, various restrictions have been placed on the rights of press, speech and sometimes assembly.

These ideas found their final expression in the United States Constitution's first ten amendments, known as the Bill of Rights. In 1789, the first Congress passed these first amendments and by December 1791, three-fourths of the states at that time had ratified them. The Bill of Rights protects certain liberties and basic rights. James Madison who wrote the amendments said that the Bill of Rights does not give Americans these rights. People, Madison said, already have these rights. They are natural rights that belong to all human beings. The Bill of Rights simply prevents the governments from taking away these rights.

Skill 6.4 **Recognize major accomplishments of the early presidential administrations, and examine the development of political parties.**

George Washington (1789-1797) faced a number of challenges during his two terms as President. There were boundary disputes with Spain over the Southeast and wars with the Indians on the western frontier.

The French Revolution and the ensuing war between France and England created great turmoil within the new nation. Thomas Jefferson, Secretary of State, was pro-French and believed the U.S. should enter the fray. Alexander Hamilton, Secretary of the Treasury, was pro-British and wanted to support England. Washington took a neutral course, believing the U.S. was not strong enough to be engaged in a war. Washington did not interfere with the powers of the Congress in establishing foreign policy. Two political parties were beginning to form by the end of his first term. In his farewell address he encouraged Americans to put an end to regional differences and exuberant party spirit. He also warned the nation against long-term alliances with foreign nations.

John Adams, of the Federalist Party, was elected President in 1796. When he assumed office, the war between England and France was in full swing. The British were seizing American ships that were engaging in trade with France. France, however, was refusing to receive the American envoy and had suspended economic relationships. The people were divided in their loyalties to either France or England. Adams focused on France and the diplomatic crisis known as the XYZ Affair. During his administration, Congress appropriated money to build three new frigates and additional ships, authorized the creation of a provisional army, and passed the Alien and Sedition Acts which were intended to drive foreign agents from the country and to maintain dominance over the Republican Party. When the war ended, Adams sent a peace mission to France. This angered the Republicans. The Election of 1800 pitted a unified and effective Republican Party against a divided and ineffective Federalist Party.

Under President John Adams, a minor diplomatic upset occurred with the government of France. By this time, the two major political parties called Federalists and Democratic-Republicans had fully developed. Hamilton and his mostly northern followers had formed the Federalist Party, which favored a strong central government and was sympathetic to Great Britain and its interests. The Democratic-Republican Party had been formed by Jefferson and his mostly Southern followers and they wanted a weak central government and stronger relations with and support of France. In 1798, the Federalists, in control of Congress, passed the **Alien and Sedition Acts** written to silence vocal opposition. These acts made it a crime to voice any criticism of the President or Congress and unfairly treated all foreigners.

The legislatures of Kentucky and Virginia protested these laws, claiming they attacked freedoms and challenging their constitutionality. These Resolutions stated mainly that the states had created the federal government, which was considered merely as an agent for the states and was limited to certain powers and could be criticized by the states, if warranted. They went further stating that states' rights included the power to declare any act of Congress null and void if the states felt it unconstitutional. The controversy died down as the Alien and Sedition Acts expired, one by one, but the doctrine of states' rights was not finally settled until the Civil War.

Thomas Jefferson won the election of 1800. Jefferson opposed a strong centralized government as a champion of States' Rights. He supported a strict interpretation of the Constitution. He reduced military expenditures, made budget cuts, and eliminated a tax on whiskey. At the same time, he reduced the national debt by one third. The Louisiana Purchase doubled the size of the nation. During his second term, the administration focused on keeping the U.S. out of the Napoleonic Wars. Both the French and the British were seizing American ships and trying to deny the other access to trade with the U.S. Jefferson's solution was to impose an embargo on all foreign commerce. The cost to the northeast was great and the embargo was both ineffective and unpopular.

After the U.S. purchased the Louisiana Territory, Jefferson appointed Captains **Meriwether Lewis and William Clark** to explore it, to find out exactly what had been bought. The expedition went all the way to the Pacific Ocean, returning two years later with maps, journals, and artifacts. This led the way for future explorers to make available more knowledge about the territory and resulted in the Westward Movement and the later belief in the doctrine of Manifest Destiny.

James Madison won the election of 1808 and inherited the foreign policy issues with England. During the first year of his administration, trade was prohibited with both Britain and France. In 1810, Congress authorized trade with both England and France. This directed the President that, if either nation would accept America's view of neutrality, he was to forbid trade with the other nation. Napoleon pretended to comply. Madison thus banned trade with Great Britain. The British continued to harass American ships and captured sailors and forced them to become members of the British Navy (impressment). In June of 1812, Madison asked Congress to declare war on Great Britain. The nation was really not prepared to fight a war, especially with the strong British army.

The British were successful in blockading U.S. ports and troops entered Washington and burned the White House and the Capitol. There were some notable American victories in the war, particularly Andrew Jackson's victory at New Orleans. This victory encouraged Americans to believe the war had been successful. The result was a tremendous rise in nationalism. The war ended with the **Treaty of Ghent**, in which Britain finally accepted U.S. independence. The war had been strenuously opposed by the Federalist Party, which even began to speak of secession. By the time the war was over, the party had been so deeply embarrassed and discredited that it was no longer a national political party.

The political party system in the U.S. has five main objects or lines of action:

(1) To influence government policy,
(2) To form or shape public opinion,
(3) To win elections,
(4) To choose between candidates for office,
(5) To procure salaried posts for party leaders and workers.

In domestic affairs of the new nation, the first problems dealt with finances--paying for the war debts of the Revolutionary War and other financial needs. Secretary of the Treasury Alexander Hamilton wanted the government to increase tariffs and put taxes on certain products made in the U.S., for example, liquor. This money would be used to pay war debts of the federal government as well as those of the states. There would be money available for expenses and needed internal improvements.

To provide for this, Hamilton favored a national bank. Secretary of State Thomas Jefferson, along with southern supporters, opposed many of Hamilton's suggested plans. Later, Jefferson relented and gave support to some proposals in return for Hamilton and his northern supporters agreeing to locate the nation's capital in the South. Jefferson continued to oppose a national bank but Congress set up the first one in 1791, chartered for the next 20 years. In 1794, Pennsylvania farmers, who made whiskey, their most important source of cash, refused to pay the liquor tax and started what came to be known as the **Whiskey Rebellion**. Troops sent by President Washington successfully put it down with no lives lost, thus demonstrating the growing strength of the new government.

The **Judiciary Act** set up the U.S. Supreme Court by providing for a Chief Justice and five associate justices. It also established federal district and circuit courts. One of the most important acts of Congress was the first 10 amendments to the Constitution called the **Bill of Rights** which emphasized and gave attention to the rights of individuals.

COMPETENCY 7.0 UNDERSTAND THE SIGNIFICANCE OF WESTWARD MOVEMENT IN U.S. HISTORY AND THE POLITICAL, ECONOMIC, SOCIAL, AND CULTURAL CONSEQUENCES OF TERRITORIAL EXPANSION

Skill 7.1 Describe basic characteristics of American Indian life and culture.

Though not differing greatly from each other in degree of civilization, the native peoples north of Mexico varied widely in customs, housing, dress, and religion. Among the native peoples of North America there were at least 200 languages and 1500 dialects. Each of the hundreds of tribes was somewhat influenced by its neighbors. Communication between tribes that spoke different languages was conducted primarily through a very elaborate system of sign language. Several groups of tribes can be distinguished.

The Woods Peoples occupied the area from the Atlantic to the Western plains and prairies. They cultivated corn and tobacco, fished and hunted.

The Plains Peoples, who populated the area from the Mississippi River to the Rocky Mountains, were largely wandering and warlike, hunting buffalo and other game for food. After the arrival of Europeans and the re-introduction of the horse they became great horsemen.

The Southwestern Tribes of New Mexico and Arizona included Pueblos, who lived in villages constructed of *adobe* (sun-dried brick), cliff dwellers, and nomadic tribes. These tribes had the most advanced civilizations.

The California Tribes were separated from the influence of other tribes by the mountains. They lived primarily on acorns, seeds and fish, and were probably the least advanced civilizations.

The Northwest Coast Peoples of Washington, British Columbia and Southern Alaska were not acquainted with farming, but built large wooden houses and traveled in huge cedar canoes.

The Plateau Peoples who lived between the plains and the Pacific coast were simple people who lived in underground houses or brush huts and subsisted primarily on fish.

The native peoples of America, like other peoples of the same stage of development, believed that all objects, both animate and inanimate, were endowed with certain spiritual powers. They were intensely religious, and lived every aspect of their lives as their religion prescribed. They believed a soul inhabited every living thing. Certain birds and animals were considered more powerful and intelligent than humans and capable of influence for good or evil.

Most of the tribes were divided into clans of close blood relations, whose *totem* was a particular animal from which they were often believed to have descended. The sun and the four principal directions were often objects of worship. The *shaman*, a sort of priest, was often the *medicine-man* of a tribe. Sickness was often supposed to be the result of displeasing some spirit and was treated with incantations and prayer. Many of the traditional stories resemble those of other peoples in providing answers to primordial questions and guidance for life. The highest virtue was self-control. Hiding emotions and enduring pain or torture unflinchingly was required of each. Honesty was also a primary virtue, and promises were always honored no matter what the personal cost.

The communities did not have any strict form of government, for the most part. Each individual was responsible for governing himself or herself, particularly with regard to the rights of other members of the community. The chiefs generally carried out the will of the tribe. Each tribe was a discrete unit, with its own lands. Boundaries of tribal territories were determined by treaties with neighbors. There was an organized confederation among certain tribes, often called a nation. The Iroquois confederation was often referred to as The Five Nations (later The Six Nations).

Customs varied from tribe to tribe. One consistent cultural element was the smoking of the calumet, a stone pipe, at the beginning and end of a war. In Native American communities, no individual owned land. The plots of land that were cultivated were, however, respected. Wealth was sometimes an honor, but generosity was more highly valued. Agriculture was quite advanced and irrigation was practiced in some locations. Most tribes practiced unique styles of basket work, pottery and weaving, either in terms of shape or decoration.

Skill 7.2   Recognize the role of geography, relations between settlers and indigenous populations, and government land policies in the settlement of the trans-Appalachian West.

The conclusion of the Civil War opened the floodgates for migration westward and settlement of new land. The availability of cheap land and the expectation of great opportunity prompted thousands, including immigrants, to travel across the Mississippi River and settle the Great Plains and California. The primary basis of the new western economy was farming, mining, and ranching. Both migration and the economy were facilitated by the expansion of the railroad, which largely replaced canal and river-way travel and transport as the preferred mode, and the completion of the transcontinental railroad in 1869. The increased efficiency of rail transport opened up new markets and enhanced existing ones. Agricultural, ranching and other business concerns in the West boomed and flourished with this improved connection to the markets of the East and, through them, the ports of Europe and beyond. This, of course, led to increased migration of people into all the territories of the West, seeking opportunity.

Migration and settlement were not easy. As the settlers moved west they encountered Native American tribes who believed they had a natural right to the lands upon which their ancestors had lived for generations. Resentment of the encroachment of new settlers was particularly strong among the tribes that had been ordered to relocate to "Indian Country" prior to 1860. Conflict was intense and frequent until 1867 when the government established two large tracts of land called "**reservations**" in Oklahoma and the Dakotas to which all tribes would be confined. With the war over, troops were sent west to enforce the relocation and reservation containment policies. There were frequent wars, particularly as white settlers attempted to move onto Indian lands and as the tribes resisted this confinement.

Continuing conflict led to passage of the **Dawes Act** of 1887. This was a recognition that confinement to reservations was not working. The law was intended to break up the Indian communities and bring about assimilation into white culture by deeding portions of the reservation lands to individual Indians who were expected to farm their land. The policy continued until 1934.

Armed resistance essentially came to an end by 1890, the same year in which the western frontier was demonstrated by the U.S. Census to be finally closed. The surrender of **Geronimo** and the massacre at **Wounded Knee**, led to a change of strategy by the Indians. Thereafter, the resistance strategy was to preserve their culture and traditions.

Skill 7.3 **Identify western land areas acquired by the United States during the nineteenth century.**

The next large territorial gain was under President Thomas Jefferson in 1803. In 1800, Napoleon Bonaparte of France secured the Louisiana Territory from Spain, who had held it since 1792. The vast area stretched westward from the Mississippi River to the Rocky Mountains as well as northward to Canada. An effort was made to keep the transaction a secret but the news reached the U.S. State Department. The U.S. didn't have any particular problem with Spanish control of the territory since Spain was weak and did not pose a threat. However, it was different with France. Though not the world power that Great Britain was, nonetheless France was still strong and, under Napoleon's leadership, was again acquiring an empire. President Jefferson had three major reasons for concern:

a. With the French controlling New Orleans at the mouth of the Mississippi River, as well as the Gulf of Mexico, Westerners would lose their "right of deposit" which would greatly affect their ability to trade. This was very important to the Americans who were living in the area between the river and the Appalachians. They were unable to get heavy products to eastern markets but had to float them on rafts down the Ohio and Mississippi Rivers to New Orleans to ships heading to Europe or the Atlantic coast ports. If France prohibited this; it would be a financial disaster.

b. President Jefferson also worried that if the French possessed the Louisiana Territory; America would be extremely limited in its expansion into its interior.

c. Under Napoleon Bonaparte, France was becoming more powerful and aggressive. This would be a constant worry and threat to the western border of the U.S. President Jefferson was very interested in the western part of the country and firmly believed that it was both necessary and desirable to strengthen western lands. So Jefferson wrote to the American minister to Paris, Robert R. Livingston, to make an offer to Napoleon for New Orleans and West Florida, as much as $10 million for the two. Napoleon countered the offer with the question of how much the U.S. would be willing to pay for all of Louisiana. After some discussion, it was agreed to pay $15 million and the largest land transaction in history was negotiated in 1803, resulting in the eventual formation of 15 states.

SEE ALSO 7.4

Skill 7.4 **Analyze the concept of Manifest Destiny, and examine the war with Mexico.**

As the nation extended its borders into the lands west of the Mississippi, thousands of settlers streamed into this part of the country bringing with them ideas and concepts adapting them to the development of the unique characteristics of the region. After the U.S. purchased the Louisiana Territory, Jefferson appointed Captains Meriwether Lewis and William Clark to explore it, to find out exactly what had been bought. The expedition went all the way to the Pacific Ocean, returning two years later with maps, journals, and artifacts. This led the way for future explorers to make available more knowledge about the territory and resulted in the Westward Movement and the later belief in the doctrine of Manifest Destiny.

"**Manifest Destiny**." ,as one newspaper editor termed it, was the belief that the United States was destined to control all of the land between the two oceans. , The mass migration westward put the U.S. government on a collision course with the Indians, Great Britain, Spain, and Mexico. The fur traders and missionaries ran up against the Indians in the northwest and the claims of Great Britain for the Oregon country.

In the American southwest, Spain had claimed this area since the 1540s, had spread northward from Mexico City, and, in the 1700s, had established missions, forts, villages, towns, and very large ranches. After the purchase of the Louisiana Territory in 1803, Americans began moving into Spanish territory. A few hundred American families in what is now Texas were allowed to live there but had to agree to become loyal subjects to Spain. In 1821, Mexico successfully revolted against Spanish rule, won independence, and chose to be more tolerant towards the American settlers and traders. The Mexican government encouraged and allowed extensive trade and settlement, especially in Texas. Many of the new settlers were southerners and brought with them their slaves. Slavery was outlawed in Mexico and technically illegal in Texas, although the Mexican government rather looked the other way.

With the influx of so many Americans and the liberal policies of the Mexican government, there came to be concern over the possible growth and development of an American state within Mexico. Settlement restrictions, cancellation of land grants, the forbidding of slavery and increased military activity brought everything to a head.

The order of events included the fight for Texas independence, the brief Republic of Texas, eventual annexation of Texas, statehood, and finally war with Mexico.

The Texas controversy was not the sole reason for war. Since American settlers had begun, pouring into the Southwest the cultural differences played a prominent part. Language, religion, law, customs, and government were totally different and opposite between the two groups. A clash was bound to occur.

Friction increased between land-hungry Americans swarming into western lands and the Mexican government, which controlled these lands. The clash was not only political but also cultural and economic. The Spanish influence permeated all parts of southwestern life: law, language, architecture, and customs. By this time, the doctrine of Manifest Destiny was in the hearts and on the lips of those seeking new areas of settlement and a new life.

The impact of the entire westward movement resulted in the completion of the borders of the present-day conterminous United States. Contributing factors include the bloody **war with Mexico**, the ever-growing controversy over slave versus free states affecting the balance of power or influence in the U.S. Congress, especially the Senate and finally to the Civil War itself.

Skill 7.5 Recognize general patterns of frontier life, and analyze the impact of the frontier on U.S. society.

In the West, restless pioneers moved into new frontiers seeking land, wealth, and opportunity. Many were from the South and were slave owners, bringing their slaves with them. Life on the frontier had marked differences. All facets of daily living--clothing, food, housing, economic and social activities--were all connected to what was needed to sustain life and survive in the wilderness. Everything was produced practically themselves. They were self-sufficient and extremely individualistic and independent. There were little, if any, levels of society or class distinctions as they considered themselves to be the equal to all others, regardless of station in life. The roots of equality, independence, individual rights and freedoms were strong and well developed. People were not judged by their fancy dress, expensive house, eloquent language, or titles following their names.

COMPETENCY 8.0 UNDERSTAND THE CAUSES, COURSE, AND CONSEQUENCES OF THE CIVIL WAR AND THE CONTINUING INFLUENCE OF THE CIVIL WAR AND RECONSTRUCTION PERIOD ON U.S. SOCIETY

Skill 8.1 Analyze the impact of slavery on U.S. society, and understand the role of sectionalism in American life.

As the new country began to stretch its boundaries, physically, new territories and opportunities were opened. New concepts like regionalism and sectionalism began to take on more meaning.

Regionalism can be defined as the political division of an area into partially autonomous regions or to loyalty to the interests of a particular region. **Sectionalism** is generally defined as excessive devotion to local interests and customs.

When the United States declared independence from England, the founding fathers created a political point of view that created a national unity while respecting the uniqueness and individual rights of each of the thirteen colonies or states. The colonies had been populated and governed by England and other countries. Some came to America in search of religious freedom, others for a fresh start and others for economic opportunity. Each colony had a particular culture and identity.

As the young nation grew, territories came to be defined as states. The states began to acquire their own particular cultures and identities. In time regional interests and cultures also began to take shape. Religious interests, economic life, and geography began to be understood as definitive of particular regions. The northeast tended toward industrial development. The south tended to rely upon agriculture. The west was an area of untamed open spaces where people settled and practiced agriculture and animal husbandry.

Each of these regions came to be defined, at least to some extent, on the basis of the way people made their living and the economic and social institutions that supported them. In the industrialized north, the factory system tended to create a division between the tycoons of business and industry and the poor industrial workers. The conditions in which the labor force worked were far from ideal – the hours were long, the conditions bad, and the pay was small.

The south was characterized by cities that were centers of social and commercial life. The agriculture that supported the region was practiced on "plantations" that were owned by the wealthy and worked by slaves or indentured servants.

MIDDLE LEVEL SOCIAL STUDIES

The west was a vast expanse to be explored and tamed. Life on a western ranch was distinctly different from either life in the industrial north or the agricultural south. The challenges of each region were also distinctly different. The role of children in the economy was different; the role of women was different; the importance of trade was different. And religion was called upon to support each unique regional lifestyle.

The regional differences between North and South came to a head over the issue of slavery. The rise of the abolitionist movement in the North, the publication of ***Uncle Tom's Cabin***, and issues of trade and efforts by the national government to control trade for the regions coalesced around the issue of slavery in a nation that was founded on the principle of the inalienable right of every person to be free. As the South defended its lifestyle and its economy and the right of the states to be self-determining, the North became stronger in its criticism of slavery. The result was a growing **sectionalism**.

Skill 8.2   Recognize major political developments and military campaigns of the war years.

The first serious clash between North and South occurred during 1819-1820 when James Monroe was in office as President and it was concerning admitting Missouri as a state. In 1819, the U.S. consisted of 21 states: 11 free states and 10 slave states. The Missouri Territory allowed slavery and if admitted would cause an imbalance in the number of U.S. Senators. Alabama had already been admitted as a slave state and that had balanced the Senate with the North and South each having 22 senators. The first Missouri Compromise resolved the conflict by approving admission of Maine as a free state along with Missouri as a slave state, thus continuing to keep a balance of power in the Senate with the same number of free and slave states.

An additional provision of this compromise was that with the admission of Missouri, slavery would not be allowed in the rest of the Louisiana Purchase territory north of latitude 36 degrees 30'. This was acceptable to the Southern Congressmen since it was not profitable to grow cotton on land north of this latitude line anyway. It was thought that the crisis had been resolved but in the next year, it was discovered that in its state constitution, Missouri discriminated against the free blacks. Anti-slavery supporters in Congress went into an uproar, determined to exclude Missouri from the Union. Henry Clay, known as the **Great Compromiser**, then proposed a second **Missouri Compromise**, which was acceptable to everyone. His proposal stated that the Constitution of the United States guaranteed protections and privileges to citizens of states and Missouri's proposed constitution could not deny these to any of its citizens. The acceptance in 1820 of this second compromise opened the way for Missouri's statehood--a temporary reprieve only.

Congress took up consideration of new territories between Missouri and present-day Idaho. Again, heated debate over permitting slavery in these areas flared up. Those opposed to slavery used the Missouri Compromise to prove their point showing that the land being considered for territories was part of the area the Compromise had designated as banned to slavery. On May 25, 1854, Congress passed the infamous **Kansas-Nebraska Act** that nullified the provision creating the territories of Kansas and Nebraska. This provided for the people of these two territories to decide for themselves whether or not to permit slavery to exist there. Feelings were so deep and divided that any further attempts to compromise would meet with little, if any, success. Political and social turmoil swirled everywhere. Kansas was called "Bleeding Kansas" because of the extreme violence and bloodshed throughout the territory because two governments existed there, one pro-slavery and the other anti-slavery.

The Supreme Court in 1857 handed down a decision guaranteed to cause explosions throughout the country. **Dred Scott** was a slave whose owner had taken him from slave state Missouri, then to free state Illinois, into Minnesota Territory, free under the provisions of the Missouri Compromise, then finally back to slave state Missouri. Abolitionists pursued the dilemma by presenting a court case, stating that since Scott had lived in a free state and free territory, he was in actuality a free man. Two lower courts had ruled before the Supreme Court became involved, one ruling in favor and one against. The Supreme Court decided that residing in a free state and free territory did not make Scott a free man because Scott (and all other slaves) were not U.S. citizens or state citizens of Missouri. Therefore, he did not have the right to sue in state or federal courts. The Court went a step further and ruled that the old Missouri Compromise was now unconstitutional because Congress did not have the power to prohibit slavery in the Territories.

Anti-slavery supporters were stunned. They had just recently formed the new Republican Party and one of its platforms was keeping slavery out of the Territories. Now, according to the decision in the Dred Scott case, this basic party principle was unconstitutional. The only way to ban slavery in new areas was by a Constitutional amendment, requiring ratification by three-fourths of all states. At this time, this was out of the question because the supporters would be unable to get a majority due to Southern opposition.

In 1858, Abraham Lincoln and Stephen A. Douglas were running for the office of U.S. Senator from Illinois and participated in a series of debates, which directly affected the outcome of the 1860 Presidential Election. Douglas, a Democrat, was up for re-election and knew that if he won this race, he had a good chance of becoming President in 1860. Lincoln, a Republican, was not an abolitionist but he believed that slavery was wrong morally and he firmly believed in and supported the Republican Party principle that slavery must not be allowed to extend any further.

Douglas, on the other hand, originated the doctrine of "**popular sovereignty**" and was responsible for supporting and getting through Congress the inflammatory Kansas-Nebraska Act. In the course of the debates, Lincoln challenged Douglas to show that popular sovereignty reconciled with the Dred Scott decision. Either way he answered Lincoln, Douglas would lose crucial support from one group or the other. If he supported the Dred Scott decision, Southerners would support him but he would lose Northern support. If he stayed with popular sovereignty, Northern support would be his but Southern support would be lost. His reply to Lincoln, stating that Territorial legislatures could exclude slavery by refusing to pass laws supporting it, gave him enough support and approval to be re-elected to the Senate. But it cost him the Democratic nomination for President in 1860.

Southerners came to the realization that Douglas supported and was devoted to popular sovereignty but not necessarily to the expansion of slavery. On the other hand, two years later, Lincoln received the nomination of the Republican Party for President.

Faced with two opposite choices, Congress opted to compromise. The state of California was admitted as a "free" state. Texas, a slave state, agreed to alter its border and was compensated for its loss of territory. In the New Mexico Territory, which included the area that is now New Mexico, Arizona and Utah, no specific prohibition on slavery was implemented. In addition, the Fugitive Slave law was passed, which required all citizens to assist in the return of runaway slaves to their owners. This group of acts is called the **Compromise of 1850**. It was aimed at balancing the competing claims of the slave-owning southern states, and the free northern states.

In 1859, abolitionist **John Brown** and his followers seized the federal arsenal at Harper's Ferry in what is now West Virginia. His purpose was to take the guns stored in the arsenal, give them to slaves nearby, and lead them in a widespread rebellion. Colonel Robert E. Lee of the United States Army captured him and his men and after a trial with a guilty verdict, he was hanged. Most Southerners felt that the majority of Northerners approved of Brown's actions but in actuality, most of them were stunned and shocked. Southern newspapers took great pains to quote a small but well-known minority of abolitionists who applauded and supported Brown's actions. This merely served to widen the gap between the two sections.

The final straw came with the election of Lincoln to the Presidency the next year. Due to a split in the Democratic Party, there were four candidates from four political parties. With Lincoln receiving a minority of the popular vote and a majority of electoral votes, the Southern states, one by one, voted to secede from the Union, as they had promised they would do if Lincoln and the Republicans were victorious. The die was cast.

In the decade leading up to the **Civil War**, tension between the northern and southern states intensified over the issue of slavery. The United States had acquired new territories in the southwest as a result of the Mexican-American War in the late 1840s. In 1850, as the nation was poised to expand, Congress took up the question of whether slavery would be allowed in the new territories.

South Carolina was the first state to **secede** from the Union and the first shots of the war were fired on Fort Sumter in Charleston Harbor. Both sides quickly prepared for war. The North had more in its favor: a larger population; superiority in finances and transportation facilities; manufacturing, agricultural, and natural resources. The North possessed most of the nation's gold, had about 92% of all industries, and almost all known supplies of copper, coal, iron, and various other minerals. Most of the nation's railroads were in the North and mid-West, men and supplies could be moved wherever needed; food could be transported from the farms of the mid-West to workers in the East and to soldiers on the battlefields. Trade with nations overseas could go on as usual due to control of the navy and the merchant fleet. The Northern states numbered 24 and included western (California and Oregon) and border (Maryland, Delaware, Kentucky, Missouri, and West Virginia) states.

The Southern states numbered eleven and included South Carolina, Georgia, Florida, Alabama, Mississippi, Louisiana, Texas, Virginia, North Carolina, Tennessee, and Arkansas, making up the Confederacy. Although outnumbered in population, the South was completely confident of victory. They knew that all they had to do was fight a defensive war and protect their own territory. The North had to invade and defeat an area almost the size of Western Europe. They believed the North would tire of the struggle and give up. Another advantage of the South was that a number of its best officers had graduated from the U.S. Military Academy at West Point and had had long years of army experience. Many had exercised varying degrees of command in the Indian wars and the war with Mexico. Men from the South were conditioned to living outdoors and were more familiar with horses and firearms than many men from northeastern cities. Since cotton was such an important crop, Southerners felt that British and French textile mills were so dependent on raw cotton that they would be forced to help the Confederacy in the war.

The South had specific reasons and goals for fighting the war, more so than the North. The major aim of the Confederacy never wavered: to win independence, the right to govern themselves as they wished, and to preserve slavery. The Northerners were not as clear in their reasons for conducting war. At the beginning, most believed, along with Lincoln, that preservation of the Union was paramount. Only a few extremely fanatical abolitionists looked on the war as a way to end slavery. However, by war's end, more and more northerners had come to believe that freeing the slaves was just as important as restoring the Union.

The war strategies for both sides were relatively clear and simple. The South planned a defensive war, wearing down the North until it agreed to peace on Southern terms. The only exception was to gain control of Washington, D.C., go North through the Shenandoah Valley into Maryland and Pennsylvania in order to drive a wedge between the Northeast and mid-West, interrupt the lines of communication, and end the war quickly. The North had three basic strategies:

1. blockade the Confederate coastline in order to cripple the South;
2. seize control of the Mississippi River and interior railroad lines to split the Confederacy in two;
3. seize the Confederate capital of Richmond, Virginia, driving southward joining up with Union forces coming east from the Mississippi Valley.

The South won decisively until the Battle of Gettysburg, July 1 - 3, 1863. Until Gettysburg, Lincoln's commanders, McDowell and McClellan, were less than desirable,. Lee, on the other hand, had many able officers, Jackson and Stuart depended on heavily by him. Jackson died at Chancellorsville and was replaced by Longstreet. Lee decided to invade the North and depended on J.E.B. Stuart and his cavalry to keep him informed of the location of Union troops and their strengths. Four things worked against Lee at Gettysburg:

1) The Union troops gained the best positions and the best ground first, making it easier to make a stand there.

2) Lee's move into Northern territory put him and his army a long way from food and supply lines. They were more or less on their own.

3) Lee thought that his Army of Northern Virginia was invincible and could fight and win under any conditions or circumstances.

4) Stuart and his men did not arrive at Gettysburg until the end of the second day of fighting and by then, it was too little too late. He and the men had had to detour around Union soldiers and he was delayed getting the information Lee needed.

Consequently, he made the mistake of failing to listen to Longstreet and following the strategy of regrouping back into Southern territory to the supply lines. Lee felt that regrouping was retreating and almost an admission of defeat.

He was convinced the army would be victorious. Longstreet was concerned about the Union troops occupying the best positions and felt that regrouping to a better position would be an advantage. He was also very concerned about the distance from supply lines.

It was not the intention of either side to fight at Gettysburg but the fighting began when a Confederate brigade, who were looking for shoes, stumbled into a unit of Union cavalry. The third and last day Lee launched the final attempt to break Union lines. General George Pickett sent his division of three brigades under Generals Garnet, Kemper, and Armistead against Union troops on Cemetery Ridge under command of General Winfield Scott Hancock. Union lines held and Lee and the defeated Army of Northern Virginia made their way back to Virginia. Although Lincoln's commander George Meade successfully turned back a Confederate charge, he and the Union troops failed to pursue Lee and the Confederates. This battle was the turning point for the North. After this, Lee never again had the troop strength to launch a major offensive.

The day after Gettysburg, on July 4, Vicksburg, Mississippi surrendered to Union General Ulysses Grant, thus severing the western Confederacy from the eastern part. In September 1863, the Confederacy won its last important victory at Chickamauga. In November, the Union victory at Chattanooga made it possible for Union troops to go into Alabama and Georgia, splitting the eastern Confederacy in two. Lincoln gave Grant command of all Northern armies in March of 1864. Grant led his armies into battles in Virginia while Phil Sheridan and his cavalry did as much damage as possible. In a skirmish at a place called Yellow Tavern, Virginia, Sheridan's and Stuart's forces met, with Stuart being fatally wounded. The Union won the Battle of Mobile Bay and in May 1864,

William Tecumseh Sherman began his march to successfully demolish Atlanta, then on to Savannah. He and his troops turned northward through the Carolinas to Grant in Virginia. On April 9, 1865, Lee formally surrendered to Grant at Appomattox Courthouse, Virginia.

The Civil War took more American lives than any other war in history. The South lost one-third of its' soldiers in battle compared to about one-sixth for the North. More than half of the total deaths were caused by disease and the horrendous conditions of field hospitals. Both sides paid a tremendous economic price but the South suffered more severely from direct damages. Destruction was pervasive with towns, farms, trade, industry, lives and homes of men, women, children all destroyed and an entire Southern way of life was lost. The deep resentment, bitterness, and hatred that remained for generations gradually lessened as the years went by but legacies of it surface and remain to this day. The South had no voice in the political, social, and cultural affairs of the nation, lessening to a great degree the influence of the more traditional Southern ideals. The Northern Yankee Protestant ideals of hard work, education, and economic freedom became the standard of the United States and helped influence the development of the nation into a modem, industrial power.

The effects of the Civil War were tremendous. It changed the methods of waging war and has been called the first modern war. It introduced weapons and tactics that, when improved later, were used extensively in wars of the late 1800s and 1900s. Civil War soldiers were the first to fight in trenches, first to fight under a unified command, first to wage a defense called "major cordon defense", a strategy of advance on all fronts. They were also the first to use repeating and breech loading weapons. Observation balloons were first used during the war along with submarines, ironclad ships, and mines. Telegraphy and railroads were put to use first in the Civil War. It was considered a modern war because of the vast destruction and was "total war", involving the use of all resources of the opposing sides. There was probably no *way* it could have ended other than total defeat and unconditional surrender of one side or the other.

Skill 8.3   Examine the political and social conflicts of the

Reconstruction era.

Following the Civil War, the nation was faced with repairing the torn Union and readmitting the Confederate states. **Reconstruction** refers to this period between 1865 and 1877 when the federal and state governments debated and implemented plans to provide civil rights to freed slaves and to set the terms under which the former Confederate states might once again join the Union.

Planning for Reconstruction began early in the war, in 1861. Abraham Lincoln's Republican Party in Washington favored the extension of voting rights to black men, but was divided as to how far to extend the right. Moderates, such as Lincoln, wanted only literate blacks and those who had fought for the Union to be allowed to vote. Radical Republicans wanted to extend the vote to all black men. Conservative Democrats did not want to give black men the vote at all. In the case of former Confederate soldiers, moderates wanted to allow all but former leaders to vote, while the radicals wanted to require an oath from all eligible voters that they had never borne arms against the US, which would have excluded all former rebels. On the issue of readmission into the Union, moderates favored a much lower standard, with the radicals demanding nearly impossible conditions for rebel states to return.

Lincoln's moderate plan for Reconstruction was actually part of his effort to win the war. Lincoln and the moderates felt that if it remained easy for states to return to the Union, and if moderate proposals on black suffrage were made, that Confederate states involved in the hostilities might be swayed to re-join the Union rather than continue fighting. The radical plan was to ensure that Reconstruction did not actually start until after the war was over.

Executive proclamation and constitutional amendment officially ended slavery ended, although there remained deep prejudice and racism, still raising its ugly head today. Also, the Union was preserved and the states were finally truly united. Sectionalism, especially in the area of politics, remained strong for another 100 years but not to the degree and with the violence as existed before 1861. It has been noted that the Civil War may have been American democracy's greatest failure for, from 1861 to 1865, calm reason, basic to democracy, fell to human passion. Yet, democracy did survive. The victory of the North established that no state has the right to end or leave the Union. Because of unity, the U.S. became a major global power. Lincoln never proposed to punish the South. He was most concerned with restoring the South to the Union in a program that was flexible and practical rather than rigid and unbending. In fact he never really felt that the states had succeeded in leaving the Union but that they had left the 'family circle" for a short time. His plans consisted of two major steps:

All Southerners taking an oath of allegiance to the Union promising to accept all federal laws and proclamations dealing with slavery would receive a full pardon. The only ones excluded from this were men who had resigned from civil and military positions in the federal government to serve in the Confederacy, those who were part of the Confederate government, those in the Confederate army above the rank of lieutenant, and Confederates who were guilty of mistreating prisoners of war and blacks.

A state would be able to write a new constitution, elect new officials, and return to the Union fully equal to all other states on certain conditions: a minimum number of persons (at least 10% of those who were qualified voters in their states before secession from the Union who had voted in the 1860 election) must take an oath of allegiance.

After the Civil War the Emancipation Proclamation in 1863 and the 13th Amendment in 1865 ended slavery in the United States, but these measures did not erase the centuries of racial prejudices among whites that held blacks to be inferior in intelligence and morality. These prejudices, along with fear of economic competition from newly freed slaves, led to a series of state laws that permitted or required businesses, landlords, school boards and others to physically segregate blacks and whites in their everyday lives.

In 1865 Abraham Lincoln was assassinated leaving his Vice President Andrew Johnson to oversee the beginning of the actual implementation of Reconstruction. Johnson struck a moderate pose, and was willing to allow former confederates to keep control of their state governments. These governments quickly enacted Black Codes that denied the vote to blacks and granted them only limited civil rights.

The economic and social chaos in the South after the war was unbelievable with starvation and disease rampant, especially in the cities. The U.S. Army provided some relief of food and clothing for both white and blacks but the major responsibility fell to the Freedmen's Bureau. Though the bureau agents to a certain extent helped southern whites, their main responsibility was to the freed slaves. They were to assist the freedmen to become self-supporting and protect them from being taken advantage of by others. Northerners looked on it as a real, honest effort to help the South out of the chaos it was in. Most white Southerners charged the bureau with causing racial friction, deliberately encouraging the freedmen to consider former owners as enemies.

In 1866, the radical Republicans won control of Congress and passed the Reconstruction Acts, which placed the governments of the southern states under the control of the federal military. With this backing, the Republicans began to implement their radical policies such as granting all black men the vote, and denying the vote to former confederate soldiers. Congress had passed the 13th, 14th and 15th amendments granting citizenship and civil rights to blacks, and made ratification of these amendments a condition of readmission into the Union by the rebel states. The Republicans found support in the south among Freedmen, as former slaves were called, white southerners who had not supported the Confederacy, called Scalawags, and northerners who had moved to the south, known as Carpetbaggers.

Military control continued throughout Grant's administration, despite growing conflict both inside and outside the Republican Party. Conservatives in Congress and in the states opposed the liberal policies of the Republicans. Some Republicans became concerned over corruption issues among Grant's appointees and dropped support for him.

Segregation laws were foreshadowed in the Black Codes, strict laws proposed by some southern states during the Reconstruction period that sought to essentially recreate the conditions of pre-war servitude. Under these codes, blacks were to remain subservient to their white employers, and were subject to fines and beatings if they failed to work. Freedmen, as newly freed slaves were called, were afforded some civil rights protection during the Reconstruction period, however beginning around 1876, so called Redeemer governments began to take office in southern states after the removal of Federal troops that had supported Reconstruction goals. The Redeemer-state legislatures began passing segregation laws that came to be known as Jim Crow laws.

The Jim Crow laws varied from state to state, but the most significant of them required separate school systems and libraries for blacks and whites and separate ticket windows, waiting rooms and seating areas on trains and, later, other public transportation. Restaurant owners were permitted or sometimes required to provide separate entrances and tables and counters for blacks and whites, so that the two races not see one another while dining.

Public parks and playgrounds were constructed for each race. Landlords were not allowed to mix black and white tenants in apartment houses in some states. The Jim Crow laws were given credibility in 1896 when the Supreme Court handed down its decision in the case *Plessy vs. Ferguson.* In 1890, Louisiana had passed a law requiring separate train cars for blacks and whites. To challenge this law, in 1892 Homer Plessy, a man who had a black great grandparent and so was considered legally "black" in that state, purchased a ticket in the white section and took his seat. Upon informing the conductor that he was black, he was told to move to the black car. He refused and was arrested. His case was eventually elevated to the Supreme Court.

The Court ruled against Plessy, thereby ensuring that the Jim Crow laws would continue to proliferate and be enforced. The Court held that segregating races was not unconstitutional as long as the facilities for each were identical. This became known as the "separate but equal" principle. In practice, facilities were seldom equal. Black schools were not funded at the same level, for instance. Streets and parks in black neighborhoods were not maintained.

Paralleling the development of segregation legislation in the mid-19th Century was the appearance of organized groups opposed to any integration of blacks into white society. The most notable of these was the Ku Klux Klan.

First organized in the Reconstruction south, the KKK was a loose group made up mainly of former Confederate soldiers who opposed the Reconstruction government and espoused a doctrine of white supremacy. KKK members intimidated and sometimes killed their proclaimed enemies. The first KKK was never completely organized, despite having nominal leadership. In 1871, President Grant took action to use federal troops to halt the activities of the KKK, and actively prosecuted them in federal court. Klan activity waned, and the organization disappeared.

The 13th Amendment abolished slavery and involuntary servitude, except as punishment for crime. The amendment was proposed on January 31, 1865. It was declared ratified by the necessary number of states on December 18, 1865. The Emancipation Proclamation had freed slaves held in states that were considered to be in rebellion. This amendment freed slaves in states and territories controlled by the Union. The Supreme Court has ruled that this amendment does not bar mandatory military service.

The 14th Amendment provides for Due Process and Equal Protection under the Law. It was proposed on June 13, 1866 and ratified on July 28, 1868. The drafters of the Amendment took a broad view of national citizenship. The law requires that states provide equal protection under the law to all persons (not just all citizens). This amendment also came to be interpreted as overturning the Dred Scott case (which said that blacks were not and could not become citizens of the U.S.).

The full potential of interpretation of this amendment was not realized until the 1950s and 1960s, when it became the basis of ending segregation in the Supreme Court case *Brown v. Board of Education*. This amendment includes the stipulation that all children born on American soil, with very few exceptions, are U.S. citizens. There have been recommendations that this guarantee of citizenship be limited to exclude the children of illegal immigrants and tourists, but this has not yet occurred. There is no provision in this amendment for loss of citizenship.

After the Civil War, many Southern states passed laws that attempted to restrict the movements of blacks and prevent them from bringing lawsuits or testifying in court. In the *Slaughterhouse Cases* (1871) the Supreme Court ruled that the Amendment applies only to rights granted by the federal government. In the *Civil Rights Cases*, the Court held that the guarantee of rights did not outlaw racial discrimination by individuals and organizations. In the next few decades the Court overturned several laws barring blacks from serving on juries or discriminating against the Chinese immigrants in regulating the laundry businesses.

The second section of the amendment establishes the "one man, one vote" apportionment of congressional representation. This ended the counting of blacks as 3/5 of a person. Section 3 prevents the election to Congress or the Electoral College of anyone who has engaged in insurrection, rebellion or treason. Section 4 stipulated that the government would not pay "damages" for the loss of slaves or for debts incurred by the Confederate government (e.g., with English or French banks).

The Fifteenth Amendment grants voting rights regardless of race, color or previous condition of servitude. It was ratified on February 3, 1870.

All three of these Constitutional Amendments were part of the Reconstruction effort to create stability and rule of law to provide, protect, and enforce the rights of former slaves throughout the nation.

Skill 8.4   Analyze the effect of war and Reconstruction on U.S. economic growth, political structures, and social relations.

The post-Reconstruction era represents a period of great transformation and expansion for the United States, both economically and geographically, particularly for the South, recovering from the devastation of the Civil War and migration west of the Mississippi River. Great numbers of former slaves moved west, away from their former masters and lured by the promise of land. White migration was also spurred by similar desires for land and resources, leading to boom economies of cotton, cattle and grain starting in Kansas and spreading westward.

Although industrial production grew fastest in the South during this period, it was still predominantly agricultural, which featured land tenancy and sharecropping, which did not really advance the remaining freed slaves economically since most of the land was still owned by the large plantation landowners who retained their holdings from before the Civil War. The economic chasm dividing white landowners and black freedmen only widened as the tenants sank further into debt to their landlords.

Westward movement of significant populations from the eastern United States originated with the discovery of gold in the West in the 1840s and picked up greater momentum after the Civil War. Settlers were lured by what they perceived as unpopulated places with land for the taking. However, when they arrived, they found that the lands were populated by earlier settlers of Spanish descent and Native Americans, who did not particularly welcome the newcomers. These original and earlier inhabitants frequently clashed with those who were moving west. Despite having signed treaties with the United States government years earlier, virtually all were ignored and broken as westward settlement accelerated and the government was called upon to protect settlers who were en route and when they had reached their destinations. This led to a series of wars between the United States and the various Native American Nations that were deemed hostile. Although the bloodshed during these encounters was great, it paled compared to the number of Native Americans who died from epidemics of deadly diseases for which they had no resistance. Eventually, the government sought to relocate inconveniently located peoples to Indian reservations, and to Oklahoma, which was lacked the resources they need and was geographically remote from their home range. The justification for this westward expansion, at the expense of the previous inhabitants was that it was America's "Manifest Destiny" to "tame" and settle the continent from coast-to-coast.

Another major factor affecting the opening of the West to migration of Americans and displacement of native peoples was the expansion of the railroad. The transcontinental railroad was completed in 1869, joining the west coast with the existing rail infrastructure terminating at Omaha, Nebraska, its westernmost point. This not only enabled unprecedented movement of people and goods, it also hastened the near extinction of bison, which the Indians of the Great Plains, in particular, depended on for their survival.

Once the American West was subdued and firmly under United States control did the United States start looking beyond its shores. Overseas markets were becoming important as American industry produced goods more efficiently and manufacturing capacity grew. Out of concern for the protection of shipping, the United States modernized and built up the Navy, which by 1900 ranked third in the world, which gave it the means to become an imperial power. The first overseas possessions were Midway Island and Alaska, purchased back in 1867 as championed by William Henry Seward.

By the 1880s, Secretary of State James G. Blaine pushed for expanding U.S. trade and influence to Central and South America and in the 1890s, President Grover Cleveland invoked the Monroe Doctrine to intercede in Latin American affairs when it looked like Great Britain was going to exert its influence and power in the Western Hemisphere. In the Pacific, the United States lent its support to American sugar planters who overthrew the Kingdom of Hawaii and eventually annexed it as U.S. territory.

The event that proved a turning point was the Spanish-American War in 1898 that used the explosion of the USS Maine as a pretext for the United States to invade Cuba, when the underlying reason was the ambition for empire and economic gain. The war with Spain also triggered the dispatch of the fleet under Admiral George Dewey to the Philippines, followed up by sending Army troops. Victory over the Spanish proved fruitful for American territorial ambitions. Although Congress passed legislation renouncing claims to annex Cuba, in a rare moment of idealism, the United States gained control of the island of Puerto Rico, a permanent deep-water naval harbor at Guantanamo Bay, Cuba, the Philippines and various other Pacific islands formerly possessed by Spain. The decision to occupy the Philippines, rather than grant it immediate independence, led to a guerrilla war, the "Philippines Insurrection" that lasted until 1902. U.S. rule over the Philippines lasted until 1942, but unlike the guerrilla war years, American rule was relatively benign.

COMPETENCY 9.0   **UNDERSTAND MAJOR POLITICAL, MILITARY, SOCIAL, ECONOMIC, AND CULTURAL DEVELOPMENTS IN THE UNITED STATES FROM 1877 TO 1919.**

Skill 9.1   **Analyze factors related to the industrialization of the U.S. economy, and examine the effect of industrialization on U.S. social and political life.**

There was a marked degree of industrialization before and during the Civil War, but at war's end, industry in America was small. After the war, dramatic changes took place. Machines replaced hand labor, extensive nationwide railroad service made possible the wider distribution of goods, invention of new products made available in large quantities, and large amounts of money from bankers and investors for expansion of business operations. American life was definitely affected by this phenomenal industrial growth. Cities became the centers of this new business activity resulting in mass population movements there and tremendous growth. This new boom in business resulted in huge fortunes for some Americans and extreme poverty for many others. The discontent this caused resulted in a number of new reform movements from which came measures controlling the power and size of big business and helping the poor.

Of course, industry before, during, and after the Civil War was centered mainly in the North, especially the tremendous industrial growth after. The late 1800s and early 1900s saw the increasing buildup of military strength and the U.S. becoming a world power.

The use of machines in industry enabled workers to produce a large quantity of goods much faster than by hand. With the increase in business, hundreds of workers were hired, assigned to perform a certain job in the production process. This was a method of organization called "division of labor" and by its increasing the rate of production, businesses lowered prices for their products making the products affordable for more people. As a result, sales and businesses were increasingly successful and profitable.

A great variety of new products or inventions became available such as: the typewriter, the telephone, barbed wire, the electric light, the phonograph, and the gasoline automobile. From this list, the one that had the greatest effect on America's economy was the automobile.

The increase in business and industry was greatly affected by the many rich natural resources that were found throughout the nation. The industrial machines were powered by the abundant water supply. The construction industry as well as products made from wood depended heavily on lumber from the forests. Coal and iron ore in abundance were needed for the steel industry, which profited and increased from the use of steel in such things as skyscrapers, automobiles, bridges, railroad tracks, and machines.

Other minerals such as silver, copper, and petroleum played a large role in industrial growth, especially petroleum, from which gasoline was refined as fuel for the increasingly popular automobile.

Skill 9.2 Identify major causes and effects of immigration to the United States, and evaluate the importance of cultural diversity in the continuing development of U.S. society.

The Irish Famine of 1845-1849 is alternately referred to as the Irish Potato Famine, The Great Famine or the Great Hunger. The immediate cause of the famine was the appearance of "the blight." This was the destruction of the potato crops due to a fungus. The potato was the primary food source for much of the population of Ireland at the time. Deaths were not officially recorded, but are believed to be in the 500,000 to one million range during the five years from 1846 to 1851. Although estimates vary, the number of people who emigrated from Ireland is in the neighborhood of two million.

The famine was more than potato blight. It was the culmination of a biological, political, social and economic catastrophe that can be attributed to contributing factors on the parts of both the British and the Irish. The famine essentially changed Irish culture and tradition forever.

The food value of the potato made it the single staple in the Irish food system. British laws (the Popery Act) prohibited Irish Catholics from passing family landholdings to a single son. This meant that land was subdivided among the male descendents in the family. The number of surviving male heirs was increasing, combining with the opportunity to own land, this led to sons marrying earlier and producing large families. With the legal restrictions on inheritance of land, this eventually meant that at the time when family size was increasing, the size of the land available to them was decreasing.

Ireland's economic/social vehicle for assistance to the poor was inadequate to meet the needs of the starving thousands. The program was funded by taxes charged to landholders on the basis of the number of tenants on the estate. As poverty and starvation increased, so did the financial need. This resulted in increasing tax rates on the landholders. To remain solvent, many landowners evicted tenants in an effort to reduce the tax bill. But this left more people poor and in need of assistance, which led to another increase in tax rates. In an effort to find an escape route from this vicious circle, some landowners paid passage to other countries rather than evict tenants. The ships on which they took passage came to be called "coffin ships." Many of these emigrants died during the voyage to North America. Many of the landowners who attempted to care for their tenants went bankrupt in the process. Ten percent of the estates were bankrupt by 1850. There were many charitable donations from around the world, but they were not adequate to solve such a large problem.

The responses of those leading the government of the United Kingdom were completely inadequate. It is believed that in 1851 the actual population of Ireland was 6.6 million. By 1911, it was only 4.4 million.

The Irish who emigrated to the U.S. for the most part became residents of cities. With no money, they were forced to remain in the port cities at which they arrived. By 1850, the Irish accounted for ¼ of the population of Boston, New York City, Philadelphia and Baltimore.

Between 1870 and 1916, more than 25 million immigrants came into the United States adding to the phenomenal population growth taking place. This tremendous growth aided business and industry in two ways: (1) The number of consumers increased creating a greater demand for products thus enlarging the markets for the products. (2) With increased production and expanding business, more workers were available for newly created jobs. The completion of the nation's transcontinental railroad in 1869 contributed greatly to the nation's economic and industrial growth. Some examples of the benefits of using the railroads include raw materials were shipped quickly by the mining companies and finished products were sent to all parts of the country. Many wealthy industrialists and railroad owners saw tremendous profits steadily increasing due to this improved method of transportation. Another impact of interstate railroad expansion was the standardization of time zones, in order to maintain the reliability and accuracy of train schedules across vast east-west routes.

Innovations in new industrial processes and technology grew at a pace unmatched at any other time in American history. Thomas Edison was the most prolific inventor of that time, using a systematic and efficient method to invent and improve on current technology in a profitable manner. The abundance of resources, together with growth of industry and the pace of capital investments led to the growth of cities. Populations were shifting from rural agricultural areas to urban industrial areas and by the early 1900's, a third of the nation's population lived in cities. Industry needed workers in its factories, mills and plants and rural workers were being displaced by advances in farm machinery and their increasing use and other forms of automation.

The dramatic growth of population in cities was fueled by growing industries, more efficient transportation of goods and resources, and the people who migrated to those new industrial jobs, either from rural areas of the United States or immigrants from foreign lands. Increased urban populations, often packed into dense tenements, often without adequate sanitation or clean water, led to public health challenges that required cities to establish sanitation, water and public health departments to cope with and prevent epidemics. Political organizations also saw the advantage of mobilizing the new industrial working class and created vast patronage programs that sometimes became notorious for corruption in big-city machine politics, like Tammany Hall in New York.

Skill 9.3   Describe the U.S. rise to world power and the effects of this development on the economy, culture, and foreign policy of the United States.

During the period of 1823 to the 1890s, the major interests and efforts of the American people were concentrated on expansion, settlement, and development of the continental United States. The Civil War, 1861-1865, preserved the Union and eliminated the system of slavery. From 1865 onward, the focus was on taming the West and developing industry. During this period, travel and trade between the United States and Europe were continuous. By the 1890s, American interests turned to areas outside the boundaries of the United States. The West was developing into a major industrial area and people in the United States became very interested in selling their factory and farm surplus to overseas markets. In fact, some Americans desired getting and controlling land outside the U.S. boundaries. Before the 1890s, the U.S. had little, if anything to do with foreign affairs, was not a strong nation militarily, and had inconsequential influence on international political affairs. In fact, the Europeans looked on the American diplomats as inept and bungling in their diplomatic efforts and activities. However, all of this changed and the Spanish-American War of 1898 saw the entry of the United States as a world power.

During the 1890s, Spain controlled such overseas possessions as Puerto Rico, the Philippines, and Cuba. Cubans rebelled against Spanish rule and the U.S. government found itself besieged by demands from Americans to assist the Cubans in their revolt. When the U.S. battleship Maine blew up off the coast of Havana, Cuba, Americans blamed the Spaniards for it and demanded American action against Spain. Two months later, Congress declared war on Spain and the U.S. quickly defeated them. The peace treaty gave the U.S. possession of Puerto Rico, the Philippines, Guam and Hawaii, which was annexed during the war. This success enlarged and expanded the U.S. role in foreign affairs.

Under the administration of Theodore Roosevelt, the U.S. armed forces were built up, greatly increasing its strength. Roosevelt's foreign policy was summed up in the slogan of "Speak softly and carry a big stick," backing up the efforts in diplomacy with a strong military. During the years before the outbreak of World War I, evidence of U.S. emergence as a world power could be seen in a number of actions. Using the Monroe Doctrine of non-involvement of Europe in the affairs of the Western Hemisphere, President Roosevelt forced Italy, Germany, and Great Britain to remove their blockade of Venezuela. He gained the rights to construct the Panama Canal by threatening force and assumed the finances of the Dominican Republic to stabilize it and prevent any intervention by Europeans. In 1916, under President Woodrow Wilson U.S. troops were sent to the Dominican Republic to keep order.

See also Skill 10.1

Skill 9.4 Compare the participants, goals, and accomplishments of the Populist and Progressive movements.

The tremendous change that resulted from the Industrial Revolution led to a demand for reform that would control the power wielded by big corporations. The gap between the industrial moguls and the working people was growing. This disparity between rich and poor resulted in a public outcry for reform at the same time that there was an outcry for governmental reform that would end the political corruption and elitism of the day.

This fire was fueled by the writings on investigative journalists – the "muckrakers" – who published scathing exposes of political and business wrongdoing and corruption. The result was the rise of a group of politicians and reformers who supported a wide array of **populist** causes. The period 1900 to 1917 came to be known as the **Progressive Era**. Although these leaders came from many different backgrounds and were driven by different ideologies, they shared a common fundamental belief that government should be eradicating social ills and promoting the common good and the equality guaranteed by the Constitution.

The reforms initiated by these leaders and the spirit of **Progressivism** were far-reaching. Politically, many states enacted the initiative and the referendum. The adoption of the recall occurred in many states. Several states enacted legislation that would undermine the power of political machines. On a national level the two most significant political changes were (1) the ratification of the 19th amendment, which required that all U.S. Senators be chosen by popular election, and (2) the ratification of the 19th Amendment, which granted women the right to vote.

Major economic reforms of the period included aggressive enforcement of the Sherman Antitrust Act; passage of the Elkins Act and the Hepburn Act, which gave the Interstate Commerce Commission greater power to regulate the railroads; the Pure Food and Drug Act prohibited the use of harmful chemicals in food; The Meat Inspection Act regulated the meat industry to protect the public against tainted meat; over two thirds of the states passed laws prohibiting child labor; workmen's compensation was mandated; and the Department of Commerce and Labor was created.

Responding to concern over the environmental effects of the timber, ranching, and mining industries, Roosevelt set aside 238 million acres of federal lands to protect them from development. Wildlife preserves were established, the national park system was expanded, and the National Conservation Commission was created. The Newlands Reclamation Act also provided federal funding for the construction of irrigation projects and dams in semi-arid areas of the country.
The Wilson Administration carried out additional reforms. The Federal Reserve Act created a national banking system, providing a stable money supply.

The Sherman Act and the Clayton Antitrust Act defined unfair competition, made corporate officers liable for the illegal actions of employees, and exempted labor unions from antitrust lawsuits. The Federal Trade Commission was established to enforce these measures. Finally, the 16th Amendment was ratified, establishing an income tax. This measure was designed to relieve the poor of a disproportionate burden in funding the federal government and make the wealthy pay a greater share of the nation's tax burden.

TEACHER CERTIFICATION STUDY GUIDE

COMPETENCY 10.0 UNDERSTAND MAJOR POLITICAL, MILITARY, SOCIAL, ECONOMIC, AND CULTURAL DEVELOPMENTS IN THE UNITED STATES FROM 1920 TO THE PRESENT

Skill 10.1 Examine major political developments, economic trends, and social movements in the United States since World War I.

During the period of 1823 to the 1890s, the major interests and efforts of the American people were concentrated on expansion, settlement, and development of the continental United States. The Civil War, 1861-1865, preserved the Union and eliminated the system of slavery. From 1865 onward, the focus was on taming the West and developing industry. During this period, travel and trade between the United States and Europe were continuous. By the 1890s, American interests turned to areas outside the boundaries of the United States. The West was developing into a major industrial area and people in the United States became very interested in selling their factory and farm surplus to overseas markets. In fact, some Americans desired getting and controlling land outside the U.S. boundaries. Before the 1890s, the U.S. had little, if anything to do with foreign affairs, was not a strong nation militarily, and had inconsequential influence on international political affairs. In fact, the Europeans looked on the American diplomats as inept and bungling in their diplomatic efforts and activities. However, all of this changed and the Spanish-American War of 1898 saw the entry of the United States as a world power.

During the 1890s, Spain controlled such overseas possessions as Puerto Rico, the Philippines, and Cuba. Cubans rebelled against Spanish rule and the U.S. government found itself besieged by demands from Americans to assist the Cubans in their revolt. When the U.S. battleship Maine blew up off the coast of Havana, Cuba, Americans blamed the Spaniards for it and demanded American action against Spain. Two months later, Congress declared war on Spain and the U.S. quickly defeated them. The peace treaty gave the U.S. possession of Puerto Rico, the Philippines, Guam and Hawaii, which was annexed during the war. This success enlarged and expanded the U.S. role in foreign affairs.

Causes attributed to the United States' participation in World War I included, the surge of nationalism, the increasing strength of military capabilities, massive colonization for raw materials needed for industrialization and manufacturing, and military and diplomatic alliances. The initial spark, which started the conflagration, was the assassination of Austrian Archduke Francis Ferdinand and his wife in Sarajevo.

MIDDLE LEVEL SOCIAL STUDIES

In Europe, Italy and Germany were each totally united into one nation from many smaller states. There were revolutions in Austria and Hungary, the Franco-Prussian War, the dividing of Africa among the strong European nations, interference and intervention of Western nations in Asia, and the breakup of Turkish dominance in the Balkans.

In Africa, France, Great Britain, Italy, Portugal, Spain, Germany, and Belgium controlled the entire continent except Liberia and Ethiopia. In Asia and the Pacific Islands, only China, Japan, and present-day Thailand (Siam) kept their independence. The others were controlled by the strong European nations.

Under the administration of Theodore Roosevelt, the U.S. armed forces greatly increased its strength. Roosevelt's foreign policy was summed up in the slogan of "Speak softly and carry a big stick," backing up the efforts in diplomacy with a strong military. During the years before the outbreak of World War I, evidence of U.S. emergence as a world power could be seen in a number of actions. In the spirit of the Monroe Doctrine of non-involvement of Europe in the affairs of the Western Hemisphere, President Roosevelt forced Italy, Germany, and Great Britain to remove their blockade of Venezuela. In addition he gained the rights to construct the Panama Canal by threatening force, assumed the finances of the Dominican Republic to stabilize it and prevent any intervention by Europeans and in 1916 under President Woodrow Wilson, to keep order, U.S. troops were sent to the Dominican Republic.

In Europe, war broke out in 1914, eventually involving nearly 30 nations, and ended in 1918. One of the major causes of the war was the tremendous surge of nationalism during the 1800s and early 1900s. People of the same nationality or ethnic group sharing a common history, language or culture began uniting or demanding the right of unification, especially in the empires of Eastern Europe, such as Russian Ottoman and Austrian-Hungarian Empires. Getting stronger and more intense were the beliefs of these peoples in loyalty to common political, social, and economic goals considered to be before any loyalty to the controlling nation or empire.

Emotions ran high and minor disputes magnified into major ones and sometimes quickly led to threats of war. Especially sensitive to these conditions was the area of the states on the Balkan Peninsula. Along with the imperialistic colonization for industrial raw materials, military build-up (especially by Germany), and diplomatic and military alliances, the conditions for one tiny spark to set off the explosion were in place. In July 1914, a Serbian national assassinated the Austrian heir to the throne and his wife and war began a few weeks later. There were a few attempts to keep war from starting, but these efforts were futile.

At the same time, Great Britain intercepted and decoded a secret message from Germany to Mexico urging Mexico to go to war against the U.S. The publishing of this information along with continued German destruction of American ships resulted in the eventual entry of the U.S. into the conflict, the first time the country prepared to fight in a conflict not on American soil. Though unprepared for war, governmental efforts and activities resulted in massive defense mobilization with America's economy directed to the war effort.

Though America made important contributions of war materials, its greatest contribution to the war was manpower, soldiers desperately needed by the Allies.

Some ten months before the war ended, President Wilson had proposed a program called the Fourteen Points as a method of bringing the war to an end with an equitable peace settlement. In these Points he had five points setting out general ideals; there were eight pertaining to immediately working to resolve territorial and political problems; and the fourteenth point counseled establishing an organization of nations to help keep world peace.

When Germany agreed in 1918 to an armistice, it assumed that the peace settlement would be drawn up on the basis of these Fourteen Points. However, the peace conference in Paris ignored these points and Wilson had to be content with efforts at establishing the League of Nations. Italy, France, and Great Britain, having suffered and sacrificed far more in the war than America, wanted retribution. The treaties punished severely the Central Powers, taking away arms and territories and requiring payment of reparations. Germany was punished more than the others and, according to one clause in the treaty, was forced to assume the responsibility for causing the war.

Pre-war empires lost tremendous amounts of territories as well as the wealth of natural resources in them. New, independent nations were formed and some predominately ethnic areas came under control of nations of different cultural backgrounds. Some national boundary changes overlapped and created tensions and hard feelings as well as political and economic confusion. The wishes and desires of every national or cultural group could not possibly be realized and satisfied, resulting in disappointments for both; those who were victorious and those who were defeated. Germany received harsher terms than expected from the treaty which weakened its post-war government. Along with the worldwide depression of the 1930s, the stage was set for the rise of Adolf Hitler and his Nationalist Socialist Party and World War II.

World War I saw the introduction of such warfare as use of tanks, airplanes, machine guns, submarines, poison gas, and flame throwers. Fighting on the Western front was characterized by a series of trenches that were used throughout the war until 1918. U.S. involvement in the war did not occur until 1916. When it began in 1914, President Woodrow Wilson declared that the U.S. was neutral and most Americans were opposed to any involvement anyway. In 1916, Wilson was reelected to a second term based on the slogan proclaiming his efforts at keeping America out of the war. For a few months after, he put forth most of his efforts to stopping the war but German submarines began unlimited warfare against American merchant shipping.

President Wilson lost in his efforts to get the U.S. Senate to approve the peace treaty. The Senate at the time was a reflection of American public opinion and its rejection of the treaty was a rejection of Wilson. The approval of the treaty would have made the U.S. a member of the League of Nations but Americans had just come off a bloody war to ensure that democracy would exist throughout the world. Americans just did not want to accept any responsibility that resulted from its new position of power and were afraid that membership in the League of Nations would embroil the U.S. in future disputes in Europe.

Skill 10.2 Identify the causes of the Great Depression, and evaluate the effects of the New Deal on U.S. society.

The end of World War I and the decade of the 1920s saw tremendous changes in the United States, signifying the beginning of its development into its modern society today. The shift from farm to city life was occurring in tremendous numbers. Social changes and problems were occurring at such a fast pace that it was extremely difficult and perplexing for many Americans to adjust to them. Politically the 18th Amendment to the Constitution, the so-called Prohibition Amendment, prohibited selling alcoholic beverages throughout the U.S. resulting in problems affecting all aspects of society. The passage of the 19th Amendment gave to women the right to vote in all elections. The decade of the 1920s also showed a marked change in roles and opportunities for women with more and more of them seeking and finding careers outside the home. They began to think of themselves as the equal of men and not as much as housewives and mothers.

The influence of the automobile, the entertainment industry, and the rejection of the morals and values of pre-World War I life, resulted in the fast-paced "**Roaring Twenties**". There were significant effects on events leading to the depression-era 1930s and another world war. Many Americans greatly desired the pre-war life and supported political policies and candidates in favor of the return to what was considered normal. It was desired to end government's strong role and adopt a policy of isolating the country from world affairs, a result of the war.

Prohibition of the sale of alcohol had caused the increased activities of bootlegging and the rise of underworld gangs and the illegal speakeasies, the jazz music and dances they promoted. The customers of these clubs were considered "modern," reflected by extremes in clothing, hairstyles, and attitudes towards authority and life. Movies and, to a certain degree, other types of entertainment, along with increased interest in sports figures and the accomplishments of national heroes, such as Lindbergh, influenced Americans to admire, emulate, and support individual accomplishments.

As wild and uninhibited modern behavior became, this decade witnessed an increase in a religious tradition known as "revivalism," emotional preaching. Although law and order were demanded by many Americans, the administration of President Warren G. Harding was marked by widespread corruption and scandal, not unlike the administration of Ulysses S. Grant, except Grant was honest and innocent. The decade of the 20s also saw the resurgence of such racist organizations as the Ku Klux Klan.

The U.S. economy experienced a tremendous period of boom. Restrictions on business because of war no longer existed and the conservatives in control adopted policies that helped and encouraged big business. To keep foreign goods from competing with American goods, tariffs were raised to the highest level. New products were developed by American manufacturers and many different items became readily available to the people. These included refrigerators, radios, washing machines, and, most importantly, the automobile.

The 1929 Stock Market Crash was the powerful event that is generally interpreted as the beginning of the Great Depression in America. Although the crash of the Stock Market was unexpected, it was not without identifiable causes. The 1920s had been a decade of social and economic growth and hope. But the attitudes and actions of the 1920s regarding wealth, production, and investment created several trends that quietly set the stage for the 1929 disaster.

The legislative and executive branches of the Coolidge administration tended to favor business and the wealthy. The Revenue Act of 1926 reduced income taxes for the wealthy very significantly. This bill lowered taxes such that a person with a million-dollar income saw his/her taxes reduced from $600,000 to $200,000. Despite the rise of labor unions, even the Supreme Court ruled in ways that further widened the gap between the rich and the middle class.

The majority of the population did not have enough money to buy what was necessary to meet their needs. The concept of buying on credit caught on very quickly. Buying on credit, however, creates artificial demand for products people cannot ordinarily afford. This has two effects: first, at some point there is less need to purchase products (because they have already been bought), and second, at some point paying for previous purchases makes it impossible to purchase new products. This exacerbated the problem of a surplus of goods.

The economy also relied on investment and luxury spending by the rich in the 1920s. Luxury spending, however, only occurs when people are confident with regard to the economy and the future. Should these people lose confidence, that luxury spending would come to an abrupt halt. This is precisely what happened when the stock market crashed in 1929. Investing in business produces returns for the investor. During the 1920s, investing was very healthy. Investors, however, began to expect greater returns on their investments. This led many to make speculative investments in risky opportunities.

Two industries, automotive and radio, drove the economy in the 1920s. During this decade, the government tended to support new industries rather than agriculture. During WWI, the government had subsidized farms and paid ridiculously high prices for grains. Farmers had been encouraged to buy and farm more land and to use new technology to increase production. The nation was feeding much of Europe during and in the aftermath of the war. But when the war ended, these farm policies were cut off. Prices plummeted, farmers fell into debt, and farm prices declined. The agriculture industry was on the brink of ruin before the stock market crash.

The concentration of production and economic stability in the automotive industry and the production and sale of radios was expected to last forever. But there comes a point when the growth of an industry slows due to market saturation. When these two industries declined, due to decreased demand, they caused the collapse of other industries upon which they were dependent (e.g., rubber tires, glass, fuel, construction, etc.).

The other factor contributing to the Great Depression was the economic condition of Europe. The U.S. was lending money to European nations to rebuild. Many of these countries used this money to purchase U.S. food and manufactured goods. But they were not able to pay off their debts. While the U.S. was providing money, food, and goods to Europe, however, it was not willing to buy European goods. Trade barriers were enacted to maintain a favorable trade balance.

Risky speculative investments in the stock market was the second major factor contributing to the stock market crash of 1929 and the ensuing depression. Stock market speculation was spectacular throughout the 1920s. In 1929, shares traded on the New York Stock Exchange reached 1,124,800,410. In 1928 and 1929 stock prices doubled and tripled (RCA stock prices rose from 85 to 420 within one year). The opportunity to achieve such profits was irresistible. In much the same way that buying goods on credit became popular, buying stock on margin allowed people to invest a very small amount of money in the hope of receiving exceptional profit. This created an investing craze that drove the market higher and higher. But brokers were also charging higher interest rates on their margin loans (nearly 20%). If, however, the price of the stock dropped, the investor owed the broker the amount borrowed plus interest.

Some scholars cite several other factors as contributing to the Great Depression. First, in 1929, the Federal Reserve increased interest rates. Second, some believe that as interest rates rose and the stock market began to decline, people began to hoard money. This was certainly the case after the crash. There is a question that it was a cause of the crash.

In September 1929, stock prices began to slip somewhat, yet people remained optimistic. On Monday, October 21, prices began to fall quickly. The volume traded was so high that the tickers were unable to keep up. Investors were frightened, and they started selling very quickly. This caused further collapse. For the next two days prices stabilized somewhat. On **Black Thursday**, October 24, prices plummeted again. By this time investors had lost confidence. On Friday and Saturday an attempt to stop the crash was made by some leading bankers. But on Monday the 28th, prices began to fall again, declining by 13% in one day. The next day, **Black Tuesday, October 29**, saw 16.4 million shares traded. Stock prices fell so far, that at many times no one was willing to buy at any price.

Unemployment quickly reached 25% nation-wide. People thrown out of their homes created makeshift domiciles of cardboard, scraps of wood and tents. With unmasked reference to President Hoover, who was quite obviously overwhelmed by the situation and incompetent to deal with it, these communities were called "**Hoovervilles**." Families stood in bread lines, rural workers left the dust bowl of the plains to search for work in California, and banks failed. More than 100,000 businesses failed between 1929 and 1932. The despair that swept the nation left an indelible scar on all who endured the Depression.

When the stock market crashed, businesses collapsed. Without demand for products other businesses and industries collapsed. This set in motion a domino effect, bringing down the businesses and industries that provided raw materials or components to these industries. Hundreds of thousands became jobless. Then the jobless often became homeless. Desperation prevailed. Little has been done to assess the toll hunger, inadequate nutrition, or starvation took on the health of those who were children during this time. Indeed, food was cheap, relatively speaking, but there was little money to buy it.

Everyone who lived through the Great Depression was permanently affected in some way. Many never trusted banks again. Many people of this generation later hoarded cash so they would not risk losing everything again. Some permanently rejected the use of credit. In the immediate aftermath of the stock market crash, many urged President Herbert Hoover to provide government relief. Hoover responded by urging the nation to be patient. By the time he signed relief bills in 1932, it was too late.

In several parts of the country, economic disaster was exacerbated by natural disaster. The Florida Keys were hit by the "**Labor Day Hurricane**" in 1935. This was one of only three hurricanes in history to make landfall as a Category 5 storm. More than 400 died in the storm, including 200 WWI veterans who were building bridges for a public works project. In the Northeast, The **Great Hurricane of 1938** struck Long Island, causing more than 600 fatalities, decimating Long Island, and resulting in millions of dollars in damage to the coast from New York City to Boston.

By far the worst natural disaster of the decade came to be known as the **Dust Bowl.** Due to severe and prolonged drought in the Great Plains and previous reliance on inappropriate farming techniques, a series of devastating dust storms occurred in the 1930s that resulted in destruction, economic ruin for many, and dramatic ecological change.

Plowing the plains for agriculture removed the grass and exposed the soil. When the drought occurred, the soil dried out and became dust. Wind blew away the dust. Between 1934 and 1939 winds blew the soil to the east, all the way to the Atlantic Ocean. The dust storms, called "black blizzards" created huge clouds of dust that were visible all the way to Chicago. Topsoil was stripped from millions of acres. In Texas, Arkansas, Oklahoma, New Mexico, Kansas and Colorado over half a million people were homeless. Many of these people journeyed west in the hope of making a new life in California.

Crops were ruined, the land was destroyed, and people either lost or abandoned homes and farms. Fifteen percent of Oklahoma's population left. Because so many of the migrants were from Oklahoma, the migrants came to be called "**Okies**" no matter where they came from. Estimates of the number of people displaced by this disaster range from 300,000 or 400,000 to 2.5 million.

Hoover's bid for re-election in 1932 failed. The new president, Franklin D. Roosevelt won the White House on his promise to the American people of a "new deal." Upon assuming the office, Roosevelt and his advisers immediately launched a massive program of innovation and experimentation to try to bring the Depression to an end and get the nation back on track. Congress gave the President unprecedented power to act to save the nation. During the next eight years, the most extensive and broadly based legislation in the nation's history was enacted. The legislation was intended to accomplish three goals: relief, recovery, and reform.

The first step in the "**New Deal**" was to relieve suffering. This was accomplished through a number of job-creation projects. The second step, the recovery aspect, was to stimulate the economy. The third step was to create social and economic change through innovative legislation.

The National Recovery Administration attempted to accomplish several goals:

- Restore employment
- Increase general purchasing power
- Provide character-building activity for unemployed youth
- Encourage decentralization of industry and thus divert population from crowded cities to rural or semi-rural communities
- To develop river resources in the interest of navigation and cheap power and light
- To complete flood control on a permanent basis
- To enlarge the national program of forest protection and to develop forest resources
- To control farm production and improve farm prices
- To assist home builders and home owners
- To restore public faith in banking and trust operations
- To recapture the value of physical assets, whether in real property, securities, or other investments.

These objectives and their accomplishments implied a restoration of public confidence and courage.

Among the "alphabet organizations" set up to work out the details of the recovery plan, the most prominent were:

- **Agricultural Adjustment Administration** (AAA), designed to readjust agricultural production and prices thereby boosting farm income
- **Civilian Conservation Corps** (CCC), designed to give wholesome, useful activity in the forestry service to unemployed young men
- **Civil Works Administration** (CWA) and the **Public Works Administration** (PWA), designed to give employment in the construction and repair of public buildings, parks, and highways
- **Works Progress Administration** (WPA), whose task was to move individuals from relief rolls to work projects or private employment

The **Tennessee Valley Authority** (TVA) was of a more permanent nature, designed to improve the navigability of the Tennessee River and increase productivity of the timber and farm lands in its valley, this program built 16 dams that provided water control and hydroelectric generation.

The **Public Works Administration** employed Americans on over 34,000 public works projects at a cost of more than $4 billion. Among these projects was the construction of a highway that linked the Florida Keys and Miami, the Boulder Dam (now the Hoover Dam) and numerous highway projects.

To provide economic stability and prevent another crash, Congress passed the **Glass-Steagall Act**, which separated banking and investing. The Securities and Exchange Commission was created to regulate dangerous speculative practices on Wall Street. The Wagner Act guaranteed a number of rights to workers and unions in an effort to improve worker-employer relations. The **Social Security Act of 1935** established pensions for the aged and infirm as well as a system of unemployment insurance.

Much of the recovery program was emergency, but certain permanent national policies emerged. Government role expanded to supervise and, regulate business operations. This included protecting bank depositors and the credit system of the country, employing gold resources and currency adjustments to aid permanent restoration of normal living, and, if possible, establishing a line of subsistence below which no useful citizen would be permitted to sink.

Many of the steps taken by the Roosevelt administration had far-reaching effects. They alleviated the economic disaster of the Great Depression, they enacted controls that would mitigate the risk of another stock market crash, and they provided greater security for workers. The nation's economy, however, did not fully recover until America entered World War II.

During the first 100 days in office, the Roosevelt Administration responded to this crisis with programs designed to restore the ecological balance. One action was the formation of the **Soil Conservation Service** (now the Natural Resources Conservation Service). The story of this natural disaster and its toll in human suffering is poignantly preserved in the photographs of Dorothea Lange.

To be sure, there were negative reactions to some of the measures taken to pull the country out of the depression. There was a major reaction to the deaths of the WWI veterans in the Labor Day Hurricane, ultimately resulting in a Congressional investigation into possible negligence. The Central Valley Project ruffled feathers of farmers who lost tillable land and some water supply to the construction of the aqueduct and the Hoover Dam. Tennesseans were initially unhappy with the changes in river flow and navigation when the Tennessee Valley Authority began its construction of dams and the directing of water to form reservoirs and to power hydroelectric plants. Some businesses and business leaders were not happy with the introduction of minimum wage laws and restrictions and controls on working conditions and limitations of work hours for laborers. The numerous import/export tariffs of the period were the subject of controversy.

In the long view, however, much that was accomplished under the New Deal had positive long-term effects on economic, ecological, social and political issues for the next several decades. The Tennessee Valley Authority and the Central Valley Project in California provided a reliable source and supply of water to major cities, as well as electrical power to meet the needs of an increasingly electricity-dependent society. For the middle class and the poor, the labor regulations, the establishment of the Social Security Administration, and the separation of investment and banking have served the nation admirably for more than six decades.

The charter of the National Recovery Administration included a statement defending the right of labor unions to exist and to negotiate with employers. This was interpreted by thousands as support for unions. But the Supreme Court declared this unconstitutional. There were several major events or actions that are particularly important to the history of organized labor during this decade:

- The Supreme Court upheld the Railway Labor Act, including its prohibition of employer interference or coercion in the choice of bargaining representatives (1930).
- The Davis-Bacon Act provided employers of contractors and subcontractors on public construction should be paid the prevailing wages (1931).
- The Anti-Injunction Act prohibited Federal injunctions in most labor disputes (1932).
- Wisconsin created the first unemployment insurance act in the country (1932).
- The Wagner-Peyser Act created the United States Employment Service within the Department of Labor (1933).
- Half a million Southern mill workers walked off the job in the Great Uprising of 1934.
- The Secretary of Labor called the first National Labor Legislation Conference to get better cooperation between the Federal Government and the States in defining a national labor legislation program (1934).
- The U.S. joined the International Labor Organization (1934).
- The Wagner Act (The National Labor Relations Act) established a legal basis for unions, set collective bargaining as a matter of national policy required by the law, provided for secret ballot elections for choosing unions, and protected union members from employer intimidation and coercion. This law was later amended by the Taft-Hartley Act (1947) and by the Landrum Griffin Act (1959).
- The Guffey Act stabilized the coal industry and improved labor conditions (1935). It was later declared unconstitutional (1936).
- The Social Security Act was approved (1935).
- The Committee for Industrial Organization (CIO) was formed within the AFL to carry unionism to the industrial sector. (1935).
- The United Rubber Workers staged the first sit-down strike (1936).

- The United Auto Workers used the sit-down strike against General Motors (1936).
- The Anti-Strikebreaker Act (the Byrnes Act) made it illegal to transport or aid strikebreakers in interstate or foreign trade (1936).
- The Public Contracts Act (the Walsh-Healey Act) of 1936 established labor standards, including minimum wages, overtime pay, child and convict labor provisions and safety standards on federal contracts.
- General Motors recognized the United Auto Workers in 1937.
- US Steel recognized the Steel Workers Organizing Committee in 1937.
- The Wagner Act was upheld by the Supreme Court (1937).
- During a strike of the Steel Workers Organizing Committee against Republic Steel, police attacked a crowd gathered in support of the strike, killing ten and injuring eighty. This came to be called **The Memorial Day Massacre** (1937).
- The CIO was expelled from the AFL over charges of dual unionism or competition (1937).
- The National Apprenticeship Act established the Bureau of Apprenticeship within the Department of Labor (1937).
- The Merchant Marine Act created a Federal Maritime Labor Board (1938).
- The Fair Labor Standards Act created a $0.25 minimum wage, stipulated time-and-a-half pay for hours over 40 per week.
- The CIO becomes the Congress of Industrial Organizations.

Skill 10.3 Describe the causes, course, and consequences of World War II, and analyze the impact of the Cold War on U.S. politics and foreign relations.

The extreme form of patriotism called nationalism that had been the chief cause of World War I grew even stronger after the war ended in 1918. The political, social, and economic unrest fueled nationalism and it became an effective tool enabling dictators to gain and maintain power from the 1930s to the end of World War II in 1945. In the Soviet Union, Joseph Stalin succeeded in gaining political control and establishing a strong harsh dictatorship. Benito Mussolini and the Fascist party, promising prosperity and order in Italy, gained national support, and set up a strong government. In Japan, although the ruler was considered Emperor Hirohito, actual control and administration of government came under military officers. In Germany, the results of war, harsh treaty terms, loss of territory, great economic chaos and collapse all enabled Adolf Hitler and his Nazi party to gain complete power and control.

Germany, Italy, and Japan initiated a policy of aggressive territorial expansion with Japan being the first to conquer. In 1931, the Japanese forces seized control of Manchuria, a part of China containing rich natural resources, and in 1937 began an attack on China, occupying most of its eastern part by 1938. Italy invaded Ethiopia in Africa in 1935, having it totally under its control by 1936. The Soviet Union did not invade or take over any territory. Like Italy and Germany, the Soviet Union actively participated in the Spanish Civil War, using it as a proving ground to test tactics and weapons setting the stage for World War II.

In Germany, almost immediately after taking power, in direct violation of the World War I peace treaty, Hitler began the buildup of the armed forces. He sent troops into the Rhineland in 1936, invaded Austria in 1938 and united it with Germany, seized control of the Sudetenland in 1938 (part of western Czechoslovakia and containing mostly Germans) and the rest of Czechoslovakia in March 1939. On September 1, 1939, World War II began in Europe by invading Poland. In 1940, Germany invaded and controlled Norway, Denmark, Belgium, Luxembourg, the Netherlands, and France.

After the war began in Europe, U.S. President Franklin D. Roosevelt announced that the United States was neutral. Most Americans, although hoping for an Allied victory, wanted the U.S. to stay out of the war. President Roosevelt and his supporters, called "interventionists," favored all aid except war to the Allied nations fighting Axis aggression. They were fearful that an Axis victory would seriously threaten and endanger all democracies. On the other hand, the "isolationists" were against any U.S. aid being given to the warring nations, accusing President Roosevelt of leading the U.S. into a war very much unprepared to fight. Roosevelt's plan was to defeat the Axis nations by sending the Allied nations the equipment needed to fight; ships, aircraft, tanks, and other war materials.

In Asia, the U.S. had opposed Japan's invasion of Southeast Asia, an effort to gain Japanese control of that region's rich resources. Consequently, the U.S. stopped all important exports to Japan, whose industries depended heavily on petroleum, scrap metal, and other raw materials. Later Roosevelt refused the Japanese withdrawal of its funds from American banks. General Tojo became the Japanese premier in October 1941 and quickly realized that the U.S. Navy was powerful enough to block Japanese expansion into Asia. Deciding to cripple the Pacific Fleet, the Japanese aircraft, without warning, bombed the Fleet December 7, 1941, while at anchor in Pearl Harbor in Hawaii. Temporarily it was a success. It destroyed many aircraft and disabled much of the U.S. Pacific Fleet. In the end, it was a costly mistake as it quickly motivated the Americans to prepare for and wage war.

Military strategy in the European theater of war as developed by Roosevelt, Churchill, and Stalin was to concentrate on Germany's defeat first, then Japan's. The start was made in North Africa, pushing Germans and Italians off the continent, beginning in the summer of 1942 and ending successfully in May, 1943. Before the war, Hitler and Stalin had signed a non-aggression pact in 1939, which Hitler violated in 1941 by invading the Soviet Union. The German defeat at Stalingrad, marked a turning point in the war, was brought about by a combination of entrapment by Soviet troops and death of German troops by starvation and freezing due to the horrendous winter conditions. All this occurred at the same time the Allies were driving them out of North Africa.

The liberation of Italy began in July 1943 and ended May 2, 1945. The third part of the strategy was D-Day, June 6, 1944, with the Allied invasion of France at Normandy. At the same time, starting in January 1943, the Soviets began pushing the German troops back into Europe and they were greatly assisted by supplies from Britain and the United States. By April 1945, Allies occupied positions beyond the Rhine and the Soviets moved on to Berlin, surrounding it by April 25. Germany surrendered May 7 and the war in Europe was finally over.

Meanwhile, in the Pacific, in the six months after the attack on Pearl Harbor, Japanese forces moved across Southeast Asia and the western Pacific Ocean. By August 1942, the Japanese Empire was at its largest size and stretched northeast to Alaska's Aleutian Islands, west to Burma, south to what is now Indonesia. Invaded and controlled areas included Hong Kong, Guam, Wake Island, Thailand, part of Malaysia, Singapore, the Philippines, and bombed Darwin on the north coast of Australia.

The raid of General Doolittle's bombers on Japanese cities and the American naval victory at Midway along with the fighting in the Battle of the Coral Sea helped turn the tide against Japan. Island-hopping by U.S. Seabees and Marines and the grueling bloody battles fought resulted in gradually pushing the Japanese back towards Japan.

After victory was attained in Europe, concentrated efforts were made to secure Japan's surrender, but it took dropping two atomic bombs on the cities of Hiroshima and Nagasaki to finally end the war in the Pacific. Japan formally surrendered on September 2, 1945, aboard the U.S. battleship Missouri, anchored in Tokyo Bay. The war was finally ended.

Before war in Europe had ended, the Allies had agreed on a military occupation of Germany. It was divided into four zones each one occupied by Great Britain, France, the Soviet Union, and the United States with the four powers jointly administering Berlin. After the war, the Allies agreed that Germany's armed forces would be abolished, the Nazi Party outlawed, and the territory east of the Oder and Neisse Rivers taken away. Nazi leaders were accused of war crimes and brought to trial. After Japan's defeat, the Allies began a military occupation directed by American General Douglas MacArthur, who introduced a number of reforms eventually ridding Japan of its military institutions transforming it into a democracy. A constitution was drawn up in 1947 transferring all political rights from the emperor to the people, granting women the right to vote, and denying Japan the right to declare war. War crimes trials of 25 war leaders and government officials were also conducted. The U.S. did not sign a peace treaty until 1951. The treaty permitted Japan to rearm but took away its overseas empire.

Again, after a major world war came efforts to prevent war from occurring again throughout the world. Preliminary work began in 1943 when the U.S., Great Britain, the Soviet Union, and China sent representatives to Moscow where they agreed to set up an international organization that would work to promote peace around the earth. In 1944, the four Allied powers met again and made the decision to name the organization the United Nations. In 1945, a charter for the U. N. was drawn up and signed, taking effect in October of that year.

Major consequences of the war included horrendous death and destruction, millions of displaced persons, the gaining of strength and spread of Communism and Cold War tensions as a result of the beginning of the nuclear age. World War II ended more lives and caused more devastation than any other war.

Besides the losses of millions of military personnel, the devastation and destruction directly affected civilians, reducing cities, houses, and factories to ruin and rubble and totally wrecking communication and transportation systems. Millions of civilian deaths, especially in China and the Soviet Union, were the results of famine.

More than 12 million people were uprooted by war's end having no place to live. Those included were prisoners of war, those that survived Nazi concentration camps and slave labor camps, orphans, and people who escaped war-torn areas and invading armies. Changing national boundary lines also caused the mass movement of displaced persons.

Germany and Japan were completely defeated; Great Britain and France were seriously weakened; and the Soviet Union and the United States became the world's leading powers. Although allied during the war, the alliance fell apart as the Soviets pushed Communism in Europe and Asia. In spite of the tremendous destruction it suffered, the Soviet Union was stronger than ever. During the war, it took control of Lithuania, Estonia, and Latvia and by mid-1945 parts of Poland, Czechoslovakia, Finland, and Romania. It helped Communist governments gain power in Bulgaria, Romania, Hungary, Czechoslovakia, Poland, and North Korea. China fell to Mao Zedong's Communist forces in 1949. Until the fall of the Berlin Wall in 1989 and the dissolution of Communist governments in Eastern Europe and the Soviet Union, the United States and the Soviet Union faced off in what was called a Cold War. The possibility of the terrifying destruction by nuclear weapons loomed over both nations.

The major thrust of U.S. foreign policy from the end of World War II to 1990 was the post-war struggle between non-Communist nations, led by the United States, and the Soviet Union and the Communist nations who were its allies. It was referred to as a "Cold War" because its conflicts did not lead to a major war of fighting, or a "hot war." Both the Soviet Union and the United States embarked on an arsenal buildup of atomic and hydrogen bombs as well as other nuclear weapons. Both nations had the capability of destroying each other but because of the continuous threat of nuclear war and accidents, extreme caution was practiced on both sides. The efforts of both sides to serve and protect their political philosophies and to support and assist their allies resulted in a number of events during this 45-year period.

In 1946, Josef Stalin stated publicly that the presence of capitalism and its development of the world's economy made international peace impossible. This resulted in an American diplomat in Moscow named George F. Kennan to propose in response to Stalin, a statement of U.S. foreign policy. The idea and goal of the U.S. was to contain or limit the extension or expansion of Soviet Communist policies and activities. After Soviet efforts to make trouble in Iran, Greece, and Turkey, U.S. President Harry Truman stated what is known as the **Truman Doctrine** which committed the U.S. to a policy of intervention in order to contain or stop the spread of communism throughout the world.

After 1945, social and economic chaos continued in Western Europe, especially in Germany. Secretary of State George C. Marshall came to realize that the U.S. had greatly serious problems and to assist in the recovery, he proposed a program known as the European Recovery Program or the **Marshall Plan**. Although the Soviet Union withdrew from any participation, the U.S. continued the work of assisting Europe in regaining economic stability. In Germany, the situation was critical with the American Army shouldering the staggering burden of relieving the serious problems of the German economy. In February 1948, Britain and the U.S. combined their two zones, with France joining in June.

The Soviets were opposed to German unification and in April 1948 took serious action to either stop it or to force the Allies to give up control of West Berlin to the Soviets. The Soviets blocked all road traffic access to West Berlin from West Germany. To avoid any armed conflict, it was decided to airlift into West Berlin the needed food and supplies. From June 1948 to mid-May 1949 Allied air forces flew in all that was needed for the West Berliners, forcing the Soviets to lift the blockade and permit vehicular traffic access to the city.

The first "hot war" in the post-World War II era was the Korean War, begun June 25, 1950 and ending July 27, 1953. Troops from Communist North Korea invaded democratic South Korea in an effort to unite both sections under Communist control. The United Nations organization asked its member nations to furnish troops to help restore peace. Many nations responded and President Truman sent American troops to help the South Koreans. The war dragged on for three years and ended with a truce, not a peace treaty. Like Germany then, Korea remained divided and does so to this day.

In 1954, the French were forced to give up their colonial claims in Indochina, the present-day countries of Vietnam, Laos, and Cambodia. Afterwards, the Communist northern part of Vietnam began battling with the democratic southern part over control of the entire country. In the late 1950s and early 1960s, U.S. Presidents Eisenhower and Kennedy sent to Vietnam a number of military advisers and military aid to assist and support South Vietnam's non-Communist government. During Lyndon Johnson's presidency, the war escalated with thousands of American troops being sent to participate in combat with the South Vietnamese. The war was extremely unpopular in America and caused such serious divisiveness among its citizens that Johnson decided not to seek reelection in 1968. It was in President Richard Nixon's second term in office that the U.S. signed an agreement ending war in Vietnam and restoring peace. This was done January 27, 1973, and by March 29, the last American combat troops and American prisoners of war left Vietnam for home. It was the longest war in U.S. history and to this day carries the perception that it was a "lost war."

In 1962, during the administration of President John F. Kennedy, Premier Khrushchev and the Soviets decided, as a protective measure for Cuba against an American invasion, to install nuclear missiles on the island. In October, American U-2 spy planes photographed over Cuba what were identified as missile bases under construction. The decision in the White House was how to handle the situation without starting a war. The only recourse was removal of the missile sites and preventing more being set up. Kennedy announced that the U.S. had set up a "quarantine" of Soviet ships heading to Cuba. It was in reality a blockade but the word itself could not be used publicly as a blockade was actually considered an act of war.

A week of incredible tension and anxiety gripped the entire world until Khrushchev capitulated. Soviet ships carrying missiles for the Cuban bases turned back and the crisis eased. What precipitated the crisis was Khrushchev's underestimation of Kennedy. The President made no effort to prevent the erection of the Berlin Wall and was reluctant to commit American troops to invade Cuba and overthrow Fidel Castro. The Soviets assumed this was a weakness and decided they could install the missiles without any interference.

The Soviets were concerned about American missiles installed in Turkey aimed at the Soviet Union and about a possible invasion of Cuba. If successful, Khrushchev would demonstrate to the Russian and Chinese critics of his policy of peaceful coexistence that he was tough and not to be intimidated. At the same time, the Americans feared that if Russian missiles were put in place and launched from Cuba to the U.S., the short distance of 90 miles would not allow enough time for adequate warning. Furthermore, it would originate from a direction that radar systems could not detect. It was felt that if America gave in and allowed a Soviet presence practically at the back door that the effect on American security and morale would be devastating.

As tensions eased in the aftermath of the crisis, several agreements were made. The missiles in Turkey were removed, as they were obsolete. A telephone "hot line" was set up between Moscow and Washington to make it possible for the two heads of government to have instant contact with each other. The U.S. agreed to sell its surplus wheat to the Soviets.

Probably the highlight of the foreign policy of President Richard Nixon, after the end of the Vietnam War and withdrawal of troops, was his 1972 trip to China. When the Communists gained control of China in 1949, the policy of the U.S. government was refusal to recognize the Communist government. It regarded as the legitimate government of China to be that of Chiang Kai-shek, exiled on the island of Taiwan.

In 1971, Nixon sent Henry Kissinger on a secret trip to Peking to investigate whether or not it would be possible for America to give recognition to China. In February 1972, President and Mrs. Nixon spent a number of days in the country visiting well-known Chinese landmarks, dining with the two leaders, Mao Tse-tung and Chou En-lai. Agreements were made for cultural and scientific exchanges, eventual resumption of trade, and future unification of the mainland with Taiwan. In 1979, formal diplomatic recognition was achieved. With this one visit, the pattern of the Cold War was essentially shifted.

Skill 10.4 Assess the impact of the Vietnam War on U.S. government and society.

U.S. involvement was the second phase of three in Vietnam's history. The first phase began in 1946 when the Vietnamese fought French troops for control of the country. Vietnam prior to 1946 had been part of the French colony of Indochina (since 1861 along with Laos and Kampuchea or Cambodia). In 1954, the defeated French left and the country became divided into Communist North and Democratic South. United States' aid and influence continued as part of the U.S. "Cold War" foreign policy to help any nation threatened by Communism.

The second phase involved the U.S. commitment. The Communist Vietnamese considered the war one of national liberation, a struggle to avoid continual dominance and influence of a foreign power. A cease-fire was arranged in January 1973 and a few months later U.S. troops left for good. The third and final phase consisted of fighting between the Vietnamese but ended April 30, 1975, with the surrender of South Vietnam, the entire country being united under Communist rule.

Participants were the United States of America, Australia, New Zealand, South and North Vietnam, South Korea, Thailand, and the Philippines. With active U.S. involvement from 1957 to 1973, it was the longest war participated in by the U.S.; was tremendously destructive and completely divided the American public in their opinions and feelings about the war. Many were frustrated and angered by the fact that it was the first war fought on foreign soil in which U.S. combat forces were totally unable to achieve their goals and objectives.

Returning veterans faced not only readjustment to normal civilian life but also faced bitterness, anger, rejection, and no heroes' welcomes. Many suffered severe physical and deep psychological problems. The war set a precedent with Congress and the American people actively challenging U.S. military and foreign policy. The conflict, though tempered markedly by time, still exists and still has a definite effect on people.

The Vietnam War also divided the Democratic Party, and the 1968 Democratic National Convention in Chicago turned out to be a highly contentious and bitterly fought, both on the floor of the convention and outside, where thousands had gathered to protest the Vietnam War. Vice President Hubert H. Humphrey became the party's nominee, but he led a divided party. 1968 was a bad year for the United States and especially the Democratic Party. In Vietnam, the forces of the Viet Cong and the North Vietnamese Army (NVA) launched a coordinated and devastating offensive on January 30, on the eve of Tet, the Lunar New Year, disproving the Johnson Administration officials who claimed that the Vietnamese Communists were no longer a viable military force. Although the Tet Offensive was a tactical defeat for the Viet Cong, it no longer could field a large enough military force to match American firepower in a set-piece engagement, it was a strategic defeat for the Americans, in public relations and the political will to continue in a seemingly endless conflict. Also, the Reverend Martin Luther King, Jr., an influential leader of the Civil Rights Movement and its most eloquent spokesman, was assassinated in Memphis, Tennessee, sparking racial riots in many American cities. Also, Senator Robert F. Kennedy of New York, the late President John F. Kennedy's younger brother, was assassinated in Los Angeles after winning the California Democratic Primary. Before he died, it looked very possible that he would have won the party's nomination, running on an anti-war platform.

The Presidential Election campaign of 1964 pitted President Johnson against the Republican nominee, Senator Barry Goldwater of Arizona. Goldwater represented the "New Conservative" wing of his party, which advocated scaling back of government from Roosevelt's New Deal and the liberal social policies of the Kennedy and Johnson administrations. The Goldwater campaign also advocated a strong military to counter the "Red Menace" of the Soviet Union, the People's Republic of China and the Communist bloc nations of the Warsaw Pact. Lyndon Johnson successfully won reelection, based partly on depicting Goldwater as a warmonger who would plunge the United States into a mutually destructive thermonuclear war with the Soviet Union. This left President Johnson with a landslide victory.

Unfortunately for Lyndon B. Johnson, the war in Vietnam overshadowed his domestic programs and indelibly marked his legacy and became known as "Johnson's War". The Gulf of Tonkin Resolution was enacted in late 1964 after an incident off the coast of Vietnam involving U.S. Naval ships and North Vietnamese coastal patrol boats, and effectively gave the President the power to prosecute a war without Congress declaring it, as clearly stated in the Constitution. Soon afterward, Johnson authorized the commitment of conventional military forces to Vietnam in 1965. The war proved to be a drain on the nation's economy and a growing burden for the President as anti-war sentiment divided the nation as it hadn't seen since the Civil War. Eventually, the Vietnam quagmire became such a hindrance to his administration that Johnson declared, in a nationally televised address, that he would halt the bombing of North Vietnam and not be a candidate for the Democratic Party's nominee for the 1968 Presidential Election.

Former Vice President Richard M. Nixon defeated the current Vice President Hubert Humphrey, who had been closely identified with Johnson's Vietnam policy. One of Nixon's campaign promises included a "secret plan" to end American involvement in Vietnam. Ironically, the war dragged on for the length of his first term and he ordered a widening of the war by ordering troops to invade previously neutral Cambodia in 1970. This action led to even more dissent against the war and the killing of four students at Kent State University in Ohio, during a protest over the invasion of Cambodia.

In other international dealings, with a major role played by his National Security Advisor and later Secretary of State Henry Kissinger, Nixon undertook a bold international policy of détente with the Soviet Union and the unexpected step of opening official relations with the People's Republic of China. This was surprising in that both gave political and material support to North Vietnam given Nixon's political reputation as a staunch anti-Communist.

COMPETENCY 11.0 UNDERSTAND MAJOR POLITICAL, SOCIAL, CULTURAL, AND ECONOMIC DEVELOPMENTS, GEOGRAPHIC FEATURES, AND KEY ERAS AND EVENTS IN THE HISTORY OF THE STATE OF OKLAHOMA

Skill 11.1 Recognize the role played by American Indian peoples in the development of Oklahoma.

Archaeologists have discovered evidence of the presence of Native peoples, near present-day Anadarko, of the Clovis culture that dates to about 9000 BCE. From 500 to 1300 CE, a group called "Mound Builders" lived near the Arkansas/Oklahoma border. Artifacts indicate that these people were skilled artisans with an advanced economy. The culture was extinct by the time explorers discovered the mounds in the seventeenth and eighteenth centuries. The region was claimed by the Quapay and Osage tribes.

The **Osage** Indians settled in northeastern Oklahoma around 1796. This area soon became part of the U.S. in the Louisiana Purchase. A group of **Cherokees** settled near the Osage after migrating from the East Coast, which resulted in a struggle for territory between the two tribes, with white settlers caught in the middle. The government was able to achieve a truce with the Osage Chief Clermont that included the tribe ceding seven million acres of land to the government. Members of the tribe continued to attack and in 1825 were forced to turn over all of their land to the government. The Osage moved to the Kansas territory until it was opened to white settlers. In 1870, the government sold the remainder of the Osage lands, gave the money to the tribe, and opened a reservation for them. When oil was discovered on this reservation land, the Osage people became the wealthiest in the nation.

The **Quapaw** sold 45 million acres of land to the U.S. government before 1820 for $18,000. In 1824, the tribal chiefs were induced with $500 each and alcohol to give up the rest of their property to the government. The Quapaw then settled near the Red River on land given to them by another tribe. The tribe was dramatically thinned during the following years by crop failures. The survivors scattered. They did not reorganize until 1890 when they were granted a very small piece of land in Indian Territory. The discovery of zinc and lead on this land has brought royalties that have supported the tribe.

The lands taken from the Quapaw and the Osage became Indian Territory. This became the home of the "Five Civilized Tribes" when they were driven out of their ancestral homes in the southeastern part of the country, following the "**Trail of Tears**." These tribes were called "civilized" because they had advanced systems of government, education and law enforcement. The five tribes were: Choctaw, Chickasaw, Cherokee, Creek and Seminole.

The most tragic relocation experience was that of the Cherokee. Forced to cross Missouri and Arkansas during a harsh winter, many of the tribe died and were buried along the route. This journey came to be known as "The Trail of Tears." By 1856 the five tribes had settled in Indian Territory and each had established a national domain (not a reservation). As they built their own cultures, forming their own constitutional governments, establishing public education, building strong economies and strong legal systems, these tribes also laid the foundation that would guide them through territorial existence and into statehood and modern society.

One of the Cherokee survivors of the Trail of Tears was **Sequoyah**. Fascinated by the ability of whites to write, he studied and experimented for 12 years and eventually created "an 86-letter syllabary" for the Cherokee language. It was easy to learn and quickly become the tribe's communication standard.

After the Civil War, the western portions of Indian Territory were confiscated by the government for the settlement of other tribes who were being relocated from the western parts of the nation because their villages stood in the way of progress. These tribes included the Cheyenne, Arapaho, Kiowa, and Comanche. Among those who were resettled at this time were **Geronimo,** the great Apache warrior, and the Cheyenne Chief **Black Kettle**.

The incursion of white settlers into the Indian lands created resentment and strengthened the determination of the Indians to maintain their territorial rights. There were numerous skirmishes between the Indians and the white settlers, some of which continued into the twentieth century. The Five Civilized Tribes tried to maintain autonomy, even attempting to organize an Indian state called Sequoyah. The U.S. government rejected the idea and a plan that united the two territories into a single state prevailed in 1907. Indians and whites then united to develop the government, the economy, and the cultural assets of the new state. The Constitution of Oklahoma incorporates many elements of the constitutions of the governments of the Five Civilized Tribes and embraces equality in ways that established the patterns for other states.

Oklahoma has the largest Indian population of any state in the nation and is home to the tribal councils of more than 35 tribes.

Skill 11.2 **Identify important individuals and groups in Oklahoma history, and analyze major events that shaped Oklahoma's political, economic, and cultural development.**

Oklahoma is generally believed to have been first explored by the Spanish in the sixteenth century. Coronado crossed the western part of the state in 1541 in search of the "city of gold". It is said that a Spanish priest, Father Gilbert, led a mining expedition into the Wichita Mountains as early as 1657.

French explorers followed shortly after the settlement of Louisiana, and French trade with the Indians dates back to the early eighteenth century. The territory was included in the Louisiana Purchase, and was set apart by the United States in 1834 as an unorganized territory for the use of the Five Civilized Tribes (the Cherokees, Creeks, Seminoles, Choctaws, and Chickasaws). The tribes were forcibly removed from the southeastern states and forced to make their way to the Oklahoma Indian Territory, an event known as "The Trail of Tears."

The tribes established governments with legislative councils, governors, courts, and schools. They became very prosperous, and in the years before the Civil War, they held large numbers of slaves. At the end of the Civil War, they were forced to make new treaties with the United States. In 1866, the Creek Indians ceded part of their lands in Indian Territory to the US for $0.30 per acre and the Seminoles sold their entire holdings at $0.15 per acre.

White men were forbidden by law to settle within the Indian lands and a large amount of this land remained unoccupied. In 1879 systematic agitation led to the opening of these lands to white settlement. The agitators were called **boomers** (the source of the state's nickname). In 1880, it became necessary to use military troops to remove settlers who had crept into the territory. On April 22, 1889, nearly 2,000,000 acres of territory were declared open for settlement. The expectant pioneers had to be kept back by troops until the hour of the opening of the lands and then a mad race for the best farms and town sites followed. The area acquired a population of approximately 100,000 within twenty-four hours, single towns such as Guthrie and Oklahoma City having from 10,000 to 15,000 each, during the first few days. There were, in fact, six land runs between 1889 and 1895. Settlers came from every part of the nation, as well as such countries as Poland, Germany, Ireland and Slavic nations.

The strip of territory known as the Panhandle originally belonged to Texas, but when Texas was admitted to the Union as a slave state it was compelled to give up that part of its territory. For a time this region was a part of no state or territory and had no established law, thus frequently called "No Man's Land." It became the haven of outlaws, and was not made a part of Oklahoma until 1890.

TEACHER CERTIFICATION STUDY GUIDE

In 1891 Oklahoma's admission as a state was defeated in the U.S. Senate. Finally, in 1906, provision was made for the admission of Oklahoma and Indian Territory as one state, if approved in each territory. The union was approved, and a constitution was drafted by delegates from both territories and adopted by the people. At this time, a governor was elected and prohibition was adopted by vote of the people.

Texas settlers were raising an abundant supply of beef, but had to move the cattle to the railroads in Kansas for shipment to the East, where there was great demand for beef. Oklahoma lay between the cattle ranches and the railroad. As cattle drives crossed the plains of Oklahoma, many of the cowboys recognized the advantages of building cattle ranches closer to the railroad among the grassy plains of the state.

After the cattlemen and settlers moved into Oklahoma and the Indian Territory, outlaws soon followed. By the late 1800s, law enforcement had not been firmly established and the landscape offered a number of places to hide. Among the outlaws and the lawmen who tracked them were:

- The outlaw Bill Doolin
- Marshal Heck Thomas
- Bass Reeves, believed to be the first African American deputy marshal West of the Mississippi River
- Judge Isaac C. Parker, known as "the hanging judge"
- Belle Star

As the oil business began to grow in the early twentieth century, many people came to the state to seek their fortune and many became quite rich. The early quarter of the century was a time of some political unrest. Many diverse groups of people had settled in the state. "Black towns", populated by African Americans who chose to live separately, began to form throughout the state, perhaps partly in response to the tendency of the whites to abide by the **Jim Crow** laws which permitted separating people and carried a bias against any non-whites. One of the most deadly race riots is U.S. history occurred in 1921 in Tulsa.

The Socialist Party was somewhat successful in Oklahoma during this time. Their rejection of the Jim Crow laws and their willingness to embrace African American and Native American voters, as well as their willingness to change some of the traditional ideology when it was in their best interest, were the primary reasons for their success. The Party was crushed in the period following WWI.

During the Great Depression, drought and poor agricultural practices combined to cause the **Dust Bowl**. The crop failures and losses of farms led many to leave the state. Many relocated to California, where they tended to form their own communities and came to be called **Oakies**.

MIDDLE LEVEL SOCIAL STUDIES

After the Great Depression, the oil boom and the post-war upswing in the economy led to the rise of tribal sovereignty as well as growth of suburban areas. In 1995, Oklahoma captured the attention of the world as the scene of one of the worst acts of terrorism in U.S. history when the **Alfred P. Murrah Federal Building** in Oklahoma City was bombed.

Skill 11.3   Describe the structure, functions, and operation of Oklahoma government at the state and local levels.

The Constitution of the State of Oklahoma was adopted in 1907 when Oklahoma was admitted to the Union. It contains many provisions which in other states are the subjects of amendments and legislative enactments, such as the initiative and referendum.

The legislature, which meets biennially, consists of a Senate of not more than forty-four members, elected for four years; and a House of Representatives of not less than ninety-seven nor more than 107 members, elected for two year terms.

The executive power is vested in the governor, lieutenant governor, secretary of state, attorney-general, treasurer, superintendent of public instruction, commissioners of labor, charities and corrections and insurance, mine inspector, and state examiner, all of whom are elected for terms of four years. The governor, secretary of state, auditor, and treasurer are not eligible for immediate reelection – there must be an interval of at least one term.

The judicial department consists of a Supreme Court, district, county, and municipal courts, and justices of the peace. The Supreme Court consists of a chief justice and eight judges, elected for six years.

Each county is organized into a corporate body under three county commissioners. Cities of 2,000 or more inhabitants may frame their own governments and may exercise the initiative and referendum.

Skill 11.4   Recognize major geographic features of Oklahoma, and use this knowledge to examine relationships between the physical environment and the historical development of Oklahoma.

Oklahoma is a vast, elevated plain, tilted toward the south and southeast and broken by low mountains. The **Ozarks** of Southwestern Missouri extend into the northeast section of the state and form a wooded table-land, carved by the deep valleys of streams, but having no high peaks. Along the eastern border, long, narrow, heavily timbered ridges rise from the prairies, culminating in the southeast in the low, rugged **Washita Mountains**, covered with forests of pine and oak. The **Arbuckle Mountains** rise 600 or 700 feet above the surrounding country in the south-central part of the state. Picturesque gypsum hills break the monotony of the grassy plains in the west-central section. The **Wichita Mountains** are a straggling range of rough granite peaks, rising abruptly from the seemingly level plain in the southwestern part of the state.

With the exception of these isolated clusters of mountains, most of the southwestern part of the state is a treeless plain. It is carved by the canyons of streams and dotted with buttes and mesas. In the north and west are broad prairies, marked by few streams and mostly bare of timber, but covered with rich buffalo grass. It is here that the great cattle ranches arose. Varying with the prairie grasses are several large salt plains coated with dazzling white salt crystals and containing many salt springs. The Panhandle is a high, rough table-land, extending nearly to the foot of the Rocky Mountains. This is the area of the state's highest elevation (3,000 to 4,700 feet). The lowest part of the state is in the Red River Valley, which is a gently rolling timber land and fertile agricultural region that is 300 to 600 feet above sea level.

Oklahoma is crossed by nine rivers and a large number of smaller streams. None is of any value for navigation. All flow in a southeasterly direction, following the slope of the land. The Red River forms the entire southern boundary, and with its tributaries, drains the southern portion of the state. The Arkansas River, crossing the northeastern part of the state, is the main waterway. There are no permanent lakes and only a few salty ponds, which evaporate during the dry season.

Oklahoma has the dry climate of the Western states and the warm temperature of the South. Due to higher elevation and greater distance from the Gulf Coast, the western and central portions of the state are cooler and dryer than the eastern and southern sections. Rainfall varies from below twenty inches in the west to forty-five inches in the east and, except in the Panhandle, the climate supports agriculture.

The state offers a variety of grasses covering large areas of grazing lands that have supported pasturage for cattle and other livestock. Agriculture has traditionally been a major basis of the state's economy. The lands of various parts of the state support a variety of crops and orchards. The Forests of the eastern part of the state provide timber, as well as fruit and nut trees. Oklahoma is rich is native minerals, including oil, coal, lead and zinc, granite, marble, gypsum, salt, copper, gold, iron and silver.

DOMAIN II.   **GOVERNMENT AND ECONOMICS**

COMPETENCY 12.0   **UNDERSTAND DEMOCRATIC PRINCIPLES AND THE STRUCTURE, ORGANIZATION, AND OPERATION OF DIFFERENT LEVELS OF GOVERNMENT IN THE UNITED STATES**

Skill 12.1   **Relate democratic principles to the structure and function of government in the United States.**

The terms "**civil liberties**" and "**civil rights**" are often used interchangeably, but there are some fine distinctions between the two terms. The term civil liberties is more often used to imply that the state has a positive role to play in assuring that all its' citizens will have equal protection and justice under the law with equal opportunities to exercise their privileges of citizenship and to participate fully in the life of the nation, regardless of race, religion, sex, color or creed. The term civil rights is used more often to refer to rights that may be described as guarantees that are specified as against the state authority implying limitations on the actions of the state to interfere with citizens' liberties. Although the term "civil rights" has thus been identified with the ideal of equality and the term "civil liberties" with the idea of freedom, the two concepts are really inseparable and interacting. Equality implies the proper ordering of liberty in a society so that one individual's freedom does not infringe on the rights of others.

The beginnings of civil liberties and the idea of civil rights in the United States go back to the ideas of the ancient Greeks. This was illustrated by the early struggle for civil rights against the British and the very philosophies that led people to come to the New World in the first place. Religious freedom, political freedom, and the right to live one's life as one sees fit are basic to the American ideal. These were embodied in the ideas expressed in the Declaration of Independence and the Constitution.

The Declaration of Independence is an outgrowth of both ancient Greek ideas of democracy and individual rights and the ideas of the European Enlightenment and the Renaissance, especially the ideology of the political thinker **John Locke**. Thomas Jefferson (1743-1826) the principle author of the Declaration borrowed much from Locke's theories and writings. John Locke was one of the most influential political writers of the 17th century who put great emphasis on human rights and put forth the belief that when governments violate those rights people should rebel. He wrote the book "Two Treatises of Government" in 1690, which had tremendous influence on political thought in the American colonies and helped shaped the U.S. Constitution and Declaration of Independence.

Essentially, Jefferson applied Locke's principles to the contemporary American situation. Jefferson argued that the currently reigning King George III had repeatedly violated the rights of the colonists as subjects of the British Crown. Disdaining the colonial petition for redress of grievances (a right guaranteed by the Declaration of Rights of 1689), the King seemed bent upon establishing an "absolute tyranny" over the colonies. Such disgraceful behavior itself violated the reasons for which government had been instituted. The American colonists were left with no choice, *"it is their right, it is their duty, to throw off such a government, and to provide new guards for their future security"* so wrote Thomas Jefferson.

Yet, though his fundamental principles were derived from Locke's, Jefferson was bolder than his intellectual mentor was. He went farther in that his view of natural rights was much broader than Locke's and less tied to the idea of property rights.

For instance, though both Jefferson and Locke believed very strongly in property rights, especially as a guard for individual liberty, the famous line in the Declaration about people being endowed with the inalienable right to "life, liberty and the pursuit of happiness", was originally Locke's idea. It was "life, liberty, and *private property"*. Jefferson didn't want to tie the idea of rights to any one particular circumstance however, thus, he changed Locke's original specific reliance on property and substituted the more general idea of human happiness as being a fundamental right that is the duty of a government to protect.

Locke and Jefferson both stressed that the individual citizen's rights are prior to and more important than any obligation to the state. Government is the servant of the people. The officials of government hold their positions at the sufferance of the people. Their job is to ensure that the rights of the people are preserved and protected by that government. The citizen come first, the government comes second. The Declaration thus produced turned out to be one of the most important and historic documents that expounded the inherent rights of all peoples; a document still looked up to as an ideal and an example.

The Declaration of Independence was the founding document of the United States of America. The Declaration was intended to demonstrate the reasons that the colonies were seeking separation from Great Britain. Conceived by and written for the most part by Thomas Jefferson, it is not only important for what it says, but also for how it says it. The Declaration is in many respects a poetic document. Instead of a simple recitation of the colonists' grievances, it set out clearly the reasons why the colonists were seeking their freedom from Great Britain. They had tried all means to resolve the dispute peacefully. It was the right of a people, when all other methods of addressing their grievances have been tried and failed, to separate themselves from that power that was keeping them from fully expressing their rights to **"life, liberty, and the pursuit of happiness"**.

By 1776, the colonists and their representatives in the Second Continental Congress realized that things were past the point of no return. The Declaration of Independence was drafted and declared July 4, 1776. George Washington labored against tremendous odds to wage a victorious war. The turning point in the Americans' favor occurred in 1777 with the American victory at Saratoga. This victory decided for the French to align themselves with the Americans against the British. With the aid of Admiral deGrasse and French warships blocking the entrance to Chesapeake Bay, British General Cornwallis trapped at Yorktown, Virginia, surrendered in 1781 and the war was over. The Treaty of Paris officially ending the war was signed in 1783.

Skill 12.2   Examine the structure and operation of the federal government.

See Skill 4.1.

Skill 12.3   Compare the structures and functions of federal, state, and local government.

The various governments of the United States and of Native American tribes have many similarities and a few notable differences. They are more similar than not; and all in all, they reflect the tendency of their people to prefer a representative that has checks and balances that look after one another and the people that keep them in power.

The United States Government has three distinct branches: the Executive, the Legislative, and the Judicial. Each has its own function and its own "check" on the other two.

The Legislative Branch consists primarily of the House of Representatives and the Senate. Each house has a set number of members, the House having 435 apportioned according to national population trends and the Senate having 100 (two for each state). House members serve two-year terms; Senators serve six-year terms. Each house can initiate a bill, but that bill must be passed by a majority of both houses in order to become a law.

The House is primarily responsible for initiating spending bills; the Senate is responsible for ratifying treaties that the President might sign with other countries.

The Executive Branch has the President and Vice-President as its two main figures. The President is the commander-in-chief of the armed forces and the person who can approve or veto all bills from Congress. (Vetoed bills can become law anyway if two-thirds of each house of Congress vote to pass it over the President's objections.) The President is elected to a four-year term by the Electoral College, which usually mirrors the popular will of the people. The President can serve a total of two terms. The Executive Branch also has several departments consisting of advisors to the President. These departments include State, Defense, Education, Treasury, and Commerce, among others. Members of these departments are appointed by the President and approved by Congress.

The Judicial Branch consists of a series of courts and related entities, with the top body being the Supreme Court. The Court decides whether laws of the land are constitutional; any law invalidated by the Supreme Court is no longer in effect. The Court also regulates the enforcement and constitutionality of the Amendments to the Constitution. The Supreme Court is the highest court in the land. Cases make their way to it from federal Appeals Courts, which hear appeals of decisions made by federal District Courts. These lower two levels of courts are found in regions around the country. Supreme Court Justices are appointed by the President and confirmed by the Senate. They serve for life. Lower-court judges are elected in popular votes within their states.

State governments are mirror images of the federal government, with a few important exceptions: Governors are not technically commanders in chief of armed forces; state supreme court decisions can be appealed to federal courts; terms of state representatives and senators vary; judges, even of the state supreme courts, are elected by popular vote; governors and legislators have term limits that vary by state.

Local governments vary widely across the country, although none of them has a judicial branch per se. Some local governments consist of a city council, of which the mayor is a member and has limited powers; in other cities, the mayor is the head of the government and the city council are the chief lawmakers. Local governments also have less strict requirements for people running for office than do the state and federal governments.

The format of the governments of the various Native American tribes varies as well. Most tribes have governments along the lines of the U.S. federal or state governments.

An example is the Cherokee Nation, which has a 15-member Tribal Council as the head of the Legislative branch, a Principal Chief and Deputy Chief who head up the Executive branch and carry out the laws passed by the Tribal Council, and a Judicial branch made up of the Judicial Appeals Tribunal and the Cherokee Nation District Court. Members of the Tribunal are appointed by the Principal Chief. Members of the other two branches are elected by popular vote of the Cherokee Nation.

Skill 12.4   Analyze ways in which democracy has evolved to meet the needs of diverse groups in the United States.

Civil Rights Movement

The phrase "the civil rights movement" generally refers to the nation-wide effort made by black people and those who supported them to gain equal rights to whites and to eliminate segregation. Discussion of this movement is generally understood in terms of the period of the 1950s and 1960s.

The **key people** in the civil rights movement are:

Rosa Parks -- A black seamstress from Montgomery Alabama who, in 1955, refused to give up her seat on the bus to a white man. This event is generally understood as the spark that lit the fire of the Civil Rights Movement. She has been generally regarded as the "mother of the Civil Rights Movement."

Martin Luther King, Jr.-- the most prominent member of the Civil Rights movement. King promoted nonviolent methods of opposition to segregation. The "Letter from Birmingham Jail" explained the purpose of nonviolent action as a way to make people notice injustice. He led the march on Washington in 1963, at which he delivered the "I Have a Dream" speech. He received the 1968 Nobel Prize for Peace.

James Meredith – the first African American to enroll at the University of Mississippi.

Emmett Till – a teenage boy who was murdered in Mississippi while visiting from Chicago. The crime of which he was accused was "whistling at a white woman in a store." He was beaten and murdered, and his body was dumped in a river. His two white abductors were apprehended and tried. They were acquitted by an all-white jury. After the acquittal, they admitted their guilt, but remained free because of double jeopardy laws.

Ralph Abernathy – A major figure in the Civil Rights Movement who succeeded Martin Luther King, Jr. as head of the Southern Christian Leadership Conference

Malcolm X – a political leader and part of the Civil Rights Movement. He was a prominent Black Muslim.

Stokely Carmichael – one of the leaders of the Black Power movement that called for independent development of political and social institutions for blacks. Carmichael called for black pride and maintenance of black culture. He was head of the Student Nonviolent Coordinating Committee.

Jackie Robinson – became the first black Major League Baseball player of the modern era in 1947 and was inducted into the Baseball Hall of Fame in 1962. He was a member of six World Series teams. He actively campaigned for a number of politicians including Hubert Humphrey and Richard Nixon.

Thurgood Marshall – was the grandson of a slave and was the first African American to serve on the Supreme Court of the United States. As a lawyer he was remembered for his high success rate in arguing before the Supreme Court and for his victory in the Brown v. Board of Education case.

Key events of the Civil Rights Movement include:

Brown vs. Board of Education, 1954

The murder of Emmett Till, 1955

Rosa Parks and the Montgomery Bus Boycott, 1955-56 – After refusing to give up her seat on a bus in Montgomery, Alabama, Parks was arrested, tried, and convicted of disorderly conduct and violating a local ordinance. When word reached the black community a bus boycott was organized to protest the segregation of blacks and whites on public buses. The boycott lasted 381 days, until the ordinance was lifted.

Strategy shift to "direct action" – nonviolent resistance and civil disobedience, 1955 – 1965. This action consisted mostly of bus boycotts, sit-ins, freedom rides.

Formation of the Southern Christian Leadership Conference, 1957. This group, formed by Martin Luther King, Jr., John Duffy, Rev. C. D. Steele, Rev. T. J. Jemison, Rev. Fred Shuttlesworth, Ella Baker, A. Philip Randolph, Bayard Rustin and Stanley Levison. The group provided training and assistance to local efforts to fight segregation. Non-violence was its central doctrine and its major method of fighting segregation and racism.

The Desegregation of Little Rock, 1957. Following up on the decision of the Supreme Court in Brown vs. Board of Education, the Arkansas school board voted to integrate the school system. The NAACP chose Arkansas as the place to push integration because it was considered a relatively progressive Southern state. However, the governor called up the National Guard to prevent nine black students from attending Little Rock's Central High School.

Sit-ins – In 1960, students began to stage "sit-ins" at local lunch counters and stores as a means of protesting the refusal of those businesses to desegregate. The first was in Greensboro, NC. This led to a rash of similar campaigns throughout the South. Demonstrators began to protest parks, beaches, theaters, museums, and libraries. When arrested, the protesters made "jail-no-bail" pledges. This called attention to their cause and put the financial burden of providing jail space and food on the cities.

Freedom Rides – Activists traveled by bus throughout the deep South to desegregate bus terminals (required by federal law). These protesters undertook extremely dangerous protests. Many buses were firebombed, attacked by the KKK, and beaten. They were crammed into small, airless jail cells and mistreated in many ways. Key figures in this effort included John Lewis, James Lawson, Diane Nash, Bob Moses, James Bevel, Charles McDew, Bernard Lafayette, Charles Jones, Lonnie King, Julian Bond, Hosea Williams, and Stokely Carmichael.

The Birmingham Campaign, 1963-64. A campaign was planned to use sit-in, kneel-ins in churches, and a march to the county building to launch a voter registration campaign. The City obtained an injunction forbidding all such protests. The protesters, including Martin Luther King, Jr., believed the injunction was unconstitutional, and defied it. They were arrested. While in jail, King wrote his famous Letter from Birmingham Jail. When the campaign began to falter, the "Children's Crusade" called students to leave school and join the protests. The events became news when more than 600 students were jailed. The next day more students joined the protest. The media was present, and broadcast to the nation, vivid pictures of fire hoses being used to knock down children and dogs attacking some of them. The resulting public outrage led the Kennedy administration to intervene. About a month later, a committee was formed to end hiring discrimination, arrange for the release of jailed protesters, and establish normative communication between blacks and whites. Four months later, the KKK bombed the Sixteenth Street Baptist Church, killing 4 girls.

The March on Washington, 1963. This was a march on Washington for jobs and freedom. It was a combined effort of all major civil rights organizations. The goals of the march were: meaningful civil rights laws, a massive federal works program, full and fair employment, decent housing, the right to vote, and adequate integrated education. It was at this march that Martin Luther King, Jr. made the famous "I Have a Dream" speech.

Mississippi Freedom Summer, 1964. Students were brought from other states to Mississippi to assist local activists in registering voters, teaching in "Freedom schools" and in forming the Mississippi Freedom Democratic Party. Three of the workers disappeared – murdered by the KKK. It took six weeks to find their bodies. The national uproar forced President Johnson to send in the FBI. Johnson was able to use public sentiment to effect passage in Congress of the Civil Rights Act of 1964.

Selma to Montgomery marches, 1965. Attempts to obtain voter registration in Selma, Alabama had been largely unsuccessful due to opposition from the city's sheriff. M.L. King came to the city to lead a series of marches. He and over 200 demonstrators were arrested and jailed. Each successive march was met with violent resistance by police. In March, a group of over 600 intended to walk from Selma to Montgomery (54 miles). News media were on hand when, 6 blocks into the march, state and local law enforcement officials attacked the marchers with billy clubs, tear gas, rubber tubes wrapped in barbed wire and bull ships. They were driven back to Selma. National broadcast of the footage provoked a nation-wide response. President Johnson again used public sentiment to achieve passage of the Voting Rights Act of 1965. This law changed the political landscape of the South irrevocably.

Brown v. Board of Education, 1954 – the Supreme Court declared that Plessy v. Ferguson was unconstitutional. This was the ruling that had established "Separate but Equal" as the basis for segregation. With this decision, the Court ordered immediate desegregation.

Civil Rights Act of 1964 – bars discrimination in public accommodations, employment and education

Voting Rights Act of 1965 – suspended poll taxes, literacy tests and other voter tests for voter registration.

The 1960 election was a contest between **John F. Kennedy** and Vice President **Richard Nixon**. The country was divided. The 1960 election was a close election, with President Kennedy winning by only 100,000 votes. President Kennedy faced Cold War challenges including Vietnam and the missile crisis in Cuba. Kennedy introduced economic reforms including a minimum wage increase. The civil rights movement led by Martin Luther King, Jr. was gaining steam and led the President to propose civil rights legislation. During a political trip to Dallas, Texas on November 22, 1963 President Kennedy was assassinated by Lee Harvey Oswald, who was subsequently shot by Jack Ruby, a local nightclub owner. Vice President Lyndon Johnson became President.

A lot of conspiracy theories developed following the President's assassination. The Warren Commission, chaired by the Chief Justice of the Supreme Court was created to investigate the assassination. The Commission concluded that Oswald was the assassin and that he acted alone.

President Johnson continued President Kennedy's commitment to civil rights reform and poverty. Johnson led the passage of the **Civil Rights Act of 1964** and proposed a series of policies around the Great Society program. Great Society proposed a war on poverty, voting rights reforms, Medicare, Medicaid and other civil rights reforms.

President Johnson won reelection over Barry Goldwater. Goldwater, a conservative is often credited with the building of the conservative movement in the United States. The Johnson campaign was able to paint Goldwater as an extremist who may lead to nuclear war.

The escalation of the **Vietnam War** led to a period of discontent in the United States. Increasing opposition to the war challenged the administration. President Johnson faced opposition during the 1968 Presidential campaign first from Eugene McCarthy and then from Senator Robert F. Kennedy. President Johnson announced that he would not seek a second term. Increased civil disobedience followed the assassination of Dr. Martin Luther King, the leader of the civil rights movement. James Earl Ray pleaded guilty to the murder. Rioting occurred in several major cities.

Senator Kennedy was assassinated in June, 1968 following his victory in the California primary by Sirhan Sirhan, who opposed the Senator's position on Israel. The summer of 1968 ended with riots at the Chicago Democratic convention in opposition to the Vietnam War. Hubert Humphrey won the Democratic nomination for President but loss the election to Richard Nixon.

The **disability rights movement** was a successful effort to guarantee access to public buildings and transportation, equal access to education and employment, and equal protection under the law in terms of access to insurance, and other basic rights of American citizens. As a result of these efforts, public buildings and public transportation must be accessible to persons with disabilities. Discrimination in hiring or housing on the basis of disability is also illegal. A "prisoners' rights" movement has been working for many years to ensure the basic human rights of persons incarcerated for crimes. Immigrant rights movements have provided for employment and housing rights, as well as preventing abuse of immigrants through hate crimes. In some states, immigrant rights movements have led to bi-lingual education and public information access. Another group movement to obtain equal rights is the lesbian, gay, bisexual and transgender social movement. This movement seeks equal housing, freedom from social and employment discrimination, and equal recognition of relationships under the law.

TEACHER CERTIFICATION STUDY GUIDE

The **women's rights movement** is concerned with the freedoms of women as differentiated from broader ideas of human rights. These issues are generally different from those that affect men and boys because of biological differences or social constructs. The rights the movement has sought to protect throughout history include:

- The right to vote
- The right to work
- The right to fair wages
- The right to bodily integrity and autonomy
- The right to own property
- The right to an education
- The right to hold public office
- Marital rights
- Parental rights
- Religious rights
- The right to serve in the military
- The right to enter into legal contracts

The movement for women's rights has resulted in many social and political changes. Many of the ideas that seemed very radical merely 100 years ago are now normative.

Some of the most famous leaders in the women's movement throughout American history are:

- Abigail Adams
- Susan B. Anthony
- Gloria E. Anzaldua
- Betty Friedan
- Olympe de Gouges
- Gloria Steinem
- Harriet Tubman
- Mary Wollstonecraft
- Virginia Woolf
- Germaine Greer

Many within the women's movement are primarily committed to justice and the natural rights of all people. This has led many members of the women's movement to be involved in the Black Civil Rights Movement, the gay rights movement, and the recent social movement to protect the rights of fathers.

MIDDLE LEVEL SOCIAL STUDIES

COMPETENCY 13.0 UNDERSTAND THE U.S. ELECTION PROCESS AND THE ROLES OF POLITICAL PARTIES AND INTEREST GROUPS IN THE U.S. POLITICAL SYSTEM

Skill 13.1 Identify and describe the components of the U.S. electoral process.

The U.S. electoral process has many and varied elements, from simple voting to complex campaigning for office. Everything in between is complex and detailed.

First of all, American citizens vote. They vote for laws and statues and referenda and elected officials. They have to register in order to vote, and at that time they can declare their intended membership in a political party. America has a large list of political parties, which have varying degrees of membership. The Democratic and Republican Parties are the two with the most money and power, but other political parties abound. In some cases, people who are registered members of a political party are allowed to vote for only members of that political party. This takes place in many cases in primary elections, when, for example, a number of people are running to secure the nomination of one political party for a general election. If you are a registered Democrat, then in the primary election, you will be able to vote for only Democratic candidates; this restriction will be listed for the general election, in which the Democratic Party will expect you to vote for that party's candidate but in which you can also vote for whomever you want. A potential voter need not register for a political party, however.

Candidates affiliate themselves with political parties (or sometimes not—some candidates run unaffiliated or independent, but they usually have trouble raising enough money to adequately campaign against their opponents). Candidates then go about the business of campaigning, which includes getting the word out of their candidacy, what they believe, and what they will do if elected. All of this costs money,. As part of the campaign candidates may participate in debates, to showcase their views on important issues of the day and how those views differ from those of their opponents. Public speechesand functions, and interviews for coverage in newspapers and magazines or radio and television is part of the campaign process.

Elections take place regularly, so voters know how long it will be before the next election. Some candidates begin planning their next campaign the day after their victory or loss. Voters technically have the option to **recall** elected candidates; such a measure, however, is drastic and requires a large pile of signatures to get the motion on the ballot and then a large number of votes to have the measure approved. As such, recalls of elected candidates are relatively rare. One widely publicized recall in recent years was that of California Governor Gray Davis, who was replaced by movie star Arnold Schwarzenegger.

Another method of removing public officials from office is **impeachment**. This is also rare. Both houses of the state or federal government get involved, and both houses have to approve the impeachment measures by a large margin. In the case of the federal government, the House of Representatives votes to impeach a federal official and the Senate votes to convict or acquit. Conviction means that the official must leave office immediately; acquittal results in no penalties or fines.

The President of the United States is only partially elected by popular vote. The Constitution provides for the President's election to be through the Electoral College. Article II of the Constitution creates the Electoral College. The Founding Fathers included the Electoral College as one of the famous "checks and balances" for two reasons: 1) to give states with small populations more of an equal weight in the presidential election, and 2) they didn't trust the common man (women couldn't vote then.) to be able to make an informed decision on which candidate would make the best president.

. The large-population states had their populations reflected in the House of Representatives. New York and Pennsylvania, two of the states with the largest populations, had the highest number of members of the House of Representatives. But these two states still had only two senators, the exact same number that small-population states like Rhode Island and Delaware had. This was true as well in the Electoral College: Each state had just one vote, regardless of how many members of the House represented that state. So, the one vote that the state of New York cast would be decided by an initial vote of New York's Representatives. (If that initial vote was a tie, then that deadlock would have to be broken.)

Secondly, when the Constitution was being written, not many people knew a whole lot about government, politics, or presidential elections. A large number of people were farmers or lived in rural areas, where they were far more concerned with making a living and providing for their families than they were with who was running for which office. Many of these "common people" could not read or write, either, and wouldn't be able to read a ballot in any case. Like it or not, the Founding Fathers thought that even if these "common people" could vote, they wouldn't necessarily make the best decision for who would make the best president.

Technically, the electors do not have to vote for anyone. The Constitution does not require them to do so. And throughout the history of presidential elections, some have indeed voted for someone else. But tradition holds that the electors vote for the candidate chosen by their state, and so the vast majority of electors do just that. The Electoral College meets a few weeks after the presidential election. Mostly, their meeting is a formality. When all the electoral votes are counted, the president with the most votes wins. In most cases, the candidate who wins the popular vote also wins in the Electoral College. However, this has not always been the case.

Most recently, in 2000 in Florida, the election was decided by the Supreme Court. The Democratic Party's nominee was Vice-President Al Gore. A presidential candidate himself back in 1988, Gore had served as vice-president for both of President Bill Clinton's terms. As such, he was both a champion of Clinton's successes and a reflection of his failures. The Republican Party's nominee was George W. Bush, governor of Texas and son of former President George Bush. He campaigned on a platform of a strong national defense and an end to questionable ethics in the White House. The election was hotly contested, and many states went down to the wire, being decided by only a handful of votes. The one state that seemed to be flip-flopping as Election Day turned into Election Night was Florida. In the end, Gore won the popular vote, by nearly 540,000 votes. But he didn't win the electoral vote. The vote was so close in Florida that a recount was necessary under federal law. Eventually, the Supreme Court weighed in and stopped all the recounts. The last count had Bush winning by less than a thousand votes. That gave him Florida and the White House.

Because of these irregularities, especially the last one, many have taken up the cry to eliminate the Electoral College, which they see as archaic and capable of distorting the will of the people. After all, they argue, elections these days come down to one or two key states, as if the votes of the people in all the other states don't matter. Proponents of the Electoral College point to the tradition of the entity and all of the other elections in which the electoral vote mirrored the popular vote. Eliminating the Electoral College would no doubt take a constitutional amendment, and those are certainly hard to come by. The debate crops up every four years; in the past decade, though, the debate has lasted longer in between elections.

Skill 13.2   Examine the organization and functions of political parties in the United States.

During the colonial period, political parties, as the term is now understood, did not exist. The issues, which divided the people, were centered on the relations of the colonies to the mother country. There was initially little difference of opinion on these issues. About the middle of the 18th century, after England began to develop a harsher colonial policy, two factions arose in America. One favored the attitude of home government and the other declined to obey and demanded a constantly increasing level of self-government. The former came to be known as **Tories**, the latter as **Whigs**. During the course of the American Revolution a large number of Tories left the country either to return to England or move into Canada.

From the beginning of the Confederation, there were differences of opinion about the new government. One faction favored a loose confederacy in which the individual state would retain all powers of sovereignty except the absolute minimum required for the limited cooperation of all the states. (This approach was tried under the Articles of Confederation.) The other faction, which steadily gained influence, demanded that the central government be granted all the essential powers of sovereignty and the what should be left to the states was only the powers of local self-government. The inadequacy of the Confederation demonstrated that the latter were promoting a more effective point of view.

The first real party organization developed soon after the inauguration of Washington as President. His cabinet included people of both factions. Hamilton was the leader of the **Nationalists** – the **Federalist Party** – and Jefferson was the spokesman for the Anti-Federalists, later known as **Republicans, Democratic-Republicans**, and finally **Democrats.   (Also refer to Skill 5.5)**

The Anti-Masonic Party came into being to oppose the Freemasons who they accused of being a secret society trying to take over the country. The Free Soil Party existed for the 1848 and 1852 elections only. They opposed slavery in the lands acquired from Mexico. The Liberty Party of this period was also abolitionist.

In the mid-1850s, the slavery issue was beginning to heat up and in 1854, those opposed to slavery, the Whigs, and some Northern Democrats opposed to slavery, united to form the Republican Party. Before the Civil War, the Democratic Party was more heavily represented in the South and was thus pro-slavery for the most part. The American Party was called the "Know Nothings." They lasted from 1854 to 1858 and were opposed to Irish-Catholic immigration.

The **Constitution Union Party** was formed in 1860. It was made up of entities from other extinguished political powers. They claim to support the Constitution above all and thought this would do away with the slavery issue. The **National Union Party** of 1864 was formed only for the purpose of the Lincoln election. That was the only reason for its existence.

Other political parties came and went in the post-Civil War era. The **Liberal Republican** Party formed in 1872 to oppose Ulysses S. Grant. They thought that Grant and his administration were corrupt and sought to displace them. The Anti-Monopoly Party of 1789 was more short-lived than the previous one. It billed itself as progressive and supported things like a graduated income tax system, the direct election of senators, etc. The **Greenback Party** was formed in 1878 and advocated the use of paper money. The Populist Party was a party consisting mostly of farmers who opposed the gold standard.

The process of political parties with short life spans continued in the twentieth century. Most of this is due to the fact that these parties come into existence in opposition to some policy or politician. Once the "problem" is gone, so is the party that opposed it. The Farmer-Labor Party was a Minnesota based political party. It supported farmers and labor and social security. It had moderate success in electing officials in Minnesota and merged with the Democratic Party in 1944.The Progressive Party was formed in 1912 due to a rift in the Republican Party that occurred when Theodore Roosevelt lost the nomination. This is not the same as the Progressive Party formed in 1924 to back LaFollette of Wisconsin. The Social Democratic Party was an outgrowth of a social movement and didn't have much political success.

There have also been other parties that have had a short termed life in the years following the Great Depression. The **American Labor Party** was a socialist party that existed in New York for a while. The American Workers Party was another socialist party based on Marxism. They also were short-lived. The **Progressive Party** came into being in 1948 to run candidates for President and Vice-President. The Dixicrats or States Rights Democratic Party also formed in 1948. They were a splinter group from the Democrats who supported Strom Thurmond. They also supported Wallace 1968. There have been various Workers' Parties that have come and gone. Most of these have had left-wing tendencies.

There are other political parties but they are not as strong as the Republicans and the Democrats. The Libertarian Party represents belief in the free rights of individuals to do as they wish without the interference of government. They favor a small government so propose a much lower level of government spending and services. The Libertarians are the third largest political party in America. The Socialist Party is also a political party. They run candidates in the elections. They favor the establishment of a radical democracy in which people control production and communities for all, not for the benefit of a few.

The **Communist Party** is also a political party advocating very radical changes in American society. They are concerned with the revolutionary struggle and moving through Marx's stages of history. There are many other parties. The American First Party is conservative as is the American Party. The American Nazi Party is also active in politics. Preaching fascism, they run candidates for elections and occasionally win. The Constitution Party is also representative of conservative views. The **Reform Party** was founded by Ross Perot, after his bid for President as an Independent. The list goes on and on. Many of these parties are regional and small and not on the national scene. Many of them form for a purpose, such as an election, and then dwindle.

Skill 13.3   Recognize the role of lobbyists in the modern legislative process.

Lobbyists are a very visible and time-honored part of the political process. They wield power to varying degrees, depending on the issues involved and how much the parties they represent want to maintain the status quo or effect change.

A lobbyist is someone who works for a political cause by attempting to influence lawmakers to vote a certain way on issues of the day. For example, a lobbyist for an oil production company would urge lawmakers not to increase existing or create new taxes on oil. This urging can take many forms, among them direct communication, letter-writing or phone-in campaigns designed to stir up public sentiment for or against an issue or set of issues. Another common form of lobbying is gifts, including meals and entertainment "given" to lawmakers and paid for by lobbyists. Such "gifts" are not illegal and are intended to make the lawmakers who receive them more inclined to vote in favor of the lobbyists' interests. Lobbyists in days gone by would threaten to hurt or even kill lawmakers who didn't vote the way the lobbyists wanted them to. This kind of lobbying is very rarely found these days; instead, such threats take the form of removal of funding, refusal to support the candidate's future campaigns, and revelations of compromising information about the lawmaker.

Lobbyists also serve to make lawmakers aware of information that they might not have, including how other lawmakers view the important issues of the day. Few and far between is the lawmaker who wants to stand up for impossible causes or suggest a radical change in policy; more prevalent is the lawmaker who wants to be a part of a coalition or be a part of the status quo. Lobbyists can make available information useful to both of these kinds of lawmakers, thus furthering their chances of success. Such information usually comes with a price, however, a price that routinely is an impassioned plea or even demand to vote a certain way on a certain bill.

Not all lobbyists work for high-powered organizations. Some work for themselves or for smaller companies. These lobbyists have the same intentions and the same purposes as their more visible and well-financed colleagues, even though they might not have the same resources at their disposal.

Lobbyists also attempt to influence one another. Some issues create strange bedfellows, and lobbyists who work for different employers might find themselves on the same side of an issue and end up working together for a larger cause, to achieve a common goal.

Skill 13.4   Analyze factors that influence political processes at the local, state, and national levels.

The most basic way for citizens to participate in the political process is to **vote**. Since the passing of the 23rd Amendment in 1965, US citizens who are at least 18 years old are eligible to vote. Elections are held at regular intervals at all levels of government, allowing citizens to weigh in on local matters as well as those of national scope.

Citizens wishing to engage in the political process to a greater degree have several paths open, such as participating in local government. Counties, states, and sometimes neighborhoods are governed by locally elected boards or councils that meet publicly. Citizens are usually able to address these boards, bringing their concerns and expressing their opinions on matters being considered. Citizens may even wish to stand for local election and join a governing board, or seek support for higher office.

Supporting a political party is another means by which citizens can participate in the political process. Political parties endorse certain platforms that express general social and political goals, and support member candidates in election campaigns. Political parties make use of much volunteer labor, with supporters making telephone calls, distributing printed material and campaigning for the party's causes and candidates. Political parties solicit donations to support their efforts as well. Contributing money to a political party is another form of participation citizens can undertake.

Another form of political activity is to support an issue-related political group. Several political groups work actively to sway public opinion on various issues or on behalf of a segment of American society. These groups may have representatives who meet with state and federal legislators to "lobby" them - to provide them with information on an issue and persuade them to take favorable action.

If there's one thing that drives American politics more than any other, it's **money**. Much more often than not, the candidate who has the most money at his or her disposal has the best chance of getting or keeping political office. Money can buy so many things that are necessary to a successful campaign that it is entirely indispensable. Money drives the utilization of every other factor in the running of a campaign.

First and foremost, money is needed to pay the people who will run a candidate's campaign. A candidate cannot expect people to give up, in some cases, years of their lives without monetary compensation. Volunteers on a political campaign are plentiful, but they are not at the top levels. The faithful lieutenants of a campaign are paid performers.

Money is also needed to buy or rent all of the tangible and intangible *things* that are needed to power a political campaign: office supplies, meeting places, transportation vehicles, and many more. The inventory of these items can add up frighteningly quickly, and money can appear to disappear like water down a drain.

Of course, the expense that gets the most exposure these days is **media** advertising, specifically television advertising. This is the most expensive kind of advertising, but it also has the potential to reach the widest audience. TV ad prices can run into the hundreds of thousands of dollars, depending on when they run; but they have the potential to reach perhaps millions of viewers. Here, too, money can disappear quickly. A political campaign is also a fashion show and candidates cannot afford to go without showing their friendly faces to as wide an audience as possible on a regular basis. Other forms of advertising include radio and Web ads, signs and billboards, and good old-fashioned flyers.

The sources of all this money that is needed to run a successful political campaign are varied. A candidate might have a significant amount of money in his or her own personal coffers. In rare cases, the candidate finances the entire campaign. However, the most prevalent source of money is outside donations. A candidate's friends and family might donate funds to the campaign, as well as the campaign workers themselves. State and federal governments will also contribute to most regional or national campaigns, provided that the candidate can prove that he or she can raise a certain amount of money first. The largest source of campaign finance money, however, comes from so-called "special interests." A large company such as an oil company or a manufacturer of electronic goods will want to keep prices or tariffs down and so will want to make sure that laws lifting those prices or tariffs aren't passed.

To this end, the company will contribute money to the campaigns of candidates who are likely to vote to keep those prices or tariffs down. A candidate is not obligated to accept such a donation, of course, and further is not obligated to vote in favor of the interests of the special interest; however, doing the former might create a shortage of money and doing the latter might ensure that no further donations come from that or any other special interest. An oil company wants to protect its interests, and its leaders don't very much care which political candidate is doing that for them as long as it is being done.

Another powerful source of support for a political campaign is **special interest groups** of a political nature. These are not necessarily economic powers but rather groups whose people want to effect political change (or make sure that such change doesn't take place, depending on the status of the laws at the time). A good example of a special interest group is an anti-abortion group or a pro-choice group. The abortion issue is still a divisive one in American politics, and many groups will want to protect or defend or ban—depending on which side they're on—certain rights and practices. An anti-abortion group, for example, might pay big money to candidates who pledge to work against laws that protect the right for women to have abortions. As long as these candidates continue to assure their supporters that they will keep on fighting the fight, the money will continue to flow. This kind of social group usually has a large number of dedicated individuals who do much more than vote: They organize themselves into political action committees, attend meetings and rallies, and work to make sure that their message gets out to a wide audience. Methods of spreading the word often include media advertising on behalf of their chosen candidates. This kind of expenditure is no doubt welcomed by the candidates, who will get the benefit of the exposure but won't have to spend that money because someone else is signing the checks.

COMPETENCY 14.0 UNDERSTAND THE RIGHTS AND RESPONSIBILITIES OF INDIVIDUAL CITIZENS IN A DEMOCRATIC SOCIETY AND THE SKILLS, KNOWLEDGE, AND VALUES NECESSARY FOR SUCCESSFUL PARTICIPATION IN DEMOCRATIC SELF-GOVERNMENT

Skill 14.1 Analyze the political, legal, and personal rights guaranteed by the U.S. Constitution.

The first amendment guarantees the basic rights of freedom of religion, freedom of speech, freedom of the press, and freedom of assembly.

The next three amendments came out of the colonists' struggle with Great Britain. For example, the third amendment prevents Congress from forcing citizens to keep troops in their homes. Before the Revolution, Great Britain tried to coerce the colonists to house soldiers.

Amendments five through eight protect citizens who are accused of crimes and are brought to trial. Every citizen has the right to due process of law, (due process as defined earlier, being that the government must follow the same fair rules for everyone brought to trial.) These rules include the right to a trial by an impartial jury, the right to be defended by a lawyer, and the right to a speedy trial.

The last two amendments limit the powers of the federal government to those that are expressly granted in the Constitution, any rights not expressly mentioned in the Constitution, thus, belong to the states or to the people.

In regards to specific guarantees:

Freedom of Religion: Religious freedom has not been seriously threatened in the United States historically. The policy of the government has been guided by the premise that church and state should be separate. However, when religious practices have been at cross-purposes with attitudes prevailing in the nation at particular times, there has been restrictions placed on these practices. Some of these have been restrictions against the practice of polygamy that is supported by certain religious groups. The idea of animal sacrifice that is promoted by some religious beliefs is generally prohibited. The use of mind altering illegal substances that some use in religious rituals has been restricted. In the United States, all recognized religious institutions are tax-exempt in following the idea of separation of church and state, and therefore, there have been many quasi-religious groups that have in the past tried to take advantage of this fact. All of these issues continue, and most likely will continue to occupy both political and legal considerations for some time to come.

Freedom of Speech, Press, and Assembly: These rights historically have been given wide latitude in their practices, though there has been instances when one or the other have been limited for various reasons. The classic limitation, for instance, in regards to freedom of speech, has been the famous precept that an individual is prohibited from yelling fire! in a crowded theatre. This prohibition is an example of the state saying that freedom of speech does not extend to speech that might endanger other people. There is also a prohibition against **slander,** or the knowingly stating of a deliberate falsehood against one party by another. There are many regulations regarding freedom of the press, the most common example are the various laws against **libel**, (or the printing of a known falsehood). In times of national emergency, various restrictions have been placed on the rights of press, speech and sometimes assembly.

The legal system in recent years has also undergone a number of serious changes, some would say challenges, with the interpretation of some constitutional guarantees.

America also has a number of organizations that present themselves as champions of the fight for civil liberties and civil rights in this country. Much criticism, however, has been raised at times against these groups as to whether or not they are really protecting rights, or following a specific ideology, perhaps attempting to create "new" rights, or in many cases, looking at the strict letter of the law, as opposed to what the law actually intends.

"Rights" come with a measure of responsibility and respect for the public order, all of which must be taken into consideration.

Overall, the American experience has been one of exemplary conduct in regards to the protection of individual rights. Where there has been a lag in its practice, notably the refusal to grant full and equal rights to blacks, the fact of their enslavement, and the second class status of women for much of American history, negates the good that the country has done in other areas. Other than the American Civil War, the country has proved itself to be more or less resilient in being able, for the most part, peacefully, to change when it has not lived up to its' stated ideals in practice. What has been called "the virtual bloodless civil rights revolution" is a case in point.

Though much effort and suffering accompanied the struggle, in the end it did succeed in changing the foundation of society in such a profound way that would have been unheard of in many other countries without the strong tradition of freedom and liberty that was, and is, the underlying feature of American society.

Skill 14.2 Describe ways citizens participate in and influence the political process in the United States.

The most basic way for citizens to participate in the political process is to vote. Since the passing of the 23rd Amendment in 1965, US citizens who are at least 18 years old are eligible to vote. Elections are held at regular intervals at all levels of government, allowing citizens to weigh in on local matters as well as those of national scope.

Citizens wishing to engage in the political process to a greater degree have several paths open, such as participating in local government. Counties, states, and sometimes even neighborhoods are governed by locally-elected boards or councils which meet publicly. Citizens are usually able to address these boards, bringing their concerns and expressing their opinions on matters being considered. Citizens may even wish to stand for local election and join a governing board, or seek support for higher office.

Supporting a political party is another means by which citizens can participate in the political process. Political parties endorse certain platforms that express general social and political goals, and support member candidates in election campaigns. Political parties make use of much volunteer labor, with supporters making telephone calls, distributing printed material and campaigning for the party's causes and candidates. Political parties solicit donations to support their efforts as well. Contributing money to a political party is another form of participation citizens can undertake.

Another form of political activity is to support an issue-related political group. Several political groups work actively to sway public opinion on various issues or on behalf of a segment of American society. These groups may have representatives who meet with state and federal legislators to "lobby" them - to provide them with information on an issue and persuade them to take favorable action.

Skill 14.3 **Demonstrate the ability to identify central questions in public policy debates, and to distinguish between fact, opinion, and interpretation.**

From the earliest days of political expression in America, efforts were a collaborative affair. One of the first of the democratic movements was the Sons of Liberty, an organization that made its actions known but kept the identity of its members a secret. Famous members of this group included John and Samuel Adams. Other patriotic movements sprang up after the success of the Sons of Liberty was assured, and the overall struggle against British oppression was a collaborative effort involving thousands of people throughout the American colonies.

American political discussion built on the example of the British Parliament, which had two houses of its legislative branch of government containing representatives who had great debates on public policy before making laws. Although this process isn't anywhere near as wide open and public and spirited as it is today, the lawmakers nonetheless had their chance to make their views known on the issues of the day. Some laws, like those implementing the infamous taxes following the British and American victory in the French and Indian War, required relatively little debate, since they were so popular and were obviously wanted by the Prime Minister and other heads of the government. Other laws enjoyed spirited debate and took months to pass.

The Assemblies of the American colonies inherited this tradition and enjoyed spirited debate as well, even though they met just one or a few times a year. One of the most famous examples of both collaboration and deliberation was the Stamp Act Congress, a gathering of fed-up Americans who drafted resolutions demanding that Great Britain repeal the unpopular tax on paper and documents. The Americans who met at both of the Continental Congresses and the Constitutional Convention built on this tradition as well.

Thanks to the voluminous notes taken diligently by James Madison, we have a clear record of just how contentious at times the debate over the shape and scope of the American federal government was. Still, every interest was advanced, every argument put forward, and every chance given to repeal the main points of the government document. The result was a blueprint for government approved by the vast majority of the delegates and eventually approved by people in all of the American colonies. This ratification process has continued throughout the history of the country, through passage by both houses of Congress to ratification by state legislatures and finally to approval by a majority of the people of a majority of states.

Even in the earliest times, people having special interests were trying to influence political debates in their favor. Plenty of people who favored a strong central government or its opposite, a weak central government, could be found who were not delegates to the Constitutional Convention. No doubt these people were in communication with the delegates.

A special interest is nothing more than a subject that a person or people who pursue one issue above all others. As more people gained more money, they began to pressure their lawmakers more and more to pass laws that favored their interests. Exporters of goods from ports to destinations overseas would not want to see heavy taxes on such exports. People who owned large amounts of land wouldn't want to see a sharp increase in property taxes.. These special interests can be found today. These days, it's just more money and more ways to influence lawmakers that distinguish special interest pursuits from those made in years past. So, too, can we draw a straight line from the deliberative-collaborative traditions of today to the secret meetings and political conventions of colonial days.

Skill 14.4   Analyze factors that have expanded or limited the role of individuals in U.S. political life during the twentieth century.

A free press is essential to maintaining responsibility and civic-mindedness in government and in the rest of society. The broadcast, print, and electronic media in America serve as societal and governmental watchdogs, showcasing for the rest of America and for the world what kinds of brilliant and terrible things the rich, powerful, and elected are doing.

First and foremost, the media report on the actions taken and encouraged by leaders of the government. In many cases, these actions are common knowledge. Policy debates, discussions on controversial issues, struggles against foreign powers in economic and wartime endeavors—all are fodder for media reports. The First Amendment guarantees media in America the right to report on these things, and the media reporters take full advantage of that right and privilege in striving not only to inform the American public but also to keep the governmental leaders in check.

The most extreme kind of action that needs reporting on is an illegal one. Officials who perform illegal actions will, in most cases, find those actions part of the public record. These officials are expected to be models of society or, at the very least, following the very laws that they were elected to pass or erase. This is largely a trust issue as well: If you can't trust your elected leaders, who can you trust? Many people would answer that question with the skeptical, "No one can be trusted, especially those in government." Others would say, more simply, that greater scrutiny is needed for those in legislative power, since they are more easily able to hide questionable actions. No one is above the law, especially those charged with making those laws. If a lawmaker thinks that he or she is above the law, then in most cases he or she will be sadly mistaken to discover that that assumption is incorrect. In the vast majority of cases, lawmakers who break the law in a big way are caught and informed on, especially because of reporting done by newspapers, radio stations, magazines, and websites.

The flip side of this is that lawmakers often do positive, noteworthy, and newsworthy things that should be reported on as well. The official who spearheads a campaign to get a certain wide-ranging bill passed will want to take the appropriate credit for those efforts, making his actions known to the media so those actions can be reported to his or her constituents.

Owners of large companies and charities and especially recognizable figures in popular entertainment are continually under scrutiny for signs of questionable actions or behavior. In the same way that lawmakers are responsible for public legislative policy, many company owners are responsible for public economic policy. If a corporation is stealing money from its employees or shareholders, then those employees and shareholders and the American public at large need to know about it. Such reporting is not only informative but also usually leads to indictments, prosecutions, and jail terms for the perpetrators of such economic crimes.

Wartime presents challenging times for a country committed to a free press. Troop movements and battle plans aren't the sort of thing that need to be broadcast. Such broadcasts have a way of making their way into the hands of the very people that the country's armed forces are attempting to defeat on the battlefield. (An excellent example of this was seen by all in the lead up and prosecution of the Gulf War, when Iraqi leader Saddam Hussein and his allies and followers kept up with Allied actions by watching CNN.) The government, and especially its armed forces, has the right to refuse to provide information that is vital to national security. This right has been validated time and again by the U.S. Supreme Court and is the law of the land.

In other countries, most notably China these days, reporters are *not* free to report on everything they see, especially things that the government does not want its people to know. If such reporting is banned, then the government can conceivably conduct all sorts of activities without fear of those actions being exposed by the mainstream media..

The proliferation of TV channels has made it very difficult for a lawmaker *not* to get noticed if her or she does something remarkable these days. And, of course, we now have the Internet, a vast, heterogeneous world of opportunities. Internet opportunities include not just news websites but personal websites and blogs.

Bloggers routinely do not use editors or run their copy by anyone else before publishing it; as such, they have lower standards of professionalism overall and need to be regarded as such. What they write might be totally true; the blog, however, is known as a *log*, a chronicle of thoughts and opinions about the affairs of the day, not so much a blow-by-blow of facts and figures.

Public officials will hire one or more people or perhaps a whole department or an entire business to conduct *public relations*, which are efforts intended to make the lawmakers look good in the eyes of their constituents. A public relations person or firm will have as its overreaching goal the happiness of the lawmaker who hired her or them and will gladly write press releases, arrange media events (like tours of schools or soup kitchens), and basically do everything else to keep their employer's name in the public eye in a good way. This includes making the lawmaker's position on important issues known to the public.

Especially controversial issues will be embraced on the other side by lawmakers, and those lawmakers will want their constituents to know how they intend to vote those issues. It's also a good idea to find out what your constituents think about these issues of the day, since the fastest way to get yourself bad publicity or thrown out at re-election time is to ignore the weight of public opinion.

On the other side of the coin, members of the media will want the public to know what their lawmakers are saying and doing. Many reporters and editors consider it in the best interest of the country to report on the dealings and actions of those in government, especially if those dealings or actions are of a questionable legal or moral nature. It works both ways and the smart politicians understand the nature of that dichotomy and use it to their advantage.

TEACHER CERTIFICATION STUDY GUIDE

COMPETENCY 15.0 UNDERSTAND THE COMPONENTS, ORGANIZATION, AND OPERATION OF THE U.S. ECONOMY AND THE BASIC PRINCIPLES OF CONSUMER ECONOMICS

Skill 15.1 Recognize the basic principles and processes of capitalism.

The fact that resources are scarce is the basis for the existence of economics. Economics is defined as a study of how scarce resources are allocated to satisfy unlimited wants. Resources refer to the four factors of production: **labor, capital, land and entrepreneurship**. The fact that the supply of these resources is finite means that society cannot have as much of everything that it wants. There is a constraint on production and consumption and on the kinds of goods and services that can be produced and consumed. **Scarcity** means that choices have to be made. If society decides to produce more of one good, this means that there are fewer resources available for the production of other goods. Assume a society can produce two goods, good A and good B. The society uses resources in the production of each good. If producing one unit of good A results in an amount of resources used to produce three units of good B then producing one more unit of good A results in a decrease in three units of good B. In effect, one unit of good A "costs" three units of good B. This cost is referred to as opportunity cost. **Opportunity cost** is the value of the sacrificed alternative, the value of what had to be given up in order to have the output of good A. Opportunity cost does not just refer to production. Your opportunity cost of studying with this guide is the value of what you are not doing because you are studying, whether it is watching TV, spending time with family, working, or whatever. Every choice has an opportunity cost.

In a market economy the markets function on the basis of **supply and demand** and, if markets are free, the result is an efficient allocation of resources. The seller's supply curve represents the different quantities of a good or service the seller is willing and able to bring to the market at different prices during a given period of time. The seller has to have the good and has to be willing to sell it. If either of these isn't true, then he isn't a part of the relevant market supply. The supply curve represents the selling and production decisions of the seller and is based on the costs of production. The costs of production of a product are based on the costs of the resources used in its production. The costs of resources are based on the scarcity of the resource. The scarcer a resource is, relatively speaking the higher its price. A diamond costs more than paper because diamonds are scarcer than paper is. All of these concepts are embodied in the seller's supply curve.

The same thing is true on the buying side of the market. The buyer's preferences, tastes, income, etc. – all of his buying decisions – are embodied in the demand curve.

MIDDLE LEVEL SOCIAL STUDIES

The demand curve represents the various quantities of a good or a service the buyer is willing and able to buy at different prices during a given period of time. The buyer has to want the good and be willing and able to purchase it. He may want a Ferrari but can't afford one; therefore, he is not a part of the relevant market demand.

The demand side of the market is showing us what buyers are willing and able to purchase and the supply side of the market is showing us what sellers are willing and able to supply. But we don't know anything about what buyers and sellers actually do buy and sell without putting the two sides together. If we compare the buying decisions of buyers with the selling decisions of sellers, the place where they coincide represents the market equilibrium. This is where the demand and supply curves intersect. At this one point of intersection the buying decisions of buyers are equal to the selling decisions of sellers. The quantity that buyers want to buy at that particular price is equal to the quantity that sellers want to sell at that particular price. This is the market equilibrium. At this one point, the quantity demanded is equal to the quantity supplied. This price – quantity combination represents an efficient allocation of resources.

Firms sell their outputs in different output market structures. There are four kinds of market structures in the output market: **perfect competition, monopoly, monopolistic competition and oligopoly**. Each of these market structures differs in terms of competition. Perfect competition is the most competitive of all market structures. For the most part, perfect competition is a theoretical extreme, most closely approximated by agriculture. Products are homogenous in this market structure. The numerous firms sell a product identical to that sold by all other firms in the industry and have no control over the price. There are a large number of buyers and a large number of sellers and no one buyer or seller is large enough to affect market price. The price is determined by supply and demand and the price is a given to the firm. This means the individual firm faces a horizontal or perfectly elastic demand curve. Buyers and sellers have full market information and there are no barriers to entry. A barrier to entry is anything that makes it difficult for firms to enter or leave the industry.

The opposite of perfect competition is a monopoly. **Monopoly** is a market structure in which there is only one seller who is selling a unique product for which there are no substitutes. The firm is the only supplier of the good. The firm can control his price because the firm is equal to the industry. A monopolist becomes a monopolist and remains a monopolist because of barriers to entry, which are very high. These barriers to entry like a very high fixed cost structure, function to keep new firms from entering the industry. Monopoly in its pure form is rare and is illegal in the U.S. economy.

In between the two extremes are the two market structures that most U.S. firms fall into. **Oligopoly** is a market structure in which there are a few sellers of products that may be either homogeneous, like steel, or heterogeneous, like automobiles. There are high barriers to entry, which is why there are only a few firms in each industry. Each firm has some degree of monopoly power but not as much as a monopolist. Oligopoly is a market structure in which firms actions and reactions are dependent on one another. Each firm must consider the actions of its rivals when making any decisions. This is referred to as a mutual interdependence in decision making. If Ford offers rebates, Chrysler will also offer rebates to keep its customers. Monopolistic competition is the market structure you see in shopping centers. There are numerous firms, each selling similar products, but not identical, like brand name shoes or clothing. Products are close substitutes for one another. Each firm has a small market share since no one firm is large enough to dominate the industry. Barriers to entry are not as high as in oligopoly, which is why there are more firms. It is relatively easy for most firms to enter or leave the industry.

When products are close substitutes for one another, firms engage in advertising, or non-price competition, to try to differentiate their product from their competitors. Advertising and non-price competition occur in monopolistic competition and homogeneous oligopoly.````

Skill 15.2 Identify the functions of and describe relationships among basic components of the U.S. economic system.

Macroeconomics is concerned with a study of the economy's overall economic performance, or what is called the Gross Domestic Product or GDP. The GDP is a monetary measure of the economy's output during a specified time period and is used by all nations to measure and compare national production. Tabulating the economy's output can be measured in two ways, both of which give the same result: the expenditures approach and the incomes approach. Basically, what is spent on the national output by each sector of the economy is equal to what is earned producing the national output by each of the factors of production. The two methods have to be equal.

The macro economy consists of four broad sectors: **consumers, businesses, government** and the **foreign sector**. In the expenditures approach, GDP is determined by the amount of spending in each sector. GDP is equal to the consumption expenditures of consumers plus the investment expenditures of businesses plus spending of all three levels of government plus the net export spending in the foreign sector.

$$GDP = C + I + G + (X-M)$$

The previous formula is called the GDP identity. The computation of GDP includes only final goods and services, not the value of intermediate goods. An intermediate good is a good that is used in the production of other goods. It is an input and its value is included in the price of the final good. If the value of intermediate goods is included, there would be double counting and GDP would be overstated.

Assessing and comparing standards of living between nations is not easy. GDP itself is not an indicator of living conditions. If a nation's GDP figure is divided by its population to obtain per capita GDP, this can function somewhat as a basis for comparison between countries. But it doesn't provide information about work-leisure time or if the composition of output is right for the particular society.

Fiscal policy consists of changing the level of taxes and government spending to influence the level of economic activity. Contractionary fiscal policy consists of decreasing government spending and/or raising taxes and is intended to slow down a rapidly expanding economy and to curb inflation. Expansionary fiscal policy consists of lowering taxes and raising government spending to stimulate a sluggish economy and generate higher levels of employment. Changes take place in government revenues and expenditures when fiscal policy is used.

The **federal budget** is a statement showing government expenditures and revenues for the fiscal year. The government's budget does not have to balance. When government expenditures are equal to revenues, the budget is balanced. When government expenditures are greater than revenues, the government has a budget deficit. When government expenditures are less than revenues, the government has a budget surplus. Whenever there is a budget deficit, whenever government spends more than it receives, the budget deficit has to be financed. The government can finance its deficit by borrowing or by the process of money creation. When government borrows, it sells bonds and uses the funds acquired by the bond sales to finance its deficit. Money creation refers to increasing the reserves in the banking system. Expansionary fiscal policy, lowering taxes and increasing government spending, puts the budget in a deficit position where government is spending more than it is taking in.

If we add all of the deficits that have occurred over time and subtract from it the figures for all of the surpluses, we have the figure for the national debt.

National debt = Total Surpluses – Total Deficits

The figure for the national debt represents the amount of money that government owes to the holders of U.S. government debt obligations. These are basically Treasury bonds, notes and bills. Every time you buy an U.S. savings bond, you are helping to finance the national debt because you are loaning money to the government.

MIDDLE LEVEL SOCIAL STUDIES

Every year that the federal government has a budget deficit that is financed by borrowing, the size of the national debt increases and so do the interest payments on the debt. Whenever the government implements contractionary fiscal policy to stimulate the economy and this fiscal policy results in a budget deficit, then the size of the national debt increases.

Nations need a smoothly functioning banking system in order to experience economic growth. The **Federal Reserve Syst**em (Fed) provides the framework for the monetary system in the United States. The Fed implements monetary policy through the banking system and it is a tool used to promote economic stability at the macro level of the economy. There are three components of monetary policy: the **reserve ratio**, the **discount rate** and **open market operations**. Changes in any of these three components affect the amount of money in the banking system and thus, the level of spending in the economy.

The reserve ratio refers to the portion of deposits that banks are required to hold as vault cash or on deposit with the Fed. The purpose of this reserve ratio is to give the Fed a way to control the money supply. These funds can't be used for any other purpose. When the Fed changes the reserve ratio, it changes the money creation and lending ability of the banking system. When the Fed wants to expand the money supply it lowers the reserve ratio, leaving banks with more money to loan. This is one aspect of expansionary monetary policy. When the reserve ratio is increased, this results in banks having less money to make loans with, which is a form of contractionary monetary policy, which leads to a lower level of spending in the economy.

Another way in which monetary policy is implemented is by changing the discount rate. When banks have temporary cash shortages, they can borrow from the Fed. The interest rate on the funds they borrow is called the discount rate. Raising and lowering the discount rate is a way of controlling the money supply. Lowering the discount rate encourages banks to borrow from the Fed, instead of restricting their lending to deal with the temporary cash shortage. By encouraging banks to borrow, their lending ability is increased and this results in a higher level of spending in the economy. Lowering the discount rate is a form of expansionary monetary policy. Discouraging bank lending by raising the discount rate, then is a form of contractionary monetary policy.

The final tool of monetary policy is called open market operations. This consists of the Fed buying or selling government securities with the public or with the banking system. When the Fed sells bonds, it is taking money out of the banking system. The public and the banks pay for the bonds, thus resulting in fewer dollars in the economy and a lower level of spending. The Fed selling bonds is a form of contractionary monetary policy that leads to a lower level of spending in the economy.

MIDDLE LEVEL SOCIAL STUDIES

The Fed is expanding the money supply when it buys bonds from the public or the banking system because it is paying for those bonds with dollars that enter the income-expenditures stream. The result of the Fed buying bonds is to increase the level of spending in the economy.

Skill 15.3   Analyze domestic and global factors affecting the formulation of U.S. economic policy.

All nations have records of their international transactions. A nation's international transactions are recorded in the Balance of Payments. The Balance of Payment consists of two major accounts: the Current Account, which gives the figures for the exchange of goods, services and unilateral transfers; and the Capital Accounts which provides the figures for capital flows resulting from the exchange of real and financial assets. The Current Account contains the Balance of Trade, which are a nation's merchandise imports minus its merchandise exports. If the nation's exports are greater than its imports, it has a trade surplus. If its imports are greater than its exports, it has a trade deficit. Adding in the category of exports and imports of services gives the Balance on Goods and Services. Adding unilateral transfers, military expenditures and other miscellaneous items yields the Balance on Current Account. The Capital Accounts consists of strictly financial items in various categories. The last category is Statistical Discrepancies, which is a balancing entry so that the overall Balance of Payments always balances. This has to do with floating exchange rate regimes. It is the trade account that is watched closely today.

The exchange rates of most currencies today are determined in a floating exchange rate regime. In a clean float, supply and demand factors for each currency in terms of another are what determine the equilibrium price or the exchange rate. A clean float is a market functioning without any government interference, purely on the basis of demand and supply. Sometimes nations will intervene in the market to affect the value of their currency vis-à-vis the other currency. This situation is referred to as a managed or dirty float. A government is not required to intervene to maintain a currency value, as they were under a regime of fixed exchange rates. A government that intervenes in the currency market now does so because it wants to, not because it is required to intervene to maintain a certain exchange rate value. For example, if the U.S. government thinks the dollar is depreciating too much against the Canadian dollar, the U.S. government will buy U.S. dollars in the open market and pay for them with Canadian dollars. This increases the demand for U.S. dollars and increases the supply of Canadian dollars. The U.S. dollar appreciates, or increases in value, and the Canadian dollar depreciates, or decreases in value, in response to the government intervention. A stronger U.S. dollar means Canadian goods are cheaper for Americans, and American goods are more expensive for Canadians.

In the international economy capital flows where it earns the highest rate of return, regardless of national borders. If the interest rate is higher in London than it is in New York, dollars will be converted into pounds, which results in dollar depreciation and pound appreciation, as capital flows into London in response to the higher interest rate. The weaker dollar means that U.S. exports are more attractive to foreigners. It also means that U.S. citizens pay a higher price for imports. Markets today are truly international when it comes to capital flows. Current national and international issues and controversies involve employment and trade issues. In today's world, markets are international. Nations are all part of a global economy. No nation exists in isolationism or is totally independent of other nations. **Isolationism** is referred to as autarky or a closed economy. No one nation has all of the resources needed to be totally self-sufficient in everything it produces and consumes. Even a nation with such a well-diversified resource base like the United States has to import items like coffee, tea and other items. The United States is not as dependent on trade as are other nations but we still need to trade for goods and items that we either can't produce domestically or that we can't produce as cheaply as other nations can.

Membership in a global economy means that what one nation does affects other nations because economies are linked through international trade, commerce and finance. They all have open economies. International transactions affect the levels of income, employment and prices in each of the trading economies. The relative importance of trade is based on what percentage of Gross Domestic Product trade constitutes. In a country like the United States, trade represents only a few percent of GDP. In other nations, trade may represent over fifty percent of GDP. For those countries changes in international transactions can cause many economic fluctuations and problems.

Trade barriers are a way in which economic problems are caused in other countries. Suppose the domestic government is confronted with rising unemployment in the domestic industry due to cheaper foreign imports. Consumers are buying the cheaper foreign import instead of the higher priced domestic good. In order to protect domestic labor, government imposes a tariff; thus raising the price of the more efficiently produced foreign good. The result of the tariff is that consumers buy more of the domestic good and less of the foreign good. The problem is that the foreign good is the product of the foreign nation's labor. A decrease in the demand for the foreign good means foreign producers don't need as much labor, so they lay-off workers in the foreign country. The result of the trade barrier is that unemployment has been exported from the domestic country to the foreign country. Treaties like NAFTA are a way lowering or eliminating trade barriers on a regional basis. As trade barriers are lowered or eliminated, this causes changes in labor and output markets. Some grow; some shrink. These adjustments are taking place now for Canada, the United States and Mexico. Membership in a global economy adds another dimension to economics, in terms of aiding developing countries and in terms of national policies that are implemented.

MIDDLE LEVEL SOCIAL STUDIES   162

Skill 15.4   Examine principles of consumer economics and factors affecting economic choices in everyday contexts.

Free enterprise, individual entrepreneurship, competitive markets and consumer sovereignty are all parts of a **market economy**. Individuals have the right to make their own decisions as to what they want to do as a career. The financial incentives are there for individuals who are willing to take the risk. A successful venture earns profit. It is these financial incentives that serve to motivate inventors and small businesses. The same is true for businesses. They are free to determine what production technique they want to use and what output they want to produce within the confines of the legal system. They can make investments based on their own decisions. Nobody is telling them what to do. Competitive markets, relatively free from government interference are also a manifestation of the freedom that the U.S. economic system is based on. These markets function on the basis of supply and demand to determine output mix and resource allocation. There is no commissar dictating what is produced and how. Since consumers buy the goods and services that give them satisfaction, this means that, for the most part, they don't buy the goods and services that they don't want that don't give them satisfaction. **Consumers** are, in effect, voting for the goods and services that they want with the dollars or what is called dollar voting. Consumers are basically signaling firms as to how they want society's scarce resources used with their dollar votes. A good that society wants acquires enough dollar votes for the producer to experience profits – a situation where the firm's revenues exceed the firm's costs. The existence of profits indicate to the firm that it is producing the goods and services that consumers want and that society's scarce resources are being used in accordance with consumer preferences. When a firm does not have a profitable product, it is because that product is not tabulating enough dollar votes of consumers. Consumers don't want the good or service and they don't want society's scarce resources being used in its production.

This process where consumers vote with their dollars is called **consumer sovereignty**. Consumers are basically directing the allocation of scarce resources in the economy with the dollar spending. Firms, who are in business to earn profit, then hire resources, or inputs, in accordance with consumer preferences. This is the way in which resources are allocated in a market economy. This is the manner in which society achieves the output mix that it desires.

TEACHER CERTIFICATION STUDY GUIDE

DOMAIN III.   GEOGRAPHY AND CULTURE

COMPETENCY 16.0   UNDERSTAND MAJOR PHYSICAL FEATURES OF THE EARTH AND THE NATURAL PROCESSES THAT SHAPE THE EARTH AND INFLUENCE LIVING ORGANISMS

Skill 16.1   Demonstrate knowledge of the shape and location of major landmasses, their significant landforms, and the relationship of these landmasses to bodies of water.

A landform comprises a geomorphological unit. Landforms are categorized by characteristics such as elevation, slope, orientation, stratification, rock exposure, and soil type. Landforms by name include berms, mounds, hills, cliffs, valleys, and others. Oceans and continents exemplify highest-order landforms. Landform elements are parts of a landform that can be further identified. The generic landform elements are: pits, peaks, channels, ridges, passes, pools, planes etc, and can be often extracted from a digital elevation model using some automated or semi-automated techniques.

Elementary landforms (segments, facets, relief units) are the smallest homogeneous divisions of the land surface, at the given scale/resolution. A plateau or a hill can be observed at various scales ranging from few hundred meters to hundreds of kilometers. Hence, the spatial distribution of landforms is often fuzzy and scale-dependent as is the case for soils and geological strata. A number of factors, ranging from plate tectonics to erosion and deposition can generate and affect landforms. Biological factors can also influence landforms—see for example the role of plants in the development of dune systems and salt marshes, and the work of corals and algae in the formation of coral reefs. Weather is the condition of the air which surrounds the day-to-day atmospheric conditions including temperature, air pressure, wind and moisture or precipitation which includes rain, snow, hail, or sleet.

The earth's surface is made up of 70% water and 30% land. Physical features of the land surface include mountains, hills, plateaus, valleys, and plains. Other minor landforms include deserts, deltas, canyons, mesas, basins, foothills, marshes and swamps. Earth's water features include oceans, seas, lakes, rivers, and canals.

Mountains are landforms with rather steep slopes at least 2,000 feet or more above sea level. Mountains are found in groups called mountain chains or mountain ranges. At least one range can be found on six of the earth's seven continents. North America has the Appalachian and Rocky Mountains; South America the Andes; Asia the Himalayas; Australia the Great Dividing Range; Europe the Alps; and Africa the Atlas, Ahaggar, and Drakensburg Mountains.

MIDDLE LEVEL SOCIAL STUDIES   164

Hills are elevated landforms rising to an elevation of about 500 to 2000 feet. They are found everywhere on earth including Antarctica where they are covered by ice.

Plateaus are elevated landforms usually level on top. Depending on location, they range from being an area that is very cold to one that is cool and healthful. Some plateaus are dry because mountains that keep out any moisture surround them. Some examples include the Kenya Plateau in East Africa, which is very cool. The plateau extending north from the Himalayas is extremely dry while those in Antarctica and Greenland are covered with ice and snow.

Plains are described as areas of flat or slightly rolling land, usually lower than the landforms next to them. Sometimes called lowlands (and sometimes located along **seacoasts**) they support the majority of the world's people. Some are found inland and many have been formed by large rivers. This resulted in extremely fertile soil for successful cultivation of crops and numerous large settlements of people. In North America, the vast plains areas extend from the Gulf of Mexico north to the Arctic Ocean and between the Appalachian and Rocky Mountains. In Europe, rich plains extend east from Great Britain into central Europe on into the Siberian region of Russia. Plains in river valleys are found in China (the Yangtze River valley), India (the Ganges River valley), and Southeast Asia (the Mekong River valley).

Valleys are land areas found between hills and mountains. Some have gentle slopes containing trees and plants; others have steep walls and are referred to as canyons. One example is Arizona's Grand Canyon of the Colorado River.

Deserts are large dry areas of land receiving ten inches or less of rainfall each year. Among the better known deserts are Africa's large Sahara Desert, the Arabian Desert on the Arabian Peninsula, and the desert Outback covering roughly one third of Australia.

Deltas are areas of lowlands formed by soil and sediment deposited at the mouths of rivers. The soil is generally very fertile and most fertile river deltas are important crop-growing areas. One well-known example is the delta of Egypt's Nile River, known for its production of cotton.

Mesas are the flat tops of hills or mountains usually with steep sides. Sometimes plateaus are also called mesas. Basins are considered to be low areas drained by rivers or low spots in mountains. Foothills are generally considered a low series of hills found between a plain and a mountain range. Marshes and swamps are wet lowlands providing growth of such plants as rushes and reeds.

Oceans are the largest bodies of water on the planet. The four oceans of the earth are the **Atlantic Ocean**, one-half the size of the Pacific and separating North and South America from Africa and Europe; the **Pacific Ocean**, covering almost one-third of the entire surface of the earth and separating North and South America from Asia and Australia; the **Indian Ocean**, touching Africa, Asia, and Australia; and the ice-filled **Arctic Ocean,** extending from North America and Europe to the North Pole. The waters of the Atlantic, Pacific, and Indian Oceans also touch the shores of Antarctica.

Seas are smaller than oceans and are surrounded by land. Some examples include the Mediterranean Sea found between Europe, Asia, and Africa; and the Caribbean Sea, touching the West Indies, South and Central America. A lake is a body of water surrounded by land. The Great Lakes in North America are a good example.

Rivers, considered a nation's lifeblood, usually begin as very small streams, formed by melting snow and rainfall, flowing from higher to lower land, emptying into a larger body of water, usually a sea or an ocean. Examples of important rivers for the people and countries affected by and/or dependent on them include the Nile, Niger, and Zaire Rivers of Africa; the Rhine, Danube, and Thames Rivers of Europe; the Yangtze, Ganges, Mekong, Hwang He, and Irrawaddy Rivers of Asia; the Murray-Darling in Australia; and the Orinoco in South America. River systems are made up of large rivers and numerous smaller rivers or tributaries flowing into them. Examples include the vast Amazon Rivers system in South America and the Mississippi River system in the United States.

Canals are man-made water passages constructed to connect two larger bodies of water. Famous examples include the **Panama Canal** across Panama's isthmus connecting the Atlantic and Pacific Oceans and the **Suez Canal** in the Middle East between Africa and the Arabian Peninsula connecting the Red and Mediterranean Seas.

Skill 16.2 Analyze geological and hydrological processes that alter the earth's surface.

Plate tectonics, is a geological theory that explains **continental drift**, which is the large movements of the solid portions of the Earth's crust floating on the molten mantle. There are ten major tectonic plates, with several smaller plates. The surface of the earth can be drastically affected at the boundaries of these plates.

There are three types of plate boundaries, convergent, divergent and transform. Convergent boundaries are where plates are moving toward one another. When this happens, the two plates collide and fold up against one another, called **continental collision**, or one plate slides under the other, called **subduction**.

Continental collision can create high mountain ranges, such as the Andes and Himalayas. Subduction often results in volcanic activity along the boundary, as in the "Ring of Fire" along the northern coasts of the Pacific Ocean.

Divergent boundaries occur where plates are moving away from one another, creating **rifts** in the surface. The Mid-Atlantic Ridge on the floor of the Atlantic Ocean, and the Great Rift Valley in east Africa are examples of rifts at divergent plate boundaries. Transform boundaries are where plates are moving in opposite directions along their boundary, grinding against one another. The tremendous pressures that build along these types of boundaries often lead to earthquake activity when this pressure is released. The San Andreas Fault along the West Coast of North America is an example of a transform boundary.

Erosion is the displacement of solid earth surfaces such as rock and soil. Erosion is often a result of wind, water or ice acting on surfaces with loose particles, such as sand, loose soils, or decomposing rock. Gravity can also cause erosion on loose surfaces. Factors such as slope, soil and rock composition, plant cover, and human activity all affect erosion.

Weathering is the natural decomposition of the Earth's surface from contact with the atmosphere. It is not the same as erosion, but can be a factor in erosion. Heat, water, ice and pressure are all factors that can lead to weathering. Chemicals in the atmosphere can also contribute to weathering

Transportation is the movement of eroded material from one place to another by wind, water or ice. Examples of transportation include pebbles rolling down a streambed and boulders being carried by moving glaciers.

Deposition is the result of transportation, and occurs when the material being carried settles on the surface and is deposited. Sand dunes and moraines are formed by transportation and deposition of glacial material.

Skill 16.3 **Describe the main elements of climate and recognize characteristics of major climate zones.**

Climate is average weather or daily weather conditions for a specific region or location over a long or extended period of time. Studying the climate of an area includes information gathered on the area's monthly and yearly temperatures and its monthly and yearly amounts of precipitation. In addition, a characteristic of an area's climate is the length of its growing season.

In northern and central United States, northern China, south central and southeastern Canada, and the western and southeastern parts of the former Soviet Union is found the "climate of four seasons," the humid continental climate--spring, summer, fall, and winter. Cold winters, hot summers, and enough rainfall to grow a variety of crops are the major characteristics of this climate.

In areas where the humid continental climate is found are some of the world's best farmlands as well as important activities such as trading and mining. Differences in temperatures throughout the year are determined by the distance a place is inland, away from the coasts.

The steppe or prairie climate is located in the interiors of the large continents like Asia and North America. These dry flatlands are far from ocean breezes and are called prairies or the Great Plains in Canada and the United States and steppes in Asia. Although the summers are hot and the winters are cold, the big difference is rainfall. In the steppe climate, rainfall is light and uncertain, 10 to 20 inches a year. Where rain is more plentiful, grass grows; in areas of less, the steppes or prairies gradually become deserts. These are found in the Gobi Desert of Asia, central and western Australia, southwestern United States, and in the smaller deserts found in Pakistan, Argentina, and Africa south of the Equator.

The two major climates found in the high latitudes are **tundra** and **taiga**. The word tundra meaning marshy plain is a Russian word and aptly describes the climatic conditions in the northern areas of Russia, Europe, and Canada. Winters are extremely cold and very long. Most of the year the ground is frozen but becomes rather mushy during the very short summer months. Surprisingly less snow falls in the area of the tundra than in the eastern part of the United States. However, due to the harshness of the extreme cold, very few people live there and no crops can be raised. Despite having a small human population, many plants and animals are found there.

The taiga is the northern forest region and is located south of the tundra. The world's largest forestlands are found here along with vast mineral wealth and fur bearing animals. The climate is extreme that very few people live here, not being able to raise crops due to the extremely short growing season. The winter temperatures are colder and the summer temperatures are hotter than those in the tundra are because the taiga climate region is farther from the waters of the Arctic Ocean. The taiga is found in the northern parts of Russia, Sweden, Norway, Finland, Canada, and Alaska with most of their lands covered with marshes and swamps.

The humid **subtropical climate** is found north and south of the tropics and is moist indeed. The areas having this type of climate are found on the eastern side of their continents and include Japan, mainland China, Australia, Africa, South America, and the United States--the southeastern coasts of these areas. An interesting feature of their locations is that warm ocean currents are found there. The winds that blow across these currents bring in warm moist air all year round. Long, warm summers; short, mild winters; a long growing season allow for different crops to be grown several times a year. All contribute to the productivity of this climate type that supports more people than any of the other climates.

The **marine climate** is found in Western Europe, the British Isles, the U.S. Pacific Northwest, the western coast of Canada and southern Chile, southern New Zealand and southeastern Australia. A common characteristic of these lands is that they are either near water or surrounded by it. The ocean winds are wet and warm bringing a mild rainy climate to these areas. In the summer, the daily temperatures average at or below 70 degrees F. During the winter, because of the warming effect of the ocean waters, the temperatures rarely fall below freezing.

In northern and central United States, northern China, south central and southeastern Canada, and the western and southeastern parts of the former Soviet Union is found the **"climate of four seasons,"** the **humid continental climate**--spring, summer, fall, and winter. Cold winters, hot summers, and enough rainfall to grow a variety of crops are the major characteristics of this climate. In areas where the humid continental climate is found are some of the world's best farmlands as well as important activities such as trading and mining. Differences in temperatures throughout the year are determined by the distance a place is inland.

In certain areas of the earth there exists a type of climate unique to areas with high mountains, usually different from their surroundings. This type of climate is called a "vertical climate" because the temperatures, crops, vegetation, and human activities change and become different as one ascends the different levels of elevation. At the foot of the mountain, a hot and rainy climate is found with the cultivation of many lowland crops. As one climbs higher, the air becomes cooler, the climate changes sharply and different economic activities change, such as grazing sheep and growing corn. At the top of many mountains, snow is found year round.

Natural resources are naturally occurring substances that are considered valuable in their natural form. A commodity is generally considered a natural resource when the primary activities associated with it are extraction and purification, as opposed to creation. Thus, mining, petroleum extraction, fishing, and forestry are generally considered natural-resource industries, while agriculture is not.

Natural resources are often classified into renewable and non-renewable resources. Renewable resources are generally living resources (fish, coffee, and forests, for example), which can restock (renew) themselves if they are not over-harvested. Renewable resources can restock themselves and be used indefinitely if they are sustained. Once renewable resources are consumed at a rate that exceeds their natural rate of replacement, the standing stock will diminish and eventually run out. The rate of sustainable use of a renewable resource is determined by the replacement rate and amount of standing stock of that particular resource. Non-living renewable natural resources include soil, as well as water, wind, tides and solar radiation.

Natural resources include soil, timber, oil, minerals, and other goods taken more or less as they are from the Earth.

In recent years, the depletion of natural capital and attempts to move to sustainable development has been a major focus of development agencies. This is of particular concern in rainforest regions, which hold most of the Earth's natural biodiversity - irreplaceable genetic natural capital. Conservation of natural resources is the major focus of Natural Capitalism, environmentalism, the ecology movement, and Green Parties. Some view this depletion as a major source of social unrest and conflicts in developing nations.

MIDDLE LEVEL SOCIAL STUDIES 170

Skill 16.4 Analyze ways in which climate and other geographic factors affect plant and animal life and human societies.

Human communities subsisted initially as gatherers – gathering berries, leaves, etc. With the invention of tools it became possible to dig for roots, hunt small animals, and catch fish from rivers and oceans. Humans observed their environments and soon learned to plant seeds and harvest crops. As people migrated to areas in which game and fertile soil were abundant, communities began to develop. When people had the knowledge to grow crops and the skills to hunt game, they began to understand division of labor. Some of the people in the community tended to agricultural needs while others hunted game.

As habitats attracted larger numbers of people, environments became crowded and there was competition. The concept of division of labor and sharing of food soon came, in more heavily populated areas, to be managed. Groups of people focused on growing crops while others concentrated on hunting. Experience led to the development of skills and of knowledge that make the work easier. Farmers began to develop new plant species and hunters began to protect animal species from other predators for their own use. This ability to manage the environment led people to settle down, to guard their resources, and to manage them.

Camps soon became villages. Villages became year-round settlements. Animals were domesticated and gathered into herds that met the needs of the village. With the settled life it was no longer necessary to "travel light." Pottery was developed for storing and cooking food.

By 8000 BCE, culture was beginning to evolve in these villages. Agriculture was developed for the production of grain crops, which led to a decreased reliance on wild plants. Domesticating animals for various purposes decreased the need to hunt wild game. Life became more settled. It was then possible to turn attention to such matters as managing water supplies, producing tools, making cloth, etc.

There was both the social interaction and the opportunity to reflect upon existence. Mythologies arose and various kinds of belief systems. Rituals arose that re-enacted the mythologies that gave meaning to life.

As farming and animal husbandry skills increased, the dependence upon wild game and food gathering declined. With this change came the realization that a larger number of people could be supported on the produce of farming and animal husbandry.

Two things seem to have come together to produce cultures and civilizations: a society and culture based on agriculture and the development of centers of the community with literate social and religious structures. The members of these hierarchies then managed water supply and irrigation, ritual and religious life, and exerted their own right to use a portion of the goods produced by the community for their own subsistence in return for their management.

Sharpened skills, development of more sophisticated tools, commerce with other communities, and increasing knowledge of their environment, the resources available to them, and responses to the needs to share good, order community life, and protect their possessions from outsiders led to further division of labor and community development.

As trade routes developed and travel between cities became easier, trade led to specialization. Trade enables a people to obtain the goods they desire in exchange for the goods they are able to produce. This, in turn, leads to increased attention to refinements of technique and the sharing of ideas. The knowledge of a new discovery or invention provides knowledge and technology that increases the ability to produce goods for trade. As each community learns the value of the goods it produces and improves its ability to produce the goods in greater quantity, industry is born.

Social scientists use the term **culture** to describe the way of life of a group of people. This would include not only art, music, and literature but also beliefs, customs, languages, traditions, inventions--in short, any way of life whether complex or simple. The term **geography** is defined as the study of earth's features and living things as to their location, relationship with each other, how they came to be there, and why it is so important.

Physical geography is concerned with the locations of such earth features as climate, water, and land; how these relate to and affect each other and human activities; and what forces shaped and changed them. All three of these earth features affect the lives of all humans having a direct influence on what is made and produced, where it occurs, how it occurs, and what makes it possible.
The combination of the different climate conditions and types of landforms and other surface features work together all around the earth to give the many varied cultures their unique characteristics and distinctions.

COMPETENCY 17.0 UNDERSTAND GLOBAL AND REGIONAL PATTERNS OF CULTURE AND RELATIONSHIPS BETWEEN GEOGRAPHY AND HISTORY

Skill 17.1 Recognize major cultural groups associated with particular regions, including the United States, and significant cultural variations within and among regions.

Cultural geography studies the location, characteristics, and influence of the physical environment on different cultures around the earth. Also included in these studies are comparisons and influences of the many varied cultures. Ease of travel and up-to-the-minute, state-of-the-art communication techniques ease the difficulties of understanding cultural differences making it easier to come in contact with them.

Physical locations of the earth's surface features include the four major hemispheres and the parts of the earth's continents in them. Political locations are the political divisions, if any, within each continent. Both physical and political locations are precisely determined in two ways: (1) Surveying is done to determine boundary lines and distance from other features. (2) Exact locations are precisely determined by imaginary lines of latitude (parallels) and longitude (meridians). The intersection of these lines at right angles forms a grid, making it impossible to pinpoint an exact location of any place using any two grip coordinates.

The **Eastern Hemisphere**, located between the North and South Poles and between the Prime Meridian (0 degrees longitude) east to the International Date Line at 180 degrees longitude, consists of most of Europe, all of Australia, most of Africa, and all of Asia, except for a tiny piece of the easternmost part of Russia that extends east of 180 degrees longitude.

The Western Hemisphere, located between the North and South Poles and between the Prime Meridian (0 degrees longitude) west to the International Date Line at 180 degrees longitude, consists of all of North and South America, a tiny part of the easternmost part of Russia that extends east of 180 degrees longitude, and a part of Europe that extends west of the Prime Meridian (0 degrees longitude).

The **Northern Hemisphere**, located between the North Pole and the Equator, contains all of the continents of Europe and North America and parts of South America, Africa, and most of Asia.

The **Southern Hemisphere**, located between the South Pole and the Equator, contains all of Australia, a small part of Asia, about one-third of Africa, most of South America, and all of Antarctica.

Of the seven continents, only one contains just one entire country and is the only island continent, Australia. Its political divisions consist of six states and one territory: Western Australia, South Australia, Tasmania, Victoria, New South Wales, Queensland, and Northern Territory.

Africa is made up of 54 separate countries, the major ones being Egypt, Nigeria, South Africa, Zaire, Kenya, Algeria, Morocco, and the large island of Madagascar.

Asia consists of 49 separate countries, some of which include China, Japan, India, Turkey, Israel, Iraq, Iran, Indonesia, Jordan, Vietnam, Thailand, and the Philippines.

Europe's 43 separate nations include France, Russia, Malta, Denmark, Hungary, Greece, Bosnia and Herzegovina.
North America consists of Canada and the United States of America and the island nations of the West Indies and the "land bridge" of Middle America, including Cuba, Jamaica, Mexico, Panama, and others.

Thirteen separate nations together occupy the continent of South America, among them such nations as Brazil, Paraguay, Ecuador, and Suriname.

The continent of Antarctica has no political boundaries or divisions but is the location of a number of science and research stations managed by nations such as Russia, Japan, France, Australia, and India.

Social scientists use the term culture to describe the way of life of a group of people. This would include not only art, music, and literature but also beliefs, customs, languages, traditions, inventions--in short, any way of life whether complex or simple. The term geography is defined as the study of earth's features and living things as to their location, relationship with each other, how they came to be there, and why so important.

Physical geography is concerned with the locations of such earth features as climate, water, and land; how these relate to and affect each other and human activities; and what forces shaped and changed them. All three of these earth features affect the lives of all humans having a direct influence on what is made and produced, where it occurs, how it occurs, and what makes it possible. The combination of the different climate conditions and types of landforms and other surface features work together all around the earth to give the many varied cultures their unique characteristics and distinctions.

Cultural geography studies the location, characteristics, and influence of the physical environment on different cultures around the earth. Also included in these studies are comparisons and influences of the many varied cultures. Ease of travel and up-to-the-minute, state-of-the-art communication techniques ease the difficulties of understanding cultural differences making it easier to come in contact with them

Skill 17.2 Analyze the interactions of human societies with one another and with their physical environments.

By nature, people are essentially social creatures. They generally live in communities or settlements of some kind and of some size. Settlements are the cradles of culture, political structure, education, and the management of resources. The relative placement of these settlements or communities are shaped by the proximity to natural resources, the movement of raw materials, the production of finished products, the availability of a work force, and the delivery of finished products. Shared values, language, culture, religion, and subsistence will at least to some extent, determine the composition of communities.

Settlements begin in areas that offer the natural resources to support life – food and water. With the ability to manage the environment one finds a concentration of populations. With the ability to transport raw materials and finished products, comes mobility. With increasing technology and the rise of industrial centers, comes a migration of the workforce.

Cities are the major hubs of human settlement. Almost half of the population of the world now lives in cities. These percentages are much higher in developed regions. Established cities continue to grow. The fastest growth, however, is occurring in developing areas. In some regions there are "metropolitan areas" made up of urban and sub-urban areas. In some places cities and urban areas have become interconnected into "megalopoli" (e.g., Tokyo-Kawasaki-Yokohama).

The concentrations of populations and the divisions of these areas among various groups that constitute the cities can differ significantly. North American cities are different from European cities in terms of shape, size, population density, and modes of transportation. While in North America, the wealthiest economic groups tend to live outside the cities, the opposite is true in Latin American cities.

There are significant differences among the cities of the world in terms of connectedness to other cities. While European and North American cities tend to be well linked both by transportation and communication connections, there are other places in the world in which communication between the cities of the country may be inferior to communication with the rest of the world.

Rural areas tend to be less densely populated due to the needs of agriculture. More land is needed to produce crops or for animal husbandry than for manufacturing, especially in a city in which the buildings tend to be taller. Rural areas, however, must be connected via communication and transportation in order to provide food and raw materials to urban areas. Social policy addresses basic human needs for the sustainability of the individual and the society. The concerns of social policy, then, include food, clean water, shelter, clothing, education, health, and social security. Social policy is part of public policy, determined by the city, the state, the nation, responsible for human welfare in a particular region.

Competition for control of areas of the earth's surface is a common trait of human interaction throughout history. This competition has resulted in both destructive conflict and peaceful and productive cooperation. Societies and groups have sought control of regions of the earth's surface for a wide variety of reasons including religion, economics, politics and administration. Numerous wars have been fought through the centuries for the control of territory for each of these reasons.

At the same time, groups of people, even societies, have peacefully worked together to establish boundaries around regions or territories that served specific purposes in order to sustain the activities that support life and social organization.

Individuals and societies have divided the earth's surface through conflict for a number of reasons:

- The domination of peoples or societies, e.g., colonialism
- The control of valuable resources, e.g., oil
- The control of strategic routes, e.g., the Panama Canal

Conflicts can be spurred by religion, political ideology, national origin, language, and race. Conflicts can result from disagreement over how land, ocean or natural resources will be developed, shared, and used. Conflicts have resulted from trade, migration, and settlement rights. Conflicts can occur between small groups of people, between cities, between nations, between religious groups, and between multi-national alliances.

Today, the world is primarily divided by political/administrative interests into state sovereignties. A particular region is recognized to be controlled by a particular government, including its territory, population and natural resources. The only area of the earth's surface that today is not defined by state or national sovereignty is Antarctica.

Alliances are developed among nations on the basis of political philosophy, economic concerns, cultural similarities, religious interests, or for military defense. Some of the most notable alliances today are:

- The United Nations
- The North Atlantic Treaty Organization
- The Caribbean Community
- The Common Market
- The Council of Arab Economic Unity
- The European Union

Large companies and multi-national corporations also compete for control of natural resources for manufacturing, development, and distribution.

Throughout human history there have been conflicts on virtually every scale over the right to divide the Earth according to differing perceptions, needs and values. These conflicts have ranged from tribal conflicts to urban riots, to civil wars, to regional wars, to world wars. While these conflicts have traditionally centered on control of land surfaces, new disputes are beginning to arise over the resources of the oceans and space. On smaller scales, conflicts have created divisions between rival gangs, use zones in cities, water supply, school districts; economic divisions include franchise areas and trade zones.

Skill 17.3 Recognize relationships between the environment and the development of particular societies, including U.S. society.

Natural resources are features of the earth's surface or substances that occur naturally and are considered to have value in their original form. Natural resources that are extracted, or purified become commodities. Thus, mining, oil extraction, fishing and forestry are generally considered natural resource industries.

Natural resources are classified into renewable and non-renewable resources. Renewable resources are living resources that can renew themselves if they are not over-harvested. These include fish, coffee, forests, etc. Non-living renewable natural resources include water, wind, soil, tides and solar radiation.

The natural resources of a nation often determine its economy and its wealth. This, in turn, contributes to the nation's political influence. A nation with significant resources in raw metallic ores, petroleum deposits, coal, etc. will develop an economy and a culture based, at least to some degree, on the extraction and refinement of those raw materials. Such natural resources as rain forests provide the raw materials for the development of medicines and other products.

Civilizations require supplies of water and food products. Agricultural communities will develop in regions with arable land that can produce crops for its own needs and for other regions. The ability to move water to high-demand areas and to harness the power of water and wind to provide energy is another use of natural resources. Societies that support their economy by managing, harvesting, extracting, and utilizing natural resources develop cultural identities that reflect the means of subsistence. These societies and cultures will develop the means of sustaining and protecting both the resources and the ecosystems.

Skill 17.4 Analyze the effects of human activity on the environment in the United States and other world regions.

A **landform** comprises a geomorphological unit. Landforms are categorized by characteristics such as elevation, slope, orientation, stratification, rock exposure, and soil type. Landforms by name include berms, mounds, hills, cliffs, valleys, and others. Oceans and continents exemplify highest-order landforms. Landform elements are parts of a landform that can be further identified. The generic landform elements are: pits, peaks, channels, ridges, passes, pools, planes etc, and can be often extracted from a digital elevation model using some automated or semi-automated techniques.

Elementary landforms (segments, facets, relief units) are the smallest homogeneous divisions of the land surface, at the given scale/resolution. A plateau or a hill can be observed at various scales ranging from few hundred meters to hundreds of kilometers. Hence, the spatial distribution of landforms is often fuzzy and scale-dependent as is the case for soils and geological strata. A number of factors, ranging from plate tectonics to erosion and deposition can generate and affect landforms. Biological factors can also influence landforms—see for example the role of plants in the development of dune systems and salt marshes, and the work of corals and algae in the formation of coral reefs. **Natural resources** are naturally occurring substances that are considered valuable in their natural form. A commodity is generally considered a natural resource when the primary activities associated with it are extraction and purification, as opposed to creation. Thus, mining, petroleum extraction, fishing, and forestry are generally considered natural-resource industries, while agriculture is not.

Natural resources are often classified into **renewable** and **non-renewable resources**. Renewable resources are generally living resources (fish, coffee, and forests, for example), which can restock (renew) themselves if they are not over-harvested. Renewable resources can restock themselves and be used indefinitely if they are sustained. Once renewable resources are consumed at a rate that exceeds their natural rate of replacement, the standing stock will diminish and eventually run out. The rate of sustainable use of a renewable resource is determined by the replacement rate and amount of standing stock of that particular resource.

MIDDLE LEVEL SOCIAL STUDIES

Non-living renewable natural resources include soil, as well as water, wind, tides and solar radiation. Natural resources include soil, timber, oil, minerals, and other goods taken more or less as they are from the Earth.

In recent years, the depletion of natural capital and attempts to move to sustainable development has been a major focus of development agencies. This is of particular concern in rainforest regions, which hold most of the Earth's natural biodiversity - irreplaceable genetic natural capital. Conservation of natural resources is the major focus of Natural Capitalism, environmentalism, the ecology movement, and Green Parties. Some view this depletion as a major source of social unrest and conflicts in developing nations.

Environmental policy is concerned with the sustainability of the earth, the region under the administration of the governing group or individual or a local habitat. The concern of environmental policy is the preservation of the region, habitat or ecosystem.

Because humans, both individually and in community, rely upon the environment to sustain human life, social and environmental policy must be mutually supportable. Because humans, both individually and in community, live upon the earth, draw upon the natural resources of the earth, and affect the environment in many ways, environmental and social policy must be mutually supportive.

If modern societies have no understanding of the limitations upon natural resources or how their actions affect the environment, and they act without regard for the sustainability of the earth, it will become impossible for the earth to sustain human existence. At the same time, the resources of the earth are necessary to support the human welfare. Environmental policies must recognize that the planet is the home of humans and other species.

For centuries, social policies, economic policies, and political policies have ignored the impact of human existence and human civilization upon the environment. Human civilization has disrupted the ecological balance, contributed to the extinction of animal and plant species, and destroyed ecosystems through uncontrolled harvesting.

In an age of global warming, unprecedented demand upon natural resources, and a shrinking planet, social and environmental policies must become increasingly interdependent if the planet is to continue to support life and human civilization.

COMPETENCY 18.0 UNDERSTAND GLOBAL AND REGIONAL PATTERNS OF POPULATION MOVEMENT, RURAL/URBAN SETTLEMENT, RESOURCE DISTRIBUTION, AND LAND USE AND DEVELOPMENT

Skill 18.1 Recognize historical and contemporary patterns of human migration and population distribution in the United States and other world regions.

Environmental and geographic factors have affected the pattern of urban development in New York and the rest of the US. In turn, urban infrastructure and development patterns are interrelated factors, which affect one another.

The growth of urban areas is often linked to the advantages provided by its geographic location. Before the advent of efficient overland routes of commerce such as railroads and highways, water provided the primary means of transportation of commercial goods. Most large American cities are situated along bodies of water.

As transportation technology advanced, the supporting infrastructure was built to connect cities with one another and to connect remote areas to larger communities. The railroad, for example, allowed for the quick transport of agricultural products from rural areas to urban centers. This newfound efficiency not only further fueled the growth of urban centers, it changed the economy of rural America. Where once farmers had practiced only subsistence farming – growing enough to support one's own family – the new infrastructure meant that one could convert agricultural products into cash by selling them at market.

For urban dwellers, improvements in building technology and advances in transportation allowed for larger cities. Growth brought with it a new set of problems unique to each location. The bodies of water that had made the development of cities possible in their early days also formed natural barriers to growth. Further infrastructure in the form of bridges, tunnels and ferry routes were needed to connect central urban areas with outlying communities.

As cities grew in population, living conditions became more crowded. As roads and bridges became better, and transportation technology improved, many people began to look outside the city for living space. Along with the development of these new suburbs came the infrastructure to connect them to the city in the form of commuter railroads and highways. In the case of New York City, which is situated mainly on islands, a mass transit system became crucial early on to bring essential workers from outlying areas into the commercial centers.

The growth of suburbs had the effect in many cities of creating a type of economic segregation. Working class people who could not afford new suburban homes and perhaps an automobile to carry them to and from work were relegated to closer, more densely populated areas. Frequently, these areas had to be passed through by those on their way to the suburbs, and rail lines and freeways sometimes bisected these urban communities.

In the modern age, advancements in telecommunications infrastructure may have an impact on urban growth patterns as information can pass instantly and freely between almost any two points on the globe, allowing access to some aspects of urban life to those in remote areas.

Skill 18.2   Analyze the effect of different patterns of urban/rural settlement on the physical environment (e.g., the impact on local air quality of agricultural vs. industrial land use).

Since the dawn of agriculture, humans have modified their environment to suit their needs and to provide food and shelter. These changes always impact the environment, sometimes adversely from a human perspective.

Agriculture, for instance, often involves loosening topsoil by plowing before planting. This in turn affects how water and wind act on the soil, and can lead to erosion. In extreme cases, erosion can leave a plot of agricultural land unsuitable for use. Technological advances have led to a modern method of farming that relies less on plowing the soil before planting, but more on chemical fertilizers, pesticides and herbicides. These chemicals can find their way into groundwater, affecting the environment.

Cities are large examples of how technological change has allowed humans to modify their environment to suit their needs. At the end of the eighteenth century, advances made in England in the construction of canals were brought to New York and an ambitious project to connect Lake Erie with the Hudson River by canal was planned. The Erie Canal was built through miles of virgin wilderness, opening natural areas to settlement and commerce. Towns along the canal grew and thrived, including Buffalo, Rochester and Albany. The canal also opened westward expansion beyond the borders of New York by opening a route between the Midwest and the East Coast.

Further advances in transportation and building methods allow for larger and denser communities, which themselves impact the environment in many ways. Concentrated consumption of fuels by automobiles and home heating systems affect the quality of the air in and around cities. The lack of exposed ground means that rainwater runs off of roads and rooftops into sewer systems instead of seeping into the ground, and often makes its way into nearby streams or rivers, carrying urban debris with it.

New York City, the nation's largest city, has had considerable impact on its island environment and is making extensive use of new technology to reduce its energy use. New York City has the world's largest mass transit system, for instance, including hybrid buses that reduce emissions. New "clean" methods of energy production are being explored, such as underwater turbines that are run by tidal forces, and wind power. Cities like New York also impact the surrounding areas that supply resources such as water. A large portion of the Catskill Mountains in New York is restricted from development because the watershed supplies water to New York City

Ecology is the study of how living organisms interact with the physical aspects of their surroundings (their environment), including soil, water, air, and other living things. **Biogeography** is the study of how the surface features of the earth – form, movement, and climate – affect living things.

Three levels of environmental understanding are critical:

1. An **ecosystem** is a community (of any size) consisting of a physical environment and the organisms that live within it.

2. A **biome** is a large area of land with characteristic climate, soil, and mixture of plants and animals. Biomes are made up of groups of ecosystems. Major biomes are: desert, chaparral, savanna, tropical rain forest, temperate grassland, temperate deciduous forest, taiga, and tundra.

3. A **habitat** is the set of surroundings within which members of a species normally live. Elements of the habitat include soil, water, predators, and competitors.

Within habitats interactions between members of the species occur. These interactions occur between members of the same species and between members of different species. Interaction tends to be of three types:

1. **Competition**. Competition occurs between members of the same species or between members of different species for resources required to continue life, to grow, or to reproduce. For example, competition for acorns can occur between squirrels or it can occur between squirrels and woodpeckers. One species can either push out or cause the demise of another species if it is better adapted to obtain the resource. When a new species is introduced into a habitat, the result can be a loss of the native species and/or significant change to the habitat. For example, the introduction of the Asian plant Kudzu into the American South, has resulted in the destruction of several species because Kudzu grows and spreads very quickly and smothers everything in its path.

2. **Predation**. Predators are organisms that live by hunting and eating other organisms. The species best suited for hunting other species in the habitat will be the species that survives. Larger species that have better hunting skills reduce the amount of prey available for smaller and/or weaker species. This affects both the amount of available prey and the diversity of species that are able to survive in the habitat.

3. **Symbiosis** is a condition in which two organisms of different species are able to live in the same environment over an extended period of time without harming one another. In some cases one species may benefit without harming the other. In other cases both species benefit.

Different organisms are by nature best suited for existence in particular environments. When an organism is displaced to a different environment or when the environment changes for some reason, its ability to survive is determined by its ability to *adapt* to the new environment. Adaptation can take the form of structural change, physiological change, or behavioral modification.

Biodiversity refers to the variety of species and organisms, as well as the variety of habitats available on the earth. Biodiversity provides the life-support system for the various habitats and species. The greater the degree of biodiversity, the more species and habitats will continue to survive.

When human and other population and migration changes, climate changes, or natural disasters disrupt the delicate balance of a habitat or an ecosystem, species either adapt or become extinct.

Natural changes can occur that alter habitats – floods, volcanoes, storms, earthquakes. These changes can affect the species that exist within the habitat, either by causing extinction or by changing the environment in a way that will no longer support the life systems. Climate changes can have similar effects. Inhabiting species, however, can also alter habitats, particularly through migration. Human civilization, population growth, and efforts to control the environment can have many negative effects on various habitats. Humans change their environments to suit their particular needs and interests. This can result in changes that result in the extinction of species or changes to the habitat itself. For example, deforestation damages the stability of mountain surfaces. One particularly devastating example is in the removal of the grasses of the Great Plains for agriculture. Tilling the ground and planting crops left the soil unprotected. Sustained drought dried out the soil into dust. When windstorms occurred, the topsoil was stripped away and blown all the way to the Atlantic Ocean.

Skill 18.3 **Locate major concentrations of important natural resources in the United States and other world regions, and examine the connection between resource distribution and regional development.**

Natural resources are naturally occurring substances that are considered valuable in their natural form. A commodity is generally considered a natural resource when the primary activities associated with it are extraction and purification, as opposed to creation. Thus, mining, petroleum extraction, fishing, and forestry are generally considered natural-resource industries, while agriculture is not.

Natural resources are often classified into **renewable** and **non-renewable resources**. Renewable resources are generally living resources (fish, coffee, and forests, for example), which can restock (renew) themselves if they are not over-harvested. Renewable resources can restock themselves and be used indefinitely if they are sustained. Once renewable resources are consumed at a rate that exceeds their natural rate of replacement, the standing stock will diminish and eventually run out. The rate of sustainable use of a renewable resource is determined by the replacement rate and amount of standing stock of that particular resource. Non-living renewable natural resources include soil, water, timber, minerals wood, oxygen, wind, tides and solar radiation. Nonrenewable resources are present in finite amounts or are used faster than they can be replaced in nature. Examples of nonrenewable resources are petroleum, coal, natural gas, and minerals.

The United States has abundant natural resources. Even with a population that now tops 300 million, the possibility for coaxing more natural resources from the land and the waters is good. It is not inexhaustible, however.

Some regions of the U.S. are known for certain things. Oil can be found in great numbers in Texas, Oklahoma, Alaska, and a handful of other states. Most of these states make oil drilling and production a big business, with output reaching staggering numbers in some cases. The oil is used to power machinery and transportation devices the world over. The ideal is to achieve a balance between wringing as much oil out of the land as possible while also preserving the land the oil is found under. This balance is not always achieved; in some cases, it is never achieved or even attempted.

Another natural resource in abundance in the U.S. is natural gas. This resource is found in Texas, Oklahoma, Wyoming, Utah, Colorado, Louisiana, Arkansas, Michigan, North Carolina, Pennsylvania, and New York. Concentrations of natural gas can be found in other states as well. This resource is transported through pipes into homes and other buildings in order to provide energy for people and businesses. Like oil, natural gas comes from deep within the ground. It is both easy and difficult to get it out of the ground.

Some deposits are easier to get at than others, and some methods of extraction are simpler and more cost-effective than others. Natural gas is more "natural" in nature than oil and can be used for things that oil can and cannot: For example, natural gas now powers buses, trains, some cars, and other transportation devices. You wouldn't necessarily find powering a family's kitchen stove, however.

Coal is another natural resource found in great amounts in the U.S., whose people use it for energy. Coal can be found in 38 of the 50 U.S. states. Among the top coal-producing states are Montana, Illinois, Wyoming, West Virginia, Kentucky, Pennsylvania, Ohio, Colorado, Texas, and Indiana. A full 24 percent of the world's recoverable reserves of coal can be found within the borders of the United States. Coal can be found on the surface or underground. Both methods have their associated costs and risks, including harmful effects on the land left behind and air around the requisite coal mines.

A host of other minerals are to be found and mined in the U.S. Among them are chromium, copper, gypsum, iron oxide, phosphate, salt, selenium, silica, silicon, silver, sulfur, tin, tungsten, and zinc. In every case, these minerals are found to varying degrees in certain parts of the country. The way they are extracted from the earth varies according to the type of mineral being extracted; some are easier to extract than others, and the mining of some leaves behind horrible scars, from which the land does not easily recover.

Human use of Natural Resources

The natural resources of a nation often determine its economy and its wealth. This, in turn, contributes to the nation's political influence. A nation with significant resources in raw metallic ores, petroleum deposits, coal, etc. will develop an economy and a culture based, at least to some degree, on the extraction and refinement of those raw materials. Such natural resources as rain forests provide the raw materials for the development of medicines and other products.

Agricultural communities will develop in regions with arable land that can produce crops for its own needs and for other regions. The ability to move water to high-demand areas and to harness the power of water and wind to provide energy is another use of natural resources.

Societies that support their economy by managing, harvesting, extracting, and utilizing natural resources develop cultural identities that reflect the means of subsistence. These societies and cultures will develop the means of sustaining and protecting both the resources and the ecosystems.

Skill 18.4 Analyze factors that influence patterns of land use in the United States and other world regions.

The largest factor influencing land use is population and the growth thereof. A burgeoning population demands a lot from the land it surrounds and eventually incorporates, for food, living, and industrial use. The more people who want to live in a certain area, the more the land in that area will have to be transformed to meet that population need. In some cases, the land is simply appropriated. Naturally aerated land is perfect for farms and ranches, with an abundance of water and natural food for the crops and animals; in other cases, however, the land is transformed—agricultural land becoming industrial land, for example, or farmland being plowed over in favor of living space. In all cases, the land is being used to support the population, which is growing and expanding its needs and demands, at the expense of the land.

Geography is another influence on land use, sometimes as a limiter and sometimes as an invitation. Highly inhospitable lands are usually not all that populated because of the inherently harsh living conditions. We just don't see cities of thousands of people built into the sides of the world's tallest mountains. (The population situation is not that desperate yet; perhaps, in the future, such cities will exist out of necessity.) In the same way, a settlement in the middle of a desert will most likely becoming a growing concern (unless, of course, it is Las Vegas, which is a main exception to this rule). Geography doesn't always have to be a limiter, however. Fertile land that is excellent for farming will, in most cases, be being put to good agricultural use. Land that lends itself to good fortification will, naturally, be inhabited by people looking to defend themselves from invasion and other forms of outside influence. In even more simple terms, the very presence of a large body of water will routinely result in the human use of that water in some way, as a source of drinking water for people and animals or as a source of nourishment for crops. Rare indeed is the body of water that has not been appropriated in some form or fashion by human hands.

Geography can also form natural boundaries for settlements and civilizations. Mountain ranges and large bodies of water make effective borders between states and countries. If a civilization that has a mountain range or a river or ocean as a boundary wants to grow, it might be forced to grow upward rather than outward, at least in those locations bordered by these landforms or bodies of water. Prime examples of this are New York City and San Francisco, both of which have limited land on which to build but which use that land to the fullest by building tall skyscrapers that house myriad people and businesses.

In all of these things, necessity is the most basic thing driving land use. Growing populations *need* more land, and geographically challenged civilizations *need* to get creative in using their land.

Land-use patterns vary substantially by region. Factors that influence the use of land include difference in climate, soil make-up, topography and population dispersal. There are several different types of land use:

Cropland – Makes up 20% of US land use. This category includes land that is actively being used to grow crops as well as idle cropland. Cropland is roughly concentrated in the central regions of the contiguous United States. Cropland is the majority of land-use in the Northern Plain and the Corn Belt and the Southern Plains, Lake States, and Delta States also having cropland shares above the national average.

Grassland Pasture and Range – Makes up 26% of US land use. This category includes land used for grazing livestock, ranching and animal husbandry. Lower levels of precipitation make land in the West more suitable for grazing. The Mountain region and Southern Plains also have a majority of land in this land-use type. The Northern Plains and the Pacific region also have relative large amounts of grazing land.

Forestland – Makes up 29% of US land use. Land used to grow timber for building and fuel. This type of land-use is most prevalent in the Eastern regions such as the Northeast, Appalachian, Southeast, and Delta States. The Lake States and the Pacific region also have a large share of forest-use land because the topography and climate of these regions are conductive to growing trees.

Urban uses – 3% of land use. The Northeast and Southeast have the highest percentage of urban-use land.

Special Uses – 13% of US land use. Special uses encompasses land used for national and state parks, roads and recreational areas.

Miscellaneous Uses – 10% of US land use. This is most of other types of land including swamps, tundras, bare rock areas, marshes, etc.

Land use and development models are theories that attempt to explain the layout of urban areas, primarily in "more economically developed countries" or in "less economically developed countries".

Two primary land use models are generally applied to urban regions. These are: (1) The Burgess model (also called the concentric model), in which cities are seen to develop in a series of concentric circles with the central business district at the center, ringed by the factories and industrial usage area, ringed by the low class residential area, then the middle class residential area, and finally the high class residential area (often suburbs); and (2) The Hoyt model (also called the Sector Model), in which the central business district occupies a central area of a circle, with factories and industry occupying an elongated area that abuts the city center, and with the low class residential area surrounding the industrial area, and the middle class residential area forming a semi-circle toward the other side of the city center, and a small upper class residential sector extending from the city center out through the middle of the middle-class residential area.

In rural areas, land use will probably include agriculture, forestry, and possibly fishing. The Von Thunen Model observes a city as the center of a state or region, from which a series of concentric circles emanates, each devoted to particular rural land usage patterns: the first ring from the city would be devoted to dairy farming and intensive farming, which allows produce to reach the market quickly. The second zone would focus on forestland, which, because of its weight, needs to be relatively close to the city. The third zone would be dedicated to extensive field cropland.

The fourth zone would be dedicated to grassland. Beyond this miscellaneous land would exist.

Skill 18.5 Examine the environmental, cultural, and economic consequences of different types of land use and development

There are many environmental, cultural and economic consequences of different types of land use. Human beings have long been altering their surroundings in order to provide water, food, fiber and shelter for billions of people. However, changes to our natural landscape to create croplands, pastures, plantations and urban areas have created significant impacts on the earth's natural resources and biodiversity. Some of the consequences of different types of land use are:

Loss of natural landscape – The conversion of the world's natural landscape (forest, wetlands, waterways, etc) to agriculture, settlement and other human uses may soon undermine the capacity of the earth's ecosystems to sustain an ever-growing population. This is because in order to create profitable production, unsustainable agriculture practices have become the norm. Some of the ways humans have changed the natural landscape is through the use of chemical fertilizers, diverting water, the practice of deforestation, etc.

Loss of natural resources – By making changes to their natural landscape, humans have been able to allocate a huge portion of earth's natural resources. In many ways this use of natural resources has been unchecked; if human society does not successfully regulate the use of resources, the world will face problems with **sustaining food production, and maintaining soil conditions and water supply**.

Loss of biodiversity – By altering the earth's natural makeup, humans have vastly changed the earth's plant and animal diversity. By destroying the natural habitat of these life-forms, humans have put many of them in peril.

Change in climate – Land cover change has been a huge source of "greenhouse gases," gases that accumulate in the atmosphere and increase global temperature. Increased levels of CO_2 (deforestation), methane (rice paddies, landfills, biomass burning, cattle), and nitrous oxide (fertilizer) are of primary concern. Climate change is also a regional issue. Economic sectors that are related to land use – agriculture, livestock, timber production, and fisheries – are the most sensitive to climate change. The more a region depends on these industries, and the more land they use to support them, the more vulnerable a region is to climate change.

For centuries, social policies, economic policies, and political policies have ignored the impact of human existence and human civilization upon the environment. Human civilization has disrupted the ecological balance, contributed to the extinction of animal and plant species, and destroyed ecosystems through uncontrolled harvesting.

If modern societies have no understanding of the limitations upon natural resources or how their actions affect the environment, and they act without regard for the sustainability of the earth, it will become impossible for the earth to sustain human existence. At the same time, the resources of the earth are necessary to support the human welfare. We face the task of balancing immediate human needs with maintaining the ability of the earth to provide natural resources in the long term.

Strategies for maintaining this balance include making agricultural production more efficient, increasing open spaces in urban areas, using forestry techniques that provide food and fiber yet sustain habitats for threatened plant and animal species, etc.

The main concerns in nonrenewable resource management are conservation, allocation, and environmental mitigation. Policy makers, corporations, and governments must determine how to use and distribute scare resources. Decision makers must balance the immediate demand for resources with the need for resources in the future. This determination is often the cause of conflict and disagreement. Finally, scientists attempt to minimize and mitigate the environmental damage caused by resource extraction. Scientists devise methods of harvesting and using resources that do not unnecessarily impact the environment. After the extraction of resources from a location, scientists devise plans and methods to restore the environment to as close to its original state as possible.

COMPETENCY 19.0 UNDERSTAND CONCEPTS RELATED TO THE STRUCTURE AND ORGANIZATION OF HUMAN SOCIETY AND THE PROCESSES OF SOCIALIZATION AND SOCIAL INTERACTION

Skill 19.1 Recognize basic sociological and anthropological concepts and use that knowledge to examine general social phenomena.

SOCIOLOGY is the study of human society: the individuals, groups, and institutions making up human society. It includes every feature of human social conditions. It deals with the predominant behaviors, attitudes, and types of relationships within a society, which is defined as a group of people with a similar cultural background living in a specific geographical area. Sociology is divided into five major areas of study:

1) Population studies: General social patterns of groups of people living in a certain
2) geographical area, Social behaviors: Changes in attitudes, morale, leadership,
3) conformity, and others,
4) Social institutions: Organized groups of people performing specific functions within a society such as churches, schools, hospitals, business organizations, and governments
5) Cultural influences: Including customs, knowledge, arts, religious beliefs, and language, and
6) Social change: Such as wars, revolutions, inventions, fashions, and other events or activities.

Sociologists use three major methods to test and verify theories:

(1) Surveys;
(2) Controlled experiments; and
(3) Field observation.

Anthropology is the scientific study of human culture and humanity, the relationship between man and his culture. Anthropologists study different groups, how they relate to other cultures, and patterns of behavior, similarities and differences. Their research is two fold: cross-cultural and comparative. The major method of study is referred to as "participant observation." The anthropologist studies and learns about the people being studied by living among them and participating with them in their daily lives. Other methods may be used but this is the most characteristic method used. Margaret Mead, in the 1920s lived among the Samoans, observing their ways of life, resulting in the book "Coming of Age in Samoa." The Leakey family, Louis, his wife Mary, and son Richard, all of whom did much field work to further the study of human origins.

See also Skill 19.3 and Skill 19.4

MIDDLE LEVEL SOCIAL STUDIES

Skill 19.2   Analyze the relationship between language and culture.

Language is inextricably joined with culture. Each complements the other in various important ways, through a number of varied means.

First and foremost, language is a means for members of a society or civilization to communicate with one another. Language, be it words or syllables or pictures, is the transmittal of concepts from one person to another or to many. The back-and-forth of conversation is a way for people to share their concerns, fears, and accomplishments—not to mention the trivialities of everyday life. People use words all the time, to communicate complex and simple concepts, to have serious discussions or throwaway conversations.

Language is also a means to communicate culture to "outsiders." People from one civilization describe their culture, customs, and other particulars to "outsiders" by using language. The way they say certain things and the various elements, words, and even syllables that they emphasize say a lot about their language, their values, and their culture.

Language doesn't always mean words. One very powerful means of communicating is "body language," the nonverbal communication that augments or takes the place of words. People who speak different languages can successfully communicate with each other through body language even though neither shares the other's tongue. Body language is both facial expressions and other body movements. Sometimes, both are used in conjunction with each other to present an overall picture.

Another way that language and culture are intertwined is in the learning of a language by someone who doesn't speak it natively. For example, a native English speaker might be studying German. By learning not only the various German words for things but also the way in which German sentences are structured and the way in which German speakers think, students of the German language can gain valuable insights into the culture of Germany. The German language is put together quite logically, which is, by and large, an apt description of the German people and culture: The trains run on time, the people like to be prepared, and the sentence structure "just makes sense." (It is important to note here that non-native-English speakers often have a difficult learning English because it is so often not logical and very often an amalgam of other languages and idioms.)

German, in addition to Spanish and French, has formal and informal versions of many words as well. The proper one is used depending on how well you know someone or on how far up or down on the social ladder you are from the person to whom you are talking. English doesn't really have a corresponding construction. What that says about the civilizations that house the native speakers can be debated by experts.

Language, then, for the most part, is a mirror, a prism of a culture. Words, signals, and symbols can communicate the particulars of a culture to anyone willing to look, listen, or otherwise pay attention.

Skill 19.3   Compare the social and economic organization of preindustrial and postindustrial societies.

Social Stratification is the division of a society into different levels based on factors such as race, religion, economic standing or family heritage. Various types of social stratification may be closely related. For instance stratification by race may result in people of one race being relegated to a certain economic class as well.

The pioneering sociologist Max Weber theorized that there are three components of social stratification: class, status and political.

Social class, as Weber defined it, is based on economics and a person's relationship to the economic market e.g. a factory worker is of a different social class than a factory owner. Social status is based on non-economic factors like honor or religion. Political status is based on the relationships and influence one has in the political domain.

The economic revolutionary Karl Marx identified social stratification as the source of exploitation of one level of society by another, and based his theory of revolution and economic reform on this belief.

Mobility between social strata may differ between societies. In some societies, a person may move up or down in social class owing to changes in one's personal economic fortunes, for instance. Political status can change when prevailing political thought shifts. Some systems of stratification are quite formal, however, as in the former caste system in India. In these systems, lines between strata are more rigid, with employment, marriage and other social activities tightly defined by one's position.

Sociologists have identified five different types of institutions around which societies are structured: family, education, government, religion and economy. These institutions provide a framework for members of a society to learn about and participate in a society, and allow for a society to perpetuate its beliefs and values to succeeding generations.

The **family** is the primary social unit in most societies. It is through the family that children learn the most essential skills for functioning in their society such as language and appropriate forms of interaction. The size of the family unit varies among cultures, with some including grandparents, aunts, uncles and cousins as part of the basic family, who may all live together. The family is also related to a society's economic institutions, as families often purchase and consume goods as a unit. A family that works to produce its own food and clothing, as was the case historically in many societies, is also a unit of economic production.

Education is an important institution in a society, as it allows for the formal passing on of a culture's collected knowledge. The institution of education is connected to the family, as that is where a child's earliest education takes place. Educational traditions within a society are also closely associated with economic institutions, as some levels of employment require specific academic achievement.

A society's **governmental** institutions often embody its beliefs and values. Laws, for instance, reflect a society's values by enforcing its ideas of right and wrong. The structure of a society's government can reflect a society's ideals about the role of an individual in his society. A democracy may emphasize that an individual's rights are more important than the needs of the larger society, while a socialist governmental institution may place the needs of the whole group first in importance.

Religion is frequently the institution from which spring a society's primary beliefs and values, and can be closely related to other social institutions. Many religions have definite teachings on the structure and importance of the family, for instance. In some societies, the head of the government is also the head of the predominant religion, or the government may be operated on religious principles. Historically, formal educational institutions in many societies were primarily religious, and all religions include an educational aspect to teach their beliefs.

A society's **economic** institutions define how an individual can contribute and receive economic reward from his society. Economic institutions are usually closely tied to governmental institutions, each informing and regulating the other. They are linked to family institutions, as workers are often supporting more than one person with their wages. A society's economic institutions might affect its educational goals by creating a demand for certain skills and knowledge.

Skill 19.4   Assess the development and significance of social customs, cultural values, and norms.

Sociologists have identified three main types of norms, or ways that cultures define behavioral expectations, each associated with different consequences if they are violated. These norms are called folkways, mores and laws.

Folkways are the informal rules of etiquette and behaviors that a society follows in day-to-day practice. Forming a line at a shop counter or holding a door open for an elderly person are examples of folkways in many societies. Someone who violates a folkway - by pushing to the front of a line, for instance - might be seen as rude, but is not thought to have done anything immoral or illegal.

Mores are stronger than folkways in the consequences they carry for not observing them. Examples of mores might include honesty and integrity. Cheating on a test or lying might violate a social more, and a person who does so may be considered immoral.

Laws are formal adoptions of norms by a society with formal punishment for their violation. Laws are usually based on the mores of a society. The more that it is wrong to kill is codified in a law against murder, for example. Laws are the most formal types of social norm, as their enforcement is specifically provided for. Folkways and mores, on the other hand, are primarily enforced informally by the fellow members of a society.

The folkways, mores and laws of a society are based on the prevailing beliefs and values of that society. Beliefs and values are similar and interrelated systems.

Beliefs are those things that are thought to be true. Beliefs are often associated with religion, but beliefs can also be based on political or ideological philosophies. "All men are created equal," is an example of an ideological belief.

Values are what a society thinks are right and wrong, and are often based on and shaped by beliefs. The value that every member of the society has a right to participate in his government might be considered to be based on the belief that "All mean are created equal," for instance.

DOMAIN IV. RESEARCH SKILLS

COMPETENCY 20.0　UNDERSTAND HOW TO LOCATE, GATHER, AND ORGANIZE PRIMARY AND SECONDARY INFORMATION USING STANDARD HISTORICAL AND SOCIAL SCIENCE RESOURCES AND RESEARCH METHODOLOGIES

Skill 20.1　Compare the characteristics of materials used in historical and social science research.

We use **illustrations** of various sorts because it is often easier to demonstrate a given idea visually instead of orally. Sometimes it is even easier to do so with an illustration than a description. This is especially true in the areas of education and research because humans are visually stimulated. It is a fact that any idea presented visually in some manner is always easier to understand and to comprehend than simply getting an idea across verbally, by hearing it or reading it. Among the more common illustrations used in political and social sciences are various types of **maps, graphs and charts**.

Photographs and **globes** are useful as well, but as they are limited in what kind of information that they can show, they are rarely used. Unless, as in the case of a photograph, it is of a particular political figure or a time that one wishes to visualize.

Although maps have advantages over globes and photographs, they do have a major disadvantage. This problem must be considered as well. The major problem of all maps comes about because most maps are flat and the Earth is a sphere. It is impossible to reproduce exactly on a flat surface an object shaped like a sphere. In order to put the earth's features onto a map they must be stretched in some way. This stretching is called **distortion.**

Distortion does not mean that maps are wrong it simply means that they are not perfect representations of the Earth or its parts. **Cartographers,** or mapmakers, understand the problems of distortion. They try to design them so that there is as little distortion as possible in the maps.

Libraries of all sorts are valuable when conducting research and nowadays almost all have digitized search systems to assist in finding information on almost any subject. Even so, the Internet with powerful search engines like Google readily available can retrieve information that doesn't exist in libraries or if it does exist, is much more difficult to retrieve.

Conducting a research project once involved the use of punch cards, microfiche and other manual means of storing the data in a retrievable fashion. No more. With high-powered computers available to anyone who chooses to conduct research, the organizing of the data in a retrievable fashion has been revolutionized. Creating multi-level folders, copying and pasting into the folders, making ongoing additions to the bibliography at the very time that a source is consulted, and using search-and-find functions make this stage of the research process go much faster with less frustration and a decrease in the likelihood that important data might be overlooked.

Serious research requires high-level analytical skills when it comes to processing and interpreting data. A degree in statistics or at least a graduate-level concentration is very useful. However, a team approach to a research project will include a statistician in addition to those members who are knowledgeable in the social sciences.

Skill 20.2　Apply research procedures used in history and the social sciences.

The world of social science research has never been so open to new possibilities. Where our predecessors were unable to tread for fear of exceeding the limits of the available data, data access and data transfer, analytic routines, or computing power, today's social scientists can advance with confidence. Where once social scientists of empirical bent struggled with punch cards, chattering computer terminals, and jobs disappearing into the black hole of remote mainframe processors, often never reappearing, we now enjoy massive arrays of data, powerful personal computers on our desks, online access to data, and suites of sophisticated analytic packages. Never before has the social scientist come so well armed. Advances in technology can free social scientists from the tyranny of simplification that has often hampered attempts to grasp the complexity of the world.

Refer to the content under **Skill 21.1** for a thorough discussion of primary and secondary sources. Primary sources for a study in social sciences may be obtained one-on-one: the children in the school where you are a teacher or via electronic means. For example, government sources contain much data for social sciences research such as census statistics, employment statistics, health statistics, etc. that can be readily accessed and manipulated.

Secondary sources may also be obtained in a hands-on fashion: interviews of people who had first-hand knowledge; books, journals, etc., that record primary statistics or analyses of primary statistics. However, the best source for obtaining that information is the Internet. An excellent resource for social science information is MOST (Management of Social Transformations) at http://portal. unesco.org/shs/en/ev.php-URL_ID=3511&URL_DO=DO_TOPIC&URL_ SECTION=201.html.

In other words, how do you choose when to use words, when to use charts, when to use graphs and when to use maps and/or illustrations (photos, etc.)? This is sometimes a difficult choice to make. To a large extent, it depends on the audience. A picture is worth a thousand words to most audiences; however, for children they are vital, as they are sometimes for older people. Also, if some members of the audience are speakers of English as a second language, graphics are extremely useful in increasing understanding of principles and events.

Another factor that is important in such a choice is how complicated the information is. Charts can go a long way in simplifying even complex ideas. Maps can defog a discussion of a geographical area that is not familiar to the audience. Photographs of people, places, or happenings can bring ideas to life.

Another factor to take into consideration is retention. If an idea is reinforced by a visual, it will be remembered longer because the listener has had access to it through more than one sense.

Skill 20.3 Understand how to use maps and globes to answer social science questions.

We use **illustrations** of various sorts because it is often easier to demonstrate a given idea visually instead of orally. Sometimes it is even easier to do so with an illustration than a description. This is especially true in the areas of education and research because humans are visually stimulated. It is a fact that any idea presented visually in some manner is always easier to understand and to comprehend than simply getting an idea across verbally, by hearing it or reading it. Among the more common illustrations used in political and social sciences are various types of **maps, graphs and charts**.

Photographs and **globes** are useful as well, but as they are limited in what kind of information that they can show, they are rarely used. Unless, as in the case of a photograph, it is of a particular political figure or a time that one wishes to visualize.

Although maps have advantages over globes and photographs, they do have a major disadvantage. This problem must be considered as well. The major problem of all maps comes about because most maps are flat and the Earth is a sphere. It is impossible to reproduce exactly on a flat surface an object shaped like a sphere. In order to put the earth's features onto a map they must be stretched in some way. This stretching is called **distortion**.

Distortion does not mean that maps are wrong it simply means that they are not perfect representations of the Earth or its parts. **Cartographers,** or mapmakers, understand the problems of distortion. They try to design them so that there is as little distortion as possible in the maps.

The process of putting the features of the Earth onto a flat surface is called **projection**. All maps are really map projections. There are many different types. Each one deals in a different way with the problem of distortion. Map projections are made in a number of ways. Some are done using complicated mathematics. However, the basic ideas behind map projections can be understood by looking at the three most common types:

(1) **Cylindrical Projections** - These are done by taking a cylinder of paper and wrapping it around a globe. A light is used to project the globe's features onto the paper. Distortion is least where the paper touches the globe. For example, suppose that the paper was wrapped so that it touched the globe at the equator, the map from this projection would have just a little distortion near the equator. However, in moving north or south of the equator, the distortion would increase as you moved further away from the equator. The best known and most widely used cylindrical projection is the **Mercator Projection.** Gerard's Mercator, a Flemish mapmaker, first developed it in 1569.

(2) **Conical Projections** - The name for these maps comes from the fact that the projection is made onto a cone of paper. The cone is made so that it touches a globe at the base of the cone only. It can also be made so that it cuts through part of the globe in two different places. Again, there is the least distortion where the paper touches the globe. If the cone touches at two different points, there is some distortion at both of them. Conical projections are most often used to map areas in the **middle latitudes**. Maps of the United States are most often conical projections. This is because most of the country lies within these latitudes.

(3) **Flat-Plane Projections** - These are made with a flat piece of paper. It touches the globe at one point only. Areas near this point show little distortion. Flat-plane projections are often used to show the areas of the north and south poles. One such flat projection is called a **Gnomonic Projection**. On this kind of map all meridians appear as straight lines, Gnomonic projections are useful because any straight line drawn between points on it forms a **Great-Circle Route**.

Great-Circle Routes can best be described by thinking of a globe and when using the globe the shortest route between two points on it can be found by simply stretching a string from one point to the other. However, if the string was extended in reality, so that it took into effect the globe's curvature, it would then make a great-circle. A great-circle is any circle that cuts a sphere, such as the globe, into two equal parts. Because of distortion, most maps do not show great-circle routes as straight lines, Gnomonic projections, however, do show the shortest distance between the two places as a straight line, because of this they are valuable for navigation. They are called **Great-Circle Sailing Maps.**

Skill 20.4   Identify the uses of traditional information sources and current technologies for historical and social science research.

Historical data can come from a wide range of sources beginning with libraries, small local ones or very large university **libraries**. Records and guides are almost universally digitally organized and available for instant searching by era, topic, event, personality, or area. The **Internet** offers unheard of possibilities for finding even the most obscure information. However, even with all these resources available, nothing is more valuable than a visit to the site being researched including a visit to historical societies, local libraries, sometimes even local schools. A historian was searching for an answer to the question as to why her great-great-grandfather had enlisted in the Union army even though he lived in the Deep South. She went to the site where he grew up and found the answer in the historical records stored in the local schoolhouse for lack of a formal historical society. The residents of the little town were also able to answer her question. She would never have found that historical information if she hadn't visited the site.

The same things could be said about geographical data. It's possible to find a map of almost any area online; however, the best maps will be locally available as will knowledge and information about the development of the area. For example, a courthouse had been moved from one small town to another in a county in Tennessee for no apparent reason. However, the local old-timers can tell you. The railroad wanted to come through town, and the farmers in the area surrounding the previous courthouse didn't want to raise the $100,000 it would take; they were also concerned that the trains would scare their cows. This information is not in a history book, yet it would be very important to a study of the geography of the area.

COMPETENCY 21.0 UNDERSTAND AND APPLY METHODS FOR EVALUATING SOURCES OF SOCIAL SCIENCE INFORMATION

Skill 21.1 Recognize primary and secondary sources and their advantages and limitations.

The resources used in the study of history can be divided into two major groups: primary sources and secondary sources.

Primary sources are works, records, etc. that were created during the period being studied or immediately after it. Secondary sources are works written significantly after the period being studied and based upon primary sources. "Primary sources are the basic materials that provide the raw data and information for the historian. Secondary sources are the works that contain the explications of, and judgments on, this primary material." [Source: Norman F Cantor & Richard I. Schneider. HOW TO STUDY HISTORY, Harlan Davidson, Inc., 1967, pp. 23-24.]

Primary sources include the following kinds of materials:

- Documents that reflect the immediate, everyday concerns of people: memoranda, bills, deeds, charters, newspaper reports, pamphlets, graffiti, popular writings, journals or diaries, records of decision-making bodies, letters, receipts, snapshots, etc.
- Theoretical writings which reflect care and consideration in composition and an attempt to convince or persuade. The topic will generally be deeper and more pervasive values than is the case with "immediate" documents. These may include newspaper or magazine editorials, sermons, political speeches, philosophical writings, etc.
- Narrative accounts of events, ideas, trends, etc. written with intentionality by someone contemporary with the events described.
- Statistical data, although statistics may be misleading.
- Literature and nonverbal materials, novels, stories, poetry and essays from the period, as well as coins, archaeological artifacts, and art produced during the period.

Guidelines for the use of primary resources:

1. Be certain that you understand how language was used at the time of writing and that you understand the context in which it was produced.
2. Do not read history blindly; but be certain that you understand both explicit and implicit referenced in the material.
3. Read the entire text you are reviewing; do not simply extract a few sentences to read.
4. Although anthologies of materials may help you identify primary source materials, the full original text should be consulted.

Secondary sources include the following kinds of materials:

- Books written on the basis of primary materials about the period of time.
- Books written on the basis of primary materials about persons who played a major role in the events under consideration.
- Books and articles written on the basis of primary materials about the culture, the social norms, the language, and the values of the period.
- Quotations from primary sources.
- Statistical data on the period.
- The conclusions and inferences of other historians.
- Multiple interpretations of the ethos of the time.

Guidelines for the use of secondary sources:

1. Do not rely upon only a single secondary source.
2. Check facts and interpretations against primary sources whenever possible.
3. Do not accept the conclusions of other historians uncritically.
4. Place greatest reliance on secondary sources created by the best and most respected scholars.
5. Do not use the inferences of other scholars as if they were facts.
6. Ensure that you recognize any bias the writer brings to his/her interpretation of history.
7. Understand the primary point of the book as a basis for evaluating the value of the material presented in it to your questions.

Skill 21.2   Analyze factors affecting the reliability of source materials.

The sky is blue", "the sky looks like rain", one a fact and the other an opinion. This is because one is **readily provable by objective empirical data**, while the other is a **subjective evaluation based upon personal bias**. This means that facts are things that can be proved by the usual means of study and experimentation. We can look and see the color of the sky. Since the shade we are observing is expressed as the color blue and is an accepted norm, the observation that the sky is blue is therefore a fact. (Of course, this depends on other external factors such as time and weather conditions).

This brings us to our next idea: that it looks like rain. This is a subjective observation in that an individual's perception will differ from another. What looks like rain to one person will not necessarily look like that to another person.

This is an important concept to understand since much of what actually is studied in political science is, in reality, simply the opinions of various political theorists and philosophers. The truth of their individual philosophies is demonstrated by how well they, (when they have been tried), work in the so called "real world."

The question thus remains as to how to differentiate fact from opinion. The best and only way is to ask oneself if what is being stated can be proved from other sources, by other methods, or by the simple process of **reasoning**.

Historians use primary sources from the actual time they are studying whenever possible. Ancient Greek records of interaction with Egypt, letters from an Egyptian ruler to regional governors, and inscriptions from the Fourteenth Egyptian Dynasty are all primary sources created at or near the actual time being studied. Letters from a nineteenth century Egyptologist would not be considered primary sources, as they were created thousands of years after the fact and may not actually be about the subject being studied.

The resources used in the study of history can be divided into two major groups: **primary sources** and **secondary sources**.

Primary sources are works, records, etc. that were created during the period being studied or immediately after it. Secondary sources are works written significantly after the period being studied and based upon primary sources. "Primary sources are the basic materials that provide the raw data and information for the historian. Secondary sources are the works that contain the explications of, and judgments on, this primary material." [Source: Norman F Cantor & Richard I. Schneider. "HOW TO STUDY HISTORY," Harlan Davidson, Inc., 1967, pp. 23-24.]

Skill 21.3   Evaluate the appropriateness of evidence used to substantiate a historical or social science argument.

In other words, how do you choose when to use words, when to use charts, when to use graphs, and when to use maps and/or illustrations (photos, etc.)? This is sometimes a difficult choice to make. To a large extent, it depends on the audience. A picture is worth a thousand words to most audiences; however, for children they are vital, as they are sometimes for older people. Also, if some members of the audience are speakers of English as a second language, graphics are extremely useful in increasing understanding of principles and events.

Another factor that is important in such a choice is how complicated the information is. Charts can go a long way in simplifying even complex ideas. Maps can defog a discussion of a geographical area that is not familiar to the audience. Photographs of people, places, or happenings can bring ideas to life.

Another factor to take into consideration is retention. If an idea is reinforced by a visual, it will be remembered longer because the listener has had access to it through more than one sense.

Helping students become critical thinkers is an important objective of the social studies curriculum. The history, geography, and political science classes provide many opportunities to teach students to recognize and understand reasoning errors. Errors tend to fall into two categories: a) inadequate reasons; and b) misleading reasoning.

COMPETENCY 22.0 UNDERSTAND HOW TO FORMULATE ISSUES OR FRAME QUESTIONS

Skill 22.1 Evaluate alternative formulations of a research problem.

There are many different ways to find ideas for **research problems**. One of the most common ways is through experiencing and assessing relevant problems in a specific field. Researchers are often involved in the fields in which they choose to study, and thus encounter practical problems related to their areas of expertise on a daily basis. The can use their knowledge, expertise and research ability to examine their selected research problem. This technique is not limited to qualified researchers engaged in specific fields; it can also be used by students. For students, all that this entails is being curious about the world around them. Research ideas can come from one's background, culture, education, experiences etc.

Another way to get research ideas is by exploring literature in a specific field and coming up with a question that extends or refines previous research.

Once a **topic** is decided, a research question must be formulated. A research question is a relevant, researchable, feasible statement that identifies the information to be studied. Once this initial question is formulated, it is a good idea to think of specific issues related to the topic. This will help to create a hypothesis. A research **hypothesis** is a statement of the researcher's expectations for the outcome of the research problem. It is a summary statement of the problem to be addressed in any research document. A good hypothesis states, clearly and concisely, the researchers expected relationship between the variables which they are investigating.

Once a hypothesis is decided, the rest of the research paper should focus on analyzing a set of information or arguing a specific point. Thus, there are two types of research papers: analytical and argumentative.

Analytical papers focus on examining and understanding the various parts of a research topic and reformulating them in a new way to support your initial statement. In this type of research paper, the research question is used as both a basis for investigation as well as a topic for the paper. Once a variety of information is collected on the given topic, it is coalesced into a clear discussion

Argumentative papers focus on supporting the question or claim with evidence or reasoning. Instead of presenting research to provide information, an argumentative paper presents research in order to prove a debatable statement and interpretation.

Skill 22.2   Summarize the main points and supporting evidence of a historical, economic, sociological, political, or geographic point of view.

Suppose you are preparing for a presentation on the Civil War and you intend to focus on causes, an issue that has often been debated. If you are examining the matter of slavery as a cause, a graph of the increase in the number of slaves by area of the country for the previous 100 years would be very useful in the discussion. If you are focusing on the economic conditions that were driving the politics of the age, graphs of GDP, distribution of wealth geographically and individually, and relationship of wealth to ownership of slaves would be useful.

If you are discussing the war in Iraq, detailed maps with geopolitical elements would help clarify not only the day-to-day happenings but also the historical features that led up to it. A map showing the number of oil fields and where they are situated with regard to the various political factions and charts showing output of those fields historically would be useful.

If you are teaching the history of space travel, photos of the most famous astronauts will add interest to the discussion. Graphs showing the growth of the industry and charts showing discoveries and their relationship to the lives of everyday Americans would be helpful.

Geography and history classes are notoriously labeled by students as dull. With all the visual resources available nowadays, those classes have the potential for being the most exciting courses in the curriculum.

Varying perspectives on the study of history may be summarized by one of three definitions:

1. History is the study of what persons have done and said and thought in the past.
2. History is a creative attempt to reconstruct the lives and thoughts of particular persons who lived at specific times (biography).
3. History is the study of the social aspects of humans, both past and present.

The first definition essentially applies to the *narrative school of history.* This approach attempts to provide a general account of the most important things people have said, done, written, etc. in the past. Several schools fall within this category:

- The political-institutional school believes that what has occurred in government and law is the most important.
- The school of intellectual history (the history of ideas) finds greatest importance in the emergence of higher thought and feeling (including philosophy, art, science, literature).
- Economic historians are most concerned with the way humans have controlled the environment and made a living.
- Cultural historians focus on the development of ideas within the total context of a social, economic, and political situation.

The second definition above understands history as biography of important persons. These historians fall into one of two schools:

- Psychologizing approaches – historians who believe the motivations and actions of people in the past can be understood and explained in terms of modern psychological theories.
- Non-psychologizing approaches – historians who believe it is impossible to psychoanalyze people who are dead and that people of the past must be understood in terms of the theories of personality and motivation that were accepted at the time.

The third definition above essentially equates history with sociology. This approach believes it is possible to study history to observe forms of social change that are relevant to current social problems. This group is also divided:

- One group uses the Marxist doctrine of dialectical materialism to explain social change.
- Another group believes that each society is unique and distinctive.
- Comparative sociological historians study history to identify consistent patterns that run through all or several societies.

Skill 22.3 Determine whether specific conclusions or generalizations are supported by verifiable evidence.

Helping students become critical thinkers is an important objective of the social studies curriculum. The history, geography, and political science classes provide many opportunities to teach students to recognize and understand reasoning errors. Errors tend to fall into two categories: a) inadequate reasons; and b) misleading reasoning. Following are examples of each:

Inadequate reasons:

1. Faulty analogies: The two things being compared must be similar in all significant aspects if the reasoning is to be relied upon. If there is a major difference between the two, then the argument falls apart.
2. False cause (*Post Hoc Ergo Propter Hoc*): after this, therefore because of this. There must be a factual tie between the effect and its declared cause.
3. *Ad Hominen*: Attacking the person instead of addressing the issues.
4. Slippery Slope: The domino effect. This is usually prophetic in nature—predicting what will follow if a certain event occurs. This is only reliable when it is used in hindsight—not in predicting the future because no one is wise enough to know the future.
5. Hasty Conclusions: Leaping to conclusions when not enough evidence has been collected. A good example is the accusations made in the 1996 bombing at the summer Olympics in Atlanta. Not enough evidence had been collected and the wrong man was arrested.

Misleading reasoning:

1. The Red Herring: comes from a smoked fish being dragged across a trail to distract hunting dogs. Often used in politics—getting your opponent on the defensive about a different issue than the one under discussion.
2. *Ad Populum* or Jumping on the Bandwagon: "Everybody's doing it, so it must be right." Biggest is not necessarily best when it comes to following a crowd.
3. Appeal to Tradition: "We've always done it this way." Often used to squelch innovation.
4. The False Dilemma or the Either/Or Fallacy: No other alternative is possible except the extremes at each end. Used in politics a lot. The creative statesman finds other alternatives.

TEACHER CERTIFICATION STUDY GUIDE

Skill 22.4 **Interpret social science information presented in various formats.**

Information can be gained looking at a map that might take hundreds of words to explain otherwise. Maps reflect the great variety of knowledge covered by social sciences. To show such a variety of information, maps are made in many different ways. Because of this variety, maps must be understood in order to make the best sense of them. Once they are understood, maps provide a solid foundation for social science studies.

To apply information obtained from **graphs** one must understand the two major reasons why graphs are used:

1. To present a model or theory visually in order to show how two or more variables interrelate.
2. To present real world data visually in order to show how two or more variables interrelate.

Most often used are those known as **bar graphs** and **line graphs**. (Charts are often used for similar reasons and are explained in the next section).

Graphs themselves are most useful when one wishes to demonstrate the sequential increase, or decrease of a variable or to show specific correlations between two or more variables in a given circumstance.

Most common is the **bar graph**, because it is easy to see and understandable way of visually showing the difference in a given set of variables. However it is limited in that it can not really show the actual proportional increase, or decrease, of each given variable to each other. (In order to show a decrease, a bar graph must show the "bar" under the starting line, thus removing the ability to really show how the various different variables would relate to each other).

Thus in order to accomplish this one must use a **line graph**. Line graphs can be of two types: a **linear** or **non-linear** graph. A linear line graph uses a series of straight lines; a non-linear line graph uses a curved line. Though the lines can be either straight or curved, all of the lines are called **curves**.

A line graph uses a number line or **axis.** The numbers are generally placed in order, equal distances from one another. The number line is used to represent a number, degree or some such other variable at an appropriate point on the line. Two lines are used, intersecting at a specific point. They are referred to as the X-axis and the Y-axis.

MIDDLE LEVEL SOCIAL STUDIES

The Y-axis is a vertical line the X-axis is a horizontal line. Together they form a **coordinate system**. The difference between a point on the line of the X-axis and the Y-axis is called the **slope** of the line, or the change in the value on the vertical axis divided by the change in the value on the horizontal axis. The Y-axis number is called the **rise** and the X-axis number is called the **run**, thus the equation for slope is:

SLOPE = **RISE** - (Change in value on the vertical axis)
            RUN - (Change in value on the horizontal axis)

The slope tells the amount of increase or decrease of a given **specific** variable. When using two or more variables one can plot the amount of difference between them in any given situation. This makes presenting information on a line graph more involved. It also makes it more informative and accurate than a simple bar graph. Knowledge of the term slope and what it is and how it is measured helps us to describe verbally the pictures we are seeing visually. For example, if a curve is said to have a slope of "zero", you should picture a flat line. If a curve has a slope of "one", you should picture a rising line that makes a 45-degree angle with the horizontal and vertical axis lines.

The preceding examples are of **linear** (straight line) curves. With **non-linear** curves (the ones that really do curve) the slope of the curve is constantly changing, so as a result, we must then understand that the slope of the non-linear curved line will be at a specific point. How is this done? The slope of a non-linear curve is determined by the slope of a straight line that intersects the curve at that specific point.

In all graphs, an upward sloping line represents a direct relationship between the two variables. A downward slope represents an inverse relationship between the two variables. In reading any graph, one must always be very careful to understand what is being measured, what can be deduced and what cannot be deduced from the given graph.

To use **charts** correctly, one should remember the reasons one uses graphs. The general ideas are similar. It is usually a question as to which, a graph or chart, is more capable of adequately portraying the information one wants to illustrate. One can see the difference between them and realize that in many ways graphs and charts are interrelated. One of the most common types, because it is easiest to read and understand, even for the lay person, is the **pie-chart**.

You can see pie-charts used often, especially when one is trying to illustrate the differences in percentages among various items, or when one is demonstrating the divisions of a whole.

Posters. The power of the political poster in the 21st century seems trivial considering the barrage of electronic campaigning, mudslinging, and reporting that seems to have taken over the video and audio media in election season. Even so, the political poster has been a powerful propaganda tool, and it has been around for a long time. For example, in the 1st century AD, a poster that calls for the election of a Satrius as quinquennial has survived to this day. Nowhere have political posters been used more powerfully or effectively than in Russia in the 1920s in the campaign to promote communism. Many of the greatest Russian writers of that era were the poster writers. Those posters would not be understood at all except in the light of what was going on in the country at the time.

However, today we see them primarily at rallies and protests where they are usually hand-lettered and hand-drawn. The message is rarely subtle. Understanding the messages of posters requires little thought as a rule. However, they are usually meaningless unless the context is clearly understood. For example, a poster reading "Camp Democracy" can only be understood in the context of the protests of the Iraq War near President George W. Bush's home near Crawford, Texas. "Impeach" posters are understood in 2006 to be directed at President Bush, not a local mayor or representative.

Cartoons. The political cartoon (aka editorial) presents a message or point of view concerning people, events, or situations using caricature and symbolism to convey the cartoonist's ideas, sometimes subtly, sometimes brashly, but always quickly. A good political cartoon will have wit and humor, which is usually obtained by exaggeration that is slick and not used merely for comic effect. It will also have a foundation in truth; that is, the characters must be recognizable to the viewer and the point of the drawing must have some basis in fact even if it has a philosophical bias. The third requirement is a moral purpose.

Using political cartoons as a teaching tool enlivens lectures, prompts classroom discussion, promotes critical thinking, develops multiple talents and learning styles, and helps prepare students for standardized tests. It also provides humor. However, it may be the most difficult form of literature to teach. Many teachers who choose to include them in their social studies curricula caution that, while students may enjoy them, it's doubtful whether they are actually getting the cartoonists' messages.

The best strategy for teaching such a unit is through a subskills approach that leads students step-by-step to higher orders of critical thinking. For example, the teacher can introduce caricature and use cartoons to illustrate the principles. Students are able to identify and interpret symbols if they are given the principles for doing so and get plenty of practice, and cartoons are excellent for this. It can cut down the time it takes for students to develop these skills, and many of the students who might lose the struggle to learn to identify symbols may overcome the roadblocks through the analysis of political cartoons. Many political cartoons exist for the teacher to use in the classroom and they are more readily available than ever before.

A popular example of an editorial cartoon that provides a way to analyze current events in politics is the popular comic strip "Doonesbury" by Gary Trudeau. For example, in the time period prior to the 2004 presidential election, Alex, the media savvy teenager does her best for political participation. In January she rallies her middle school classmates to the phones for a Deanathon and by August she is luring Ralph Nader supporters into discussions on Internet chat rooms. Knowledgeable about government, active in the political process, and willing to enlist others, Alex has many traits sought by the proponents of civics education.

Bibliography

Adams, James Truslow. (2006). "The March of Democracy," Vol 1. "The Rise of the Union". New York: Charles Scribner's Sons, Publisher.

Barbini, John & Warshaw, Steven. (2006). "The World Past and Present." New York: Harcourt, Brace, Jovanovich, Publishers.

Berthon, Simon & Robinson, Andrew. (2006. "The Shape of the World." Chicago: Rand McNally, Publisher.

Bice, David A. (2006). "A Panorama of Florida II". (Second Edition). Marceline, Missouri: Walsworth Publishing Co., Inc.

Bram, Leon (Vice-President and Editorial Director). (2006). "Funk and Wagnalls New Encyclopedia." United States of America.

Burns, Edward McNall & Ralph, Philip Lee. (2006. "World Civilizations Their History and Culture" (5th ed.). New York: W.W. Norton & Company, Inc., Publishers.

Dauben, Joseph W. (2006). "The World Book Encyclopedia." Chicago: World Book Inc. A Scott Fetzer Company, Publisher.

De Blij, H.J. & Muller, Peter O. (2006). "Geography Regions and Concepts" (Sixth Edition). New York: John Wiley & Sons, Inc., Publisher.

Encyclopedia Americana. (2006). Danbury, Connecticut: Grolier Inc, Publisher.

Heigh, Christopher (Editor). (2006). "The Cambridge Historical Encyclopedia of Great Britain and Ireland." Cambridge: Cambridge University Press, Publisher.

Hunkins, Francis P. & Armstrong, David G. (2006). "World Geography People and Places." Columbus, Ohio: Charles E. Merrill Publishing Co. A Bell & Howell Company, Publishers.

Jarolimek, John; Anderson, J. Hubert & Durand, Loyal, Jr. (2006). "World Neighbors." New York: Macmillan Publishing Company. London: Collier Macmillan Publishers.

McConnell, Campbell R. (2006). "Economics-Principles, Problems, and Policies" (Tenth Edition). New York: McGraw-Hill Book Company, Publisher.

Millard, Dr. Anne & Vanags, Patricia. (2006). "The Usborne Book of World History." London: Usborne Publishing Ltd., Publisher.

Novosad, Charles (Executive Editor). (2006). "The Nystrom Desk Atlas." Chicago:Nystrom Division of Herff Jones, Inc., Publisher.

Patton, Clyde P.; Rengert, Arlene C.; Saveland, Robert N.; Cooper, Kenneth S. & Cam, Patricia T. (2006). "A World View." Morristown, N.J.: Silver Burdette Companion, Publisher.

Schwartz, Melvin & O'Connor, John R. (2006). "Exploring A Changing World." New York: Globe Book Company, Publisher.

"The Annals of America: Selected Readings on Great Issues in American History 1620-1968." (2006). United States of America: William Benton, Publisher.

Tindall, George Brown & Shi, David E. (2006). "America-A Narrative History" (Fourth Edition). New York: W.W. Norton & Company, Publisher.

Todd, Lewis Paul & Curti, Merle. (2006). "Rise of the American Nation" (Third Edition). New York: Harcourt, Brace, Jovanovich, Inc., Publishers.

Tyler, Jenny; Watts, Lisa; Bowyer, Carol; Trundle, Roma & Warrender, Annabelle (2006) 'The Usborne Book of World Geography." London: Usborne Publishing Ltd., Publisher.

Willson, David H. (2006). "A History of England." Hinsdale, Illinois: The Dryder Press, inc., Publisher

Sample Test

1. **Which of the following best describes current thinking on the major purpose of social science?**

    A. Social science is designed primarily for students to acquire facts

    B. Social science should not be taught earlier than the middle school years

    ✓C. A primary purpose of social sciences is the development of good citizens

    D. Social science should be taught as an elective

2. **Psychology is a social science because:**

    A. It focuses on the biological development of individuals

    ✓B. It focuses on the behavior of individual persons and small groups of persons

    C. It bridges the gap between the natural and the social sciences

    D. It studies the behavioral habits of lower animals

3. **A historian would be interested in:**

    A. The manner in which scientific knowledge is advanced

    B. The effects of the French Revolution on world colonial policy

    C. The viewpoint of persons who have written previous "history"

    ✓D. All of the above

4. **The sub-discipline of linguistics is usually studied under:**

    A. Geography

    B. History

    C. Anthropology

    D. Economics

5. **Which of the following is not generally considered to be a discipline within the social sciences?**

    ✓A. Geometry

    B. Anthropology

    C. Geography

    D. Sociology

MIDDLE LEVEL SOCIAL STUDIES

TEACHER CERTIFICATION STUDY GUIDE

6. **Economics is best described as:**
   A. The study of how money is used in different societies
   B. The study of how different political systems produce goods and services
   ✓ C. The study of how human beings use limited resources to supply their necessities and wants
   D. The study of how human beings have developed trading practices through the years

7. **Which of the following is most reasonably studied under the social sciences?**
   ✓ A. Political science
   B. Geometry
   C. Physics
   D. Grammar

8. **For the historian studying ancient Egypt, which of the following would be least useful?**
   A. The record of an ancient Greek historian on Greek-Egyptian interaction
   B. Letters from an Egyptian ruler to his/her regional governors
   C. Inscriptions on stele of the Fourteenth Egyptian Dynasty
   ✓ D. Letters from a nineteenth century Egyptologist to his wife

9. **A political scientist might use all of the following except:**
   A. An investigation of government documents
   ✓ B. A geological timeline
   C. Voting patterns
   D. Polling data

MIDDLE LEVEL SOCIAL STUDIES

10. A geographer wishes to study the effects of a flood on subsequent settlement patterns. Which might he or she find most useful?

    A. A film clip of the floodwaters

    B. An aerial photograph of the river's source

    ✓C. Census data taken after the flood

    D. A soil map of the A and B horizons beneath the flood area

11. A social scientist observes how individual persons react to the presence or absence of noise. This scientist is most likely a:

    A. Geographer

    B. Political Scientist

    C. Economist

    ✓D. Psychologist

12. As a sociologist, you would be most likely to observe:

    A. The effects of an earthquake on farmland

    B. The behavior of rats in sensory-deprivation experiments

    C. The change over time in Babylonian obelisk styles

    ✓D. The behavior of human beings in television focus groups

13. An economist investigates the spending patterns of low-income individuals. Which of the following would yield the most pertinent information?

    A. Prime lending rates of neighborhood banks

    B. The federal discount rate

    C. City-wide wholesale distribution figures

    ✓D. Census data and retail sales figures

TEACHER CERTIFICATION STUDY GUIDE

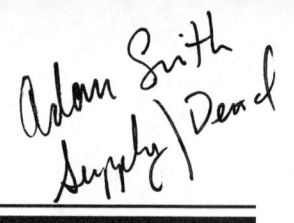

14. A teacher and a group of students take a field trip to an Indian mound to examine artifacts. This activity most closely fits under which branch of the social sciences?

    ✓ A. Anthropology

    B. Sociology

    C. Psychology

    D. Political Science

15. Which of the following is most closely identified as a sociologist?

    A. Herodotus

    B. John Maynard Keynes

    C. Emile Durkheim

    ✓ D. Arnold Toynbee

16. We can credit modern geography with which of the following?

    A. Building construction practices designed to withstand earthquakes

    ✓ B. Advances in computer cartography

    C. Better methods of linguistic analysis

    D. Making it easier to memorize countries and their capitals

17. Adam Smith is most closely identified with which of the following?

    A. The law of diminishing returns

    ✓ B. The law of supply and demand

    C. The principle of motor primacy

    D. The territorial imperative

18. Margaret Mead may be credited with major advances in the study of:

    A. The marginal propensity to consume

    B. The thinking of the Anti-Federalists

    C. The anxiety levels of non-human primates

    ✓ D. Interpersonal relationships in non-technical societies

MIDDLE LEVEL SOCIAL STUDIES 218

TEACHER CERTIFICATION STUDY GUIDE

19. The advancement of understanding in dealing with human beings has led to a number of interdisciplinary areas. Which of the following interdisciplinary studies would NOT be considered under the social sciences?

    A. Molecular biophysics ✓

    B. Peace studies

    C. African-American studies

    D. Cartographic information systems

20. Cognitive, developmental, and behavioral are three types of:

    A. Economists

    B. Political Scientists

    ✓ C. Psychologists

    D. Historians

21. A physical geographer would be concerned with which of the following groups of terms?

    ✓ A. Landform, biome, precipitation

    B. Scarcity, goods, services

    C. Nation, state, administrative subdivision

    D. Cause and effect, innovation, exploration

22. An economist might engage in which of the following activities?

    A. An observation of the historical effects of a nation's banking practices

    B. The application of a statistical test to a series of data

    C. Introduction of an experimental factor into a specified population to measure the effect of the factor

    ✓ D. An economist might engage in all of these

23. Political science is primarily concerned with _____.

    A. Elections

    B. Economic Systems

    C. Boundaries

    ✓ D. Public Policy

24. An anthropologist is studying a society's sororate and avunculate. In general, this scientist is studying the society's:

    A. Level of technology

    B. Economy

    ✓ C. Kinship practices

    D. Methods of farming

Sororate & avunculate = Kinship

MIDDLE LEVEL SOCIAL STUDIES 219

25. Of the following lists, which includes persons who have made major advances in the understanding of **psychology**?

   A. Herodotus, Thucydides, Ptolemy

   B. Adam Smith, Milton Friedman, John Kenneth Galbraith

   ✓C. Edward Hall, E.L. Thorndike, B.F. Skinner

   D. Thomas Jefferson, Karl Marx, Henry Kissinger

26. **The writing of history is called:**

   A. Public policy analysis

   ✓B. Historiography

   C. Historical perspective

   D. Historical analysis

27. If geography is the study of how human beings live in relationship to the earth on which they live, why do geographers include physical geography within the discipline?

   ✓A. The physical environment serves as the location for the activities of human beings

   B. No other branch of the natural or social sciences studies the same topics

   C. The physical environment is more important than the activities carried out by human beings

   D. It is important to be able to subdue natural processes for the advancement of humankind

Roman Empire / Modern US = federalism - similar govt system

TEACHER CERTIFICATION STUDY GUIDE

28. A historian might compare the governmental systems of the Roman Empire and the twentieth century United States with regard to which of the following commonalities?

    A. Totalitarianism

    B. Technological development

    C. Constitutional similarities

    ✓ D. Federalism

29. Capitalism and communism are alike in that they are both:

    A. Organic systems

    B. Political systems

    C. Centrally planned systems

    ✓ D. Economic systems

30. Which of the following demonstrates evidence of the interaction between physical and cultural anthropology?

    A. Tall Nilotic herdsmen are often expert warriors

    ✓ B. Until recent years the diet of most Asian peoples caused them to be shorter in stature than most other peoples

    C. Native South American peoples adopted potato production after invasion by Europeans

    D. Polynesians exhibit different skin coloration than Melanesians

31. A social scientist studies the behavior of four persons in a carpool. This is an example of:

    A. Developmental psychology

    B. Experimental psychology

    ✓ C. Social psychology

    D. Macroeconomics

MIDDLE LEVEL SOCIAL STUDIES 221

TEACHER CERTIFICATION STUDY GUIDE

32. Peace studies might include elements of all of the following disciplines except:

    A. Geography

    B. History

    C. Economics

    ✓ D. All of these might contribute to peace studies

33. Which of the following sets of terms relates to the Davisian erosion cycle?

    ✓ A. Youth, maturity, old age

    B. Atmospheric erosion, subsurface erosion, superficial erosion

    C. Fluvial, alluvial, estuarine

    D. Mississippian, Pennsylvanian, Illinoisian

34. What is a drumlin?

    A. A narrow ridge of sand, gravel, and boulders deposited by a stream flowing on, in, or under a nonmoving glacier

    B. Accumulated earth, pebbles, and stones carried by and then deposited by a glacier

    C. The active front face of a non-stagnant glacier

    D. An elongated or oval hill formed by drift material of glaciers

35. A coral island or series of islands which consists of a reef which surrounds a lagoon describes a(n):

    A. Needle

    B. Key

    ✓ C. Atoll

    D. Mauna

36. What type of cloud usually produces rain?

    A. Cirrus

    ✓ B. Cumulonimbus

    C. Altostratus

    D. Cirrostratus

MIDDLE LEVEL SOCIAL STUDIES   222

TEACHER CERTIFICATION STUDY GUIDE

37. Which of the following is NOT a type of rainfall?

    A. Convectional

    B. Cyclonic

    ✓ C. Adiabatic

    D. Frontal

38. The Mediterranean type climate [desert] is characterized by:

    ✓ A. Hot, dry summers and mild, relatively wet winters

    B. Cool, relatively wet summers and cold winters

    C. Mild summers and winters, with moisture throughout the year

    D. Hot, wet summers and cool, dry winters

39. The climate of Southern Florida is the _____ type.

    ✓ A. Humid subtropical

    B. Marine West Coast

    C. Humid continental

    D. Tropical wet-dry

40. Which of the following is an island nation?

    A. Luxembourg

    B. Finland

    C. Monaco

    ✓ D. Nauru

41. Which location may be found in Canada?

    A. 27 N   93 W

    B. 41 N   93 E

    ✓ C. 50 N   111 W

    D. 18 N   120 W

42. The highest point on the North American continent is:

    A. Mt. St. Helen's

    ✓ B. Denali

    C. Mt. Everest

    D. Pike's Peak

    Denali = "highest"   "turn package"

43. Concerning the present political map of Africa, which statement most closely applies?

   A. The modern states reflect an effort to establish political units based on ethnic groupings

   ✓ B. The international community allowed for a period of elasticity with regard to boundaries, so that a condition of relative equilibrium could develop

   C. Africans were given the task of delineating the modern states, using whatever criteria they chose

   D. The modern states reflect imposed boundaries, without regard to ethnic groupings or other indigenous considerations

44. Which of the following areas would NOT be a primary area of hog production?

   A. Midland England

   B. The Mekong delta of Vietnam

   ✓ C. Central Syria

   D. Northeast Iowa

   too hot

45. Indo-European languages are native languages to each of the following EXCEPT:

   A. Germany

   B. India

   C. Italy

   ✓ D. Finland

46. A cultural geographer is investigating the implications of <u>The Return of the Native</u> by Thomas Hardy. He or she is most likely concentrating on:

   A. The reactions of British city-dwellers to the in-migration of French professionals

   ✓ B. The activities of persons in relation to poorly drained, coarse-soiled land with low-lying vegetation

   C. The capacity of riverine lands to sustain a population of edible amphibians

   D. The propagation of new crops introduced by settlers from North America

TEACHER CERTIFICATION STUDY GUIDE

47. Which of the following is NOT considered to be an economic need:

    A. Food

    ✓ B. Transportation

    C. Shelter

    D. Clothing

48. As your income rises, you tend to spend more money on entertainment. This is an expression of the:

    ✓ A. Marginal propensity to consume

    B. Allocative efficiency

    C. Compensating differential

    D. Marginal propensity to save

49. A student buys a candy bar at lunch. The decision to buy a second candy bar relates to the concept of:

    A. Equilibrium pricing

    B. Surplus

    ✓ C. Utility

    D. Substitutability

50. If the price of Good G increases, what is likely to happen with regard to comparable Good H?

    A. The demand for Good G will stay the same

    B. The demand for Good G will increase

    ✓ C. The demand for Good H will increase

    D. The demand for Good H will decrease

51. A teacher has an extra $1,000 which she wishes to invest and wants to minimize the risk. The best choice for investment, from the following, is:

    A. Money market account

    B. Treasury bills

    C. Stock in a new company

    ✓ D. Certificate of deposit

MIDDLE LEVEL SOCIAL STUDIES 225

52. In a command economy:

   A. The open market determines how much of a good is produced and distributed

   ✓ B. The government determines how much of a good is produced and distributed

   C. Individuals produce and consume a specified good as commanded by their needs

   D. The open market determines the demand for a good, and then the government produces and distributes the good

53. In a barter economy, which of the following would not be an economic factor?

   A. Time

   B. Goods

   ✓ C. Money

   D. Services

54. Of the following, the best example of an oligopoly in the United States is:

   ✓ A. Automobile industry

   B. Electric power provision

   C. Telephone service

   D. Clothing manufacturing

55. Which best describes the economic system of the United States?

   A. Most decisions are the result of open markets, with little or no government modification or regulation

   B. Most decisions are made by the government, but there is some input by open market forces

   ✓ C. Most decisions are made by open market factors, with important regulatory functions and other market modifications the result of government activity

   D. There is joint decision making by government and private forces, with final decisions resting with the government

56. An agreement in which a company allows a business to use its name and sell its products, usually for a fee, is called a:

   A. Sole proprietorship

   B. Partnership

   C. Corporation

   ✓ D. Franchise

MIDDLE LEVEL SOCIAL STUDIES 226

57. What is a major difference between monopolistic competition and perfect competition?

   A. Perfect competition has many consumers and suppliers, while monopolistic competition does not

   ✓ B. Perfect competition provides identical products, while monopolistic competition provides similar but not identical products

   C. Entry to perfect competition is difficult, while entry to monopolistic competition is relatively easy

   D. Monopolistic competition has many consumers and suppliers, while perfect competition does not

58. Which concept is not embodied as a right in the First Amendment to the U.S. Constitution?

   A. Peaceable assembly

   ✓ B. Protection again unreasonable search and seizure

   C. Freedom of speech

   D. Petition for redress of grievances

59. In the Constitutional system of checks and balances, a primary "check" which accrues to the President is the power of:

   A. Executive privilege

   B. Approval of judges nominated by the Senate

   ✓ C. Veto of Congressional legislation

   D. Approval of judged nominated by the House of Representatives

60. According to the Constitution, any amendment must be ratified by _____ of the states to become a part of the Constitution:

   A. Three-fourths

   ✓ B. Two-thirds

   C. Three-fifths

   D. Five-sixths

61. Collectively, the first ten Amendments to the Constitution are known as the:

   A. Articles of Confederation

   B. Mayflower Compact

   ✓ C. Bill of Rights

   D. Declaration of the Rights of Man

62. In the United States, if a person is accused of a crime and cannot afford a lawyer:

   A. The person cannot be tried

   B. A court will appoint a lawyer, but the person must pay the lawyer back when able to do so

   C. The person must be tried without legal representation

   ✓ D. A court will appoint a lawyer for the person free of charge

63. Which of the following lists elements usually considered to be responsibilities of citizenship under the American system of government?

   A. Serving in public office, voluntary government service, military duty

   ✓ B. Paying taxes, jury duty, upholding the Constitution

   C. Maintaining a job, giving to charity, turning in fugitives

   D. Quartering of soldiers, bearing arms, government service

64. Consider the following passage from the Mayflower Compact: "...covenant, & combine ourselves together into a Civil body politick;" This demonstrates what theory of social organization?

   A. Darwinian

   B. Naturalistic

   C. Nonconsensual

   ✓ D. Constitutional

65. Why is the system of government in the United States referred to as a federal system?

   A. There are different levels of government

   B. There is one central authority in which all governmental power is vested

   C. The national government cannot operate except with the consent of the governed

   D. Elections are held at stated periodic times, rather than as called by the head of the government

66. Which of the following are NOT local governments in the United States?

   A. Cities

   B. Townships

   C. School boards

   D. All of these are forms of local government

67. The major expenditures of state governments in the United States go toward:

   A. Parks, education, and highways

   B. Law enforcement, libraries and highways

   C. Education, highways, and law enforcement

   D. Recreation, business regulation, and education

68. How does the government of France differ from that of the United States?

   A. France is a direct democracy, while the United States is a representative democracy

   B. France has a unitary form of national government, while the United States has a federal form of government

   C. France is a representative democracy, while the United States is a direct democracy

   D. France does not elect a President, while the United States elects a President

69. In the Presidential Election of 1888, Grover Cleveland lost to Benjamin Harrison, although Cleveland received more popular votes. How is this possible?

   A. The votes of certain states (New York, Indiana) were thrown out because of voting irregularities

   ✓ B. Harrison received more electoral votes than Cleveland

   C. None of the party candidates received a majority of votes, and the House of Representatives elected Harrison according to Constitutional procedures

   D. Because of accusations of election law violations, Cleveland withdrew his name and Harrison became President

70. How are major party candidates chosen to run for President in the United States?

   A. Caucuses of major party officeholders meet to select a state's choice for the party, and the candidate selected by the most states becomes the nominee

   B. Potential Presidential nominees seek pledges from each state party's chair and co-chair, and the candidate with the most pledges becomes the nominee

   C. Nationwide primaries are held by each party, to select delegates to a national nominating convention

   ✓ D. Each state party decides how to select delegates to a nominating convention; these selection processes may be caucuses, primaries, or any other method chosen by the state party

71. A person who receives more votes than anyone else in an election is said to have a _____ of the votes cast; a person who has over 50% of the votes in an election is said to have a _____ of the votes cast.

   A. Plurality; majority ✓

   B. Majority; minority

   C. Plurality; minority

   D. Majority; plurality

   plurality = the # of votes
   majority = % of votes

72. Which of the following developments is most closely associated with the Neolithic Age?

   A. Human use of fire

   B. First use of stone chipping instruments

   C. Domestication of plants ✓

   D. Development of metallurgical alloys

73. The Tigris-Euphrates Valley was the site of which two primary ancient civilizations?

   A. Babylonian and Assyrian ✓

   B. Sumerian and Egyptian

   C. Hyksos and Hurrian

   D. Persian and Phoenician

74. The politics of classical Athens is best described by which of the following?

   A. Limited democracy, including both slaves and free men

   B. One man dictatorial rule

   C. Universal democracy among free owners of property ✓

   D. Oligarchy with a few families controlling all decisions

   Similar to our own.

75. The _____ were fought between the Roman Empire and Carthage.

   A. Civil Wars

   B. Punic wars ✓

   C. Caesarian Wars

   D. Persian Wars

MIDDLE LEVEL SOCIAL STUDIES

76. What Holy Roman Emperor was forced to do public penance because of his conflict with Pope Gregory VII over lay investiture of the clergy?

    A. Charlemagne

    B. Henry IV

    C. Charles V

    D. Henry VIII

77. The _____ declared monophysitism (the belief that Jesus was completely divine with no admixture of humanity) to be a heresy?

    A. Council of Nicaea

    B. Diet of Worms

    C. Council of Trent

    D. Council of Chalcedon

78. The painter of the Sistine Ceiling was:

    A. Raphael

    B. Michelangelo

    C. Leonardo da Vinci

    D. Titian

79. Luther issued strong objection to all but which of the following practices of the 15th Century Roman Catholic Church?

    A. The sacrament of baptism

    B. Absolution of sins through the intermediation of a priest and through ceremony

    C. The sale of indulgences, whereby the buyer may purchase purgation of sins

    D. Imposed church control over the individual conscience

80. The first explorer to reach India by sailing around the southern tip of Africa was:

    A. Amerigo Vespucci

    B. Vasco da Gama

    C. Ferdinand Magellan

    D. John Cabot

81. Vasco Nunez de Balboa accomplished which of the following?

    A. Sighting of the Pacific Ocean from lands discovered by Europeans in the 1500's

    B. The conquest of the Inca civilization through treachery and deceit

    C. The murder of the ruler of the Aztecs and subsequent subjugation of the Empire

    D. None of the above

82. Great Britain became the center of technological and industrial development during the nineteenth century chiefly on the basis of:

    A. Central location relative to the population centers of Europe

    B. Colonial conquests and military victories over European powers

    C. Reliance on exterior sources of financing

    D. Resources of coal and production of steel

83. The years 1793-94 in France, characterized by numerous trials and executions of supposed enemies of the Revolutionary Convention, were known as the:

    A. Reign of Terror

    B. Dark Ages

    C. French Inquisition

    D. Glorious Revolution

84. In the first aggression of World War II outside the Orient, identify the aggressor nation and the nation which was invaded:

    A. Germany; Sudetenland

    B. Italy; Abyssinia

    C. Germany; Poland

    D. Italy; Yugoslavia

85. In issuing an ultimatum for Soviet ships not to enter Cuban waters in October, 1962, President John F. Kennedy, as part of his decision, used the provisions of the:

A. Monroe Doctrine

B. Declaration of the Rights of Man

C. Geneva Convention

D. Truman Doctrine

86. In 1990, Alberto Fujimori was elected president of:

A. Japan

B. Okinawa

C. South Korea

D. Peru

87. Which of the following most closely characterizes the geopolitical events of the USSR in 1991-92:

A. The USSR established greater military and economic control over the fifteen Soviet republics

B. The Baltic States (Estonia, Latvia, Lithuania) declared independence, while the remainder of the USSR remained intact.

C. Fourteen of fifteen Soviet republics declared some degree of autonomy; the USSR was officially dissolved; the Supreme Soviet rescinded the Soviet Treaty of 1922

D. All fifteen Soviet republics simultaneously declared immediate and full independence from the USSR, with no provisions for a transitional form of government

88. **Chinese civilization is generally credited with the original development of which of the following sets of technologies:**

    A. Movable type and mass production of goods

    B. Wool processing and domestication of the horse

    C. Paper and gunpowder manufacture

    D. Leather processing and modern timekeeping

89. **Extensive exports of gold and copper; elaborate court and constitution; trade links on both the Atlantic and Indian Oceans; use of heavy stone architecture; these most closely characterize the civilization of:**

    A. Mwene Mutapa

    B. Chichen Itza

    C. Great Zimbabwe

    D. Muscat and Oman

90. **Which of the following is NOT one of the Pillars of Faith of Islam?**

    A. Alms-giving (zakah)

    B. Pilgrimage (hajj)

    C. Membership in a school of law (al-madhahib)

    D. Fasting (sawm)

91. **The native metaphysical outlook of Japan, usually characterized as a religion, is:**

    A. Tao

    B. Shinto

    C. Nichiren Shoju

    D. Shaolin

92. **The Native Americans of the Eastern Woodlands lived on:**

    A. Buffalo and crops such as corn, beans, and sunflowers

    B. Chiefly farming of squash, beans, and corn

    C. A variety of game (deer, bear, moose) and crops (squash, pumpkins, corn)

    D. Wolves, foxes, polar bears, walruses, and fish

93. Apartments built out of cliff faces; shared government by adult citizens; absence of aggression toward other groups. These factors characterize the Native American group known as:

   A. Pueblos

   B. Comanches

   C. Seminoles

   D. Sioux

94. Columbus first reached Western Hemisphere lands in what is now:

   A. Florida

   B. Bermuda

   C. Puerto Rico

   D. Bahamas

95. The "Trail of Tears" relates to:

   A. The removal of the Cherokees from their native lands to Oklahoma Territory

   B. The revolt and subsequent migration of the Massachusetts Pilgrims under pressure from the Iroquois

   C. The journey of the Nez Perce under Chief Joseph before their capture by the U.S. Army

   D. The 1973 standoff between federal marshals and Native Americans at Wounded Knee, S.D.

96. Bartholomeu Dias, in seeking a route around the tip of Africa, was forced to turn back. Nevertheless, the cape he discovered near the southern tip of Africa became known as:

   A. Cape Horn

   B. Cabo Bojador

   C. Cape of Good Hope

   D. Cape Hatteras

97. The Middle Colonies of the Americas were:

   A. Maryland, Virginia, North Carolina

   B. New York, New Jersey, Pennsylvania, Delaware

   C. Rhode Island, Connecticut, New York, New Jersey

   D. Vermont and New Hampshire

98. Slavery arose in the Southern Colonies partly as a perceived economical way to:

   A. Increase the owner's wealth through human beings used as a source of exchange

   B. Cultivate large plantations of cotton, tobacco, rice, indigo, and other crops

   C. Provide Africans with humanitarian aid, such as health care, Christianity, and literacy

   D. Keep ships' holds full of cargo on two out of three legs of the "triangular trade" voyage

99. Of the following, which contributed most to penetration of western areas by colonial Americans?

   A. Development of large ships capable of sailing upstream in rivers such as the Hudson, Susquehanna, and Delaware

   B. The invention of the steamboat

   C. Improved relations with Native Americans, who invited colonial Americans to travel west to settle

   D. Improved roads, mail service, and communications

100. A major quarrel between colonial Americans and the British concerned a series of British Acts of Parliament dealing with:

   A. Taxes

   B. Slavery

   C. Native Americans

   D. Shipbuilding

101. The first shots in what was to become the American Revolution were fired in:

    A. Florida

    B. Massachusetts

    C. New York

    D. Virginia

102. The U.S. Constitution, adopted in 1789, provided for:

    A. Direct election of the President by all citizens

    B. Direct election of the President by citizens meeting a standard of wealth

    C. Indirect election of the President by electors

    D. Indirect election of the President by the U.S. Senate

103. The area of the United States was effectively doubled through purchase of the Louisiana Territory under which President?

    A. John Adams

    B. Thomas Jefferson

    C. James Madison

    D. James Monroe

104. What was a major source of contention between American settlers in Texas and the Mexican government in the 1830s and 1840s?

    A. The Americans wished to retain slavery, which had been outlawed in Mexico

    B. The Americans had agreed to learn Spanish and become Roman Catholic, but failed to do so

    C. The Americans retained ties to the United States, and Santa Ana feared the power of the U.S.

    D. All of the above were contentious issues between American settlers and the Mexican government

105. "Fifty-four Forty or Fight" refers to the desire of some nineteenth century Americans to:

   A. Explore the entire Missouri River valley to its source in the Oregon Territory

   B. Insist that Mexico cede all of Texas to the U.S. or face war

   C. Demand that American territory reach to the border of Russian America

   D. Pay only $54,040,000 for all of the Oregon Territory

106. Which President helped postpone a civil war by supporting the Compromise of 1850?

   A. Henry Clay

   B. Franklin Pierce

   C. Millard Fillmore

   D. James Buchanan

107. Which American Secretary of War oversaw the purchase of Present-day southern Arizona (the Gadsden Purchase) for the purpose of building a railroad to connect California to the rest of the United States?

   A. Henry Clay

   B. William Seward

   C. Franklin Pierce

   D. Jefferson Davis

108. A consequence of the Gold Rush of Americans to California in 1848 and 1849 was that:

   A. California spent the minimum amount of time as a territory and was admitted as a slave state

   B. California was denied admission on its first application, since most Americans felt that the settlers were too "uncivilized" to deserve statehood

   C. California was purchased from Mexico for the express purpose of gaining immediate statehood

   D. California did not go through the normal territorial stage but applied directly for statehood as a free state

109. Of the following groups of states, which were slave states?

   A. Delaware, Maryland, Missouri

   B. California, Texas, Florida

   C. Kansas, Missouri, Kentucky

   D. Virginia, West Virginia, Indiana

110. In the American Civil War, who was the first commander of the forces of the United States?

   A. Gen. Ulysses S. Grant

   B. Gen. Robert E. Lee

   C. Gen. Irwin McDowell

   D. Gen. George Meade

111. Abraham Lincoln won re-election in 1864 chiefly through:

   A. His overwhelming force of personality and appeal to all segments of the electorate

   B. His reputation as the Great Emancipator

   C. The fact that people felt sorry for him because of his difficulties

   D. His shrewd political manipulation, clever use of patronage jobs, and wide-appeal selection of cabinet members

112. How many states re-entered the Union before 1868?

State	Date of Readmission
Alabama	1868
Arkansas	1868
Florida	1868
Georgia	1870
Louisiana	1868
Mississippi	1870
North Carolina	1868
South Carolina	1868
Tennessee	1866
Texas	1870
Virginia	1870

A. 0 states

B. 1 state

C. 2 states

D. 3 states

113. The Interstate Commerce Commission (ICC) was established in reaction to abuses and corruption in what industry?

A. Textile

B. Railroad

C. Steel

D. Banking

114. Which of the following sets of inventors is correctly matched with the area in which they primarily worked?

A. Thomas Edison and George Westinghouse: transportation

B. Cyrus McCormick and George Washington Carver: household appliances

C. Alexander Graham Bell and Samuel F. B. Morse: communications

D. Isaac Singer and John Gorrie: agriculture

115. The Teapot Dome scandal related to:

A. The improper taxing of tea surpluses in Boston

B. The improper awarding of building contracts in Washington, D.C.

C. The improper sale of policy decisions by various Harding administration officials

D. The improper sale of oil reserves in Wyoming

116. Which of the following was NOT a factor in the United States' entry into World War I?

A. The closeness of the Presidential election of 1916

B. The German threat to sink all allied ships, including merchant ships

C. The desire to preserve democracy as practiced in Britain and France as compared to the totalitarianism of Germany

D. The sinking of the Lusitania and the Sussex

117. What 1924 Act of Congress severely restricted immigration in the United States?

A. Taft-Hartley Act

B. Smoot-Hawley Act

C. Fordney-McCumber Act

D. Johnson-Reed Act

118. The first territorial governor of Florida after Florida's purchase by the United States was:

A. Napoleon B. Broward

B. William P. Duval

C. Andrew Jackson

D. Davy Crockett

119. President Truman suspended Gen. Douglas MacArthur from command of Allied forces in Korea because of:

A. MacArthur's inability to make any progress against North Korea

B. MacArthur's criticism of Truman, claiming that the President would not allow him to pursue aggressive tactics against the Communists

C. The harsh treatment MacArthur exhibited toward the Japanese after World War II

D. The ability of the U.S. Navy to continue the conflict without the presence of MacArthur

120. Which of the following most closely characterizes the Supreme Court's decision in Brown v. Board of Education?

   A. Chief Justice Warren had to cast the deciding vote in a sharply divided Court

   B. The decision was rendered along sectional lines, with northerners voting for integration and southerners voting for continued segregation

   C. The decision was 7-2, with dissenting justices not even preparing a written dissent

   D. Chief Justice Warren was able to persuade the Court to render a unanimous decision

121. The economic practices under President Ronald Reagan ("Reaganomics") were characterized by:

   A. Low inflation, high unemployment, high interest rates, high national debt

   B. High inflation, low unemployment, low interest rates, low national debt

   C. Low inflation, high unemployment, low interest rates, depletion of national debt

   D. High inflation, low unemployment, high interest rates, low national debt

122. The Harlem Renaissance of the 1920s refers to:

   A. The migration of black Americans out of Harlem, and its resettlement by white Americans

   B. A movement whereby the residents of Harlem were urged to "Return to Africa"

   C. A proliferation in the arts among black Americans, centered on Harlem

   D. The discovery of lost 15th century Italian paintings in a Harlem warehouse

123. **Which of the following is most descriptive of the conflict between the U.S. government and the Seminoles between 1818 and 1858?**

   A. There was constant armed conflict between the Seminoles and the U.S. during these years

   B. Historians discern three separate phases of hostilities (1818, 1835-42, 1855-58), known collectively as the Seminole Wars

   C. On May 7, 1858, the Seminoles admitted defeat, signed a peace treaty with the U.S., and left for Oklahoma, except for fifty-one individuals

   D. The former Seminole chief Osceola helped the U.S. defeat the Seminoles and effect their removal to Oklahoma

124. **Match the railroad entrepreneur with the correct area of development:**

   A. Henry Plant: Tampa and the West Coast

   B. Cornelius Vanderbilt: Jacksonville and the Northeast

   C. Henry Flagler: Orlando and the Central Highlands

   D. J.P. Morgan: Pensacola and the Northwest

125. **Florida's space exploration industry is centered in:**

   A. Baker County

   B. Broward County

   C. Brevard County

   D. Bradford County

TEACHER CERTIFICATION STUDY GUIDE

Answer Key

1.	C	34.	D	67.	C	100.	A
2.	B	35.	C	68.	B	101.	B
3.	D	36.	B	69.	B	102.	C
4.	C	37.	C	70.	D	103.	B
5.	A	38.	A	71.	A	104.	D
6.	C	39.	A	72.	C	105.	C
7.	A	40.	D	73.	A	106.	C
8.	D	41.	C	74.	C	107.	D
9.	B	42.	B	75.	B	108.	D
10.	C	43.	B	76.	B	109.	A
11.	D	44.	C	77.	D	110.	C
12.	D	45.	D	78.	B	111.	D
13.	D	46.	B	79.	A	112.	B
14.	A	47.	B	80.	B	113.	B
15.	C	48.	A	81.	A	114.	C
16.	B	49.	C	82.	D	115.	D
17.	B	50.	C	83.	A	116.	A
18.	D	51.	D	84.	B	117.	D
19.	A	52.	B	85.	A	118.	C
20.	C	53.	C	86.	D	119.	B
21.	A	54.	A	87.	C	120.	D
22.	D	55.	C	88.	C	121.	A
23.	D	56.	D	89.	C	122.	C
24.	C	57.	B	90.	C	123.	B
25.	C	58.	B	91.	B	124.	A
26.	B	59.	C	92.	C	125.	C
27.	A	60.	A	93.	A		
28.	D	61.	C	94.	D		
29.	D	62.	D	95.	A		
30.	B	63.	B	96.	C		
31.	C	64.	D	97.	B		
32.	D	65.	A	98.	B		
33.	A	66.	D	99.	D		

MIDDLE LEVEL SOCIAL STUDIES

TEACHER CERTIFICATION STUDY GUIDE

Rationale with Sample Questions

1. **Which of the following best describes current thinking on the major purpose of social science?**

    A. Social science is designed primarily for students to acquire facts

    B. Social science should not be taught earlier than the middle school years

    C. A primary purpose of social sciences is the development of good citizens

    D. Social science should be taught as an elective

Answer: C

C. A primary purpose of social sciences is the development of good citizens. By making students aware of the importance of their place in society, how their society and others are governed, how societies develop and advance, and how cultural behaviors arise, the social sciences are currently thought to be of primary importance in (C) developing good citizens.

2. **Psychology is a social science because:**

    A. It focuses on the biological development of individuals

    B. It focuses on the behavior of individual persons and small groups of persons

    C. It bridges the gap between the natural and the social sciences

    D. It studies the behavioral habits of lower animals

Answer: B

B. It focuses on the behavior of individual persons and small groups of persons While it is true that (C) psychology draws from natural sciences, it is (B) the study of the behavior of individual persons and small groups that defines psychology as a social science. (A) The biological development of human beings and (D) the behavioral habits of lower animals are studied in the developmental and behavioral branches of psychology.

TEACHER CERTIFICATION STUDY GUIDE

3. **A historian would be interested in:**

    A. The manner in which scientific knowledge is advanced

    B. The effects of the French Revolution on world colonial policy

    C. The viewpoint of persons who have written previous "history"

    D. All of the above

Answer: D

D.   All of the above

Historians are interested in broad developments through history (A), as well as how individual events affected the time in which they happened (B). Knowing the viewpoint of earlier historians can also help explain the common thinking among historical cultures and groups (C), so all of these answers are correct (D).

4. **The sub-discipline of linguistics is usually studied under:**

    A. Geography

    B. History

    C. Anthropology

    D. Economics

Answer: C

C.   Anthropology

The fields of (A) Geography, (B) History and (D) Economics may study language as part of other subjects that affect these fields of study, but taken by itself language is a defining characteristic of a culture. (C) Anthropology studies human culture and the relationships between cultures, so linguistics is included under this social science.

MIDDLE LEVEL SOCIAL STUDIES   247

TEACHER CERTIFICATION STUDY GUIDE

5. **Which of the following is not generally considered a discipline within the social sciences?**

   A. Geometry

   B. Anthropology

   C. Geography

   D. Sociology

Answer: A

A.   Geometry

(B) Anthropology studies the culture of groups of people. (C) Geography examines the relationship between societies and the physical place on earth where they live. (D) Sociology studies the predominant attitudes, beliefs and behaviors of a society. All three of these fields are related to the social interactions of humans, and so are considered social sciences. (A) Geometry is a field of mathematics and does not relate to the social interactions of people, so it is not considered a social science.

6. **Economics is best described as:**

   A. The study of how money is used in different societies

   B. The study of how different political systems produces goods and services

   C. The study of how human beings use limited resources to supply their necessities and wants

   D. The study of how human beings have developed trading practices through the years

Answer: C
C.   The study of how human beings use limited resources to supply their necessities and wants

(A) How money is used in different societies might be of interest to a sociologist or anthropologist. (B) The study of how different political systems produce goods and services is a topic of study that could be included under the field of political science. (D) The study of historical trading practices could fall under the study of history. Only (C) is the best general description of the social science of economics as a whole.

MIDDLE LEVEL SOCIAL STUDIES

TEACHER CERTIFICATION STUDY GUIDE

7. Which of the following is most reasonably studied under the social sciences?

    A. Political science

    B. Geometry

    C. Physics

    D. Grammar

Answer: A

A.   Political science

Social sciences deal with the social interactions of people. (B) Geometry is a branch of mathematics. (C) Physics is a natural science that studies the physical world. Although it may be studied as part of linguistics, (D) grammar is not recognized as a scientific field of study in itself. Only (A) political science is considered a general field of the social sciences.

8. For the historian studying ancient Egypt, which of the following would be least useful?

    A. The record of an ancient Greek historian on Greek-Egyptian interaction

    B. Letters from an Egyptian ruler to his/her regional governors

    C. Inscriptions on stele of the Fourteenth Egyptian Dynasty

    D. Letters from a nineteenth century Egyptologist to his wife

Answer: D

D.   Letters from a nineteenth century Egyptologist to his wife

Historians use primary sources from the actual time they are studying whenever possible. (A) Ancient Greek records of interaction with Egypt, (B) letters from an Egyptian ruler to regional governors, and (C) inscriptions from the Fourteenth Egyptian Dynasty are all primary sources created at or near the actual time being studied. (D) Letters from a nineteenth century Egyptologist would not be considered primary sources, as they were created thousands of years after the fact and may not actually be about the subject being studied.

9. A political scientist might use all of the following except:

A. An investigation of government documents

B. A geological timeline

C. Voting patterns

D. Polling data

Answer: B

B.   A geological timeline

Political science is primarily concerned with the political and governmental activities of societies. (A) Government documents can provide information about the organization and activities of a government. (C) Voting patterns reveal the political behavior of individuals and groups. (D) Polling data can provide insight into the predominant political views of a group of people. (B) A geological timeline describes the changes in the physical features of the earth over time and would not be useful to a political scientist.

10. A geographer wishes to study the effects of a flood on subsequent settlement patterns. Which might he or she find most useful?

A. A film clip of the floodwaters

B. An aerial photograph of the river's source

C. Census data taken after the flood

D. A soil map of the A and B horizons beneath the flood area

Answer: C

C.   Census data taken after the flood

(A) A film clip of the flood waters may be of most interest to a historian, (B) an aerial photograph of the river's source, and (D) soil maps tell little about the behavior of the individuals affected by the flood. (C) Census surveys record the population for certain areas on a regular basis, allowing a geographer to tell if more or fewer people are living in an area over time. These would be of most use to a geographer undertaking this study.

TEACHER CERTIFICATION STUDY GUIDE

11. A social scientist observes how individual persons react to the presence or absence of noise. This scientist is most likely a:

   A. Geographer

   B. Political Scientist

   C. Economist

   D. Psychologist

Answer: D

D.   Psychologist

(D) Psychologists scientifically study the behavior and mental processes of individuals. Studying how individuals react to changes in their environment falls under this social science. (A) Geographers, (B) political scientists and (C) economists are more likely to study the reactions of groups rather than individual reactions.

12. As a sociologist, you would be most likely to observe:

   A. The effects of an earthquake on farmland

   B. The behavior of rats in sensory deprivation experiments

   C. The change over time in Babylonian obelisk styles

   D. The behavior of human beings in television focus groups

Answer: D

D.   The behavior of human beings in television focus groups.

Predominant beliefs and attitudes within human society are studied in the field of sociology. (A) The effects of an earthquake on farmland might be studied by a geographer. (B) The behavior of rats in an experiment falls under the field of behavioral psychology. (C) Changes in Babylonian obelisk styles might interest a historian. None of these answers fits easily within the definition of sociology. (D) A focus group, where people are asked to discuss their reactions to a certain product or topic, would be the most likely method for a sociologist of observing and discovering attitudes among a selected group.

13. An economist investigates the spending patterns of low-income individuals. Which of the following would yield the most pertinent information?

   A. Prime lending rates of neighborhood banks

   B. The federal discount rate

   C. Citywide wholesale distribution figures

   D. Census data and retail sales figures

Answer: D

D.   Census data and retail sales figures

(A) Local lending rates and (B) the federal discount rate might provide information on borrowing habits, but not necessarily spending habits, and give no information on income levels. (C) Citywide wholesale distribution figures would provide information on the business activity of a city, but tell nothing about consumer activities. (D) Census data records the income levels of households within a certain area, and retail sales figures for that area would give an economist data on spending, which can be compared to income levels, making this the most pertinent source.

14. A teacher and a group of students take a field trip to an Indian mound to examine artifacts. This activity most closely fits under which branch of the social sciences?

   A. Anthropology

   B. Sociology

   C. Psychology

   D. Political Science

Answer: A

A.   Anthropology

(A) Anthropology is the study of human culture and the way in which people of different cultures live. The artifacts created by people of a certain culture can provide information about the behaviors and beliefs of that culture, making anthropology the best-fitting field of study for this field trip. (B) Sociology, (C) psychology and (D) political science are more likely to study behaviors and institutions directly than through individual artifacts created by a specific culture.

15. Which of the following is most closely identified as a sociologist?

A. Herodotus

B. John Maynard Keynes

C. Emile Durkheim

D. Arnold Toynbee

Answer: C

C.   Emile Durkheim

(C) Durkheim (1858-1917) was the founder of the first sociological journal in France and the first to apply scientific methods of research to the study of human society. (A) Herodotus (ca. 484-425 BC) was an early Greek historian. (B) John Maynard Keynes (1883-1946) was a British economist who developed the field of modern theoretical macroeconomics. (D) Arnold Toynbee (1882-1853) was also a British economist who took a historical approach to the field.

16. We can credit modern geography with which of the following?

A. Building construction practices designed to withstand earthquakes

B. Advances in computer cartography

C. Better methods of linguistic analysis

D. Making it easier to memorize countries and their capitals

Answer: B

B.   Advances in computer cartography.

(B) Cartography is concerned with the study and creation of maps and geographical information and falls under the social science of geography.

TEACHER CERTIFICATION STUDY GUIDE

17. Adam Smith is most closely identified with which of the following?

    A. The law of diminishing returns

    B. The law of supply and demand

    C. The principle of motor primacy

    D. The territorial imperative

Answer: B

B.   The law of supply and demand

Adam Smith was an economist who developed the theory that value was linked to the supply of a good or service compared to the demand for it. Something in low supply but high demand will have a high value. Something in great supply but low demand is worth less. This has become known as (B) the law of supply and demand. (A) The law of diminishing returns is an economic principle described by Thomas Malthus in 1798. (C) The principle of motor primacy refers to a stage in developmental psychology. (D) The territorial imperative is a theory of the origin of property outlined by anthropologist Robert Ardrey in 1966.

18. Margaret Mead may be credited with major advances in the study of:

    A. The marginal propensity to consume

    B. The thinking of the Anti-Federalists

    C. The anxiety levels of non-human primates

    D. Interpersonal relationships in non-technical societies

Answer: D

D.   Interpersonal relationships in non-technical societies

Margaret Mead (1901-1978) was a pioneer in the field of anthropology, living among the people of Samoa, observing and writing about their culture in the book Coming of Age in Samoa in 1928. (A) The marginal propensity to consume is an economic subject. (B) The thinking of the Anti-Federalists is a topic in American history. (C) The anxiety levels of non-human primates are a subject studied in behavioral psychology.

TEACHER CERTIFICATION STUDY GUIDE

19. **The advancement of understanding in dealing with human beings has led to a number of interdisciplinary areas. Which of the following interdisciplinary studies would NOT be considered under the social sciences?**

    A. Molecular biophysics

    B. Peace studies

    C. African-American studies

    D. Cartographic information systems

Answer: A

A. Molecular biophysics

(A) Molecular biophysics is an interdisciplinary field combining the fields of biology, chemistry, and physics. These are all natural sciences and not social sciences

20. **Cognitive, developmental, and behavioral are three types of:**

    A. Economist

    B. Political Scientist

    C. Psychologist

    D. Historian

Answer: C

C. Psychologists

(C) Psychologists study mental processes (cognitive psychology), the mental development of children (developmental psychology), and observe human and animal behavior in controlled circumstances (behavioral psychology.)

21. A physical geographer would be concerned with which of the following groups of terms?

    A. Landform, biome, precipitation

    B. Scarcity, goods, services

    C. Nation, state, administrative subdivision

    D. Cause and effect, innovation, exploration

Answer: A

A.   Landform, biome, precipitation.

(A) Landform, biome, and precipitation are all terms used in the study of geography. A landform is a physical feature of the earth, such as a hill or valley. A biome is a large community of plants or animals, such as a forest. Precipitation is the moisture that falls to earth as rain or snow. (B) Scarcity, goods, and services are terms encountered in economics. (C) Nation, state, and administrative subdivision are terms used in political science. (D) Cause and effect, innovation, and exploration are terms in developmental psychology.

22. An economist might engage in which of the following activities?

    A. An observation of the historical effects of a nation's banking practices

    B. The application of a statistical test to a series of data

    C. Introduction of an experimental factor into a specified population to measure the effect of the factor

    D. An economist might engage in all of these

Answer: D

D.   An economist might engage in all of these

Economists use statistical analysis of economic data, controlled experimentation as well as historical research in their field of social science.

TEACHER CERTIFICATION STUDY GUIDE

23. **Political science is primarily concerned with _____.**

    A. Elections

    B. Economic Systems

    C. Boundaries

    D. Public Policy

Answer: D

D.   Public policy

Political science studies the actions and policies of the government of a society. (D) Public policy is the official stance of a government on an issue and is a primary source for studying a society's dominant political beliefs. (A) Elections are also an interest of political scientists but are not a primary field of study. (B) Economic systems are of interest to an economist and (C) boundaries to a geographer.

24. **An anthropologist is studying a society's sororate and avunculate. In general, this scientist is studying the society's:**

    A. Level of technology

    B. Economy

    C. Kinship practices

    D. Methods of farming

Answer: C

C.   Kinship practices

Sororate and avunculate are anthropological terms referring to interfamily relationships between sisters and between men and their sisters' sons. These are terms used to describe (C) kinship practices.

TEACHER CERTIFICATION STUDY GUIDE

25. Of the following lists, which includes persons who have made major advances in the understanding of psychology?

    A. Herodotus, Thucydides, Ptolemy

    B. Adam Smith, Milton Friedman, John Kenneth Galbraith

    C. Edward Hall, E.L. Thorndike, B.F. Skinner

    D. Thomas Jefferson, Karl Marx, Henry Kissinger

Answer: C

C.   Edward Hall, E.L. Thorndike, B.F. Skinner

Edward Hall wrote in the 1960s about the effects of overcrowding on humans, especially in large cities. E.L. Thorndike (1874-1949) was an early developer of an experimental approach to studying learning in animals and of educational psychology. B.F. Skinner (1904-1990) was a pioneer in behavioral psychology. (A) Herodotus, Thucydides, and Ptolemy were early historians. (B) Smith, Friedman, and Galbraith made significant contributions to the field of economics. (D) Jefferson, Marx, and Kissinger are figures in political science.

26. The writing of history is called:

    A. Public policy analysis

    B. Historiography

    C. Historical perspective

    D. Historical analysis

Answer: B

B.   Historiography

(B) Historiography is a term used to refer to the actual writing of history as well as the study of this type of writing. (A) Public policy analysis is part of political science. (C) Historical perspective refers to the prevailing viewpoint of a historical time, and (D) historical analysis concerns the interpretation of historical events.

MIDDLE LEVEL SOCIAL STUDIES

27. **If geography is the study of how human beings live in relationship to the earth on which they live, why do geographers include physical geography within the discipline?**

    A. The physical environment serves as the location for the activities of human beings

    B. No other branch of the natural or social sciences studies the same topics

    C. The physical environment is more important than the activities carried out by human beings

    D. It is important to be able to subdue natural processes for the advancement of humankind

Answer: A

A. The physical environment serves as the location for the activities of human beings.

Cultures will develop different practices depending on the predominant geographical features of the area in which they live. Cultures that live along a river will have a different kind of relationship to the surrounding land than those who live in the mountains, for instance. Answer (A) best describes why physical geography is included in the social science of geography. Answer (B) is false, as physical geography is also studied under other natural sciences (such as geology.) Answers (C) and (D) are matters of opinion and do not pertain to the definition of geography as a social science.

28. **A historian might compare the governmental systems of the Roman Empire and the twentieth century United States with regard to which of the following commonalities?**

    A. Totalitarianism

    B. Technological development

    C. Constitutional similarities

    D. Federalism

Answer: D

D.   Federalism

(A) Totalitarianism is a form of government where citizens are completely subservient to the state. While this was sometimes the case during the reign of the Roman Empire, it was not common to 20th century America. (B) Technological development does not necessarily address similarities in governmental systems. (C) The Roman constitution applied to the republic of Rome but not directly to the empire as a whole. (D) Federalism is a type of governmental system where several separate states join under a common government. This describes both the United States and the Roman Empire and is the best answer.

29. **Capitalism and communism are alike in that they are both:**

    A. Organic systems

    B. Political systems

    C. Centrally planned systems

    D. Economic systems

Answer: D

D.   Economic systems

While economic and (B) political systems are often closely connected, capitalism and communism are primarily (D) economic systems. Capitalism is a system of economics that allows the open market to determine the relative value of goods and services. Communism is an economic system where the market is planned by a central state. While communism is a (C) centrally planned system, this is not true of capitalism. (A) Organic systems are studied in biology, a natural science.

TEACHER CERTIFICATION STUDY GUIDE

30. **Which of the following demonstrates evidence of the interaction between physical and cultural anthropology?**

    A. Tall Nilotic herdsmen are often expert warriors

    B. Until recent years the diet of most Asian peoples caused them to be shorter in stature than most other peoples

    C. Native South American peoples adopted potato production after invasion by Europeans

    D. Polynesians exhibit different skin coloration than Melanesians

Answer: B

B. Until recent years the diet of most Asian peoples caused them to be shorter in stature than most other peoples.

Cultural anthropology is the study of culture. Physical anthropology studies human evolution and other biologically related aspects of human culture. Answers (A) and (D) describe physical attributes of members of different cultures but make no connection between these attributes and the behaviors of these cultures. Answer (C) describes a cultural behavior of Native Americans but makes no connection to any physical attributes of the people of this culture. Answer (B) draws a connection between a cultural behavior (diet) and a physical attribute (height) and is the best example demonstrating the interaction between cultural and physical anthropology.

31. **A social scientist studies the behavior of four persons in a carpool. This is an example of:**

    A. Developmental psychology

    B. Experimental psychology

    C. Social psychology

    D. Macroeconomics

Answer: C

C. Social psychology

(A) Developmental psychology studies the mental development of humans as they mature. (B) Experimental psychology uses formal experimentation with control groups to examine human behavior. (C) Social psychology is a branch of the field that investigates people's behavior as they interact within society and is the type of project described in the question. (D) Macroeconomics is a field within economics and would not apply to this project.

32. **Peace studies might include elements of all of the following disciplines except:**

    A. Geography

    B. History

    C. Economics

    D. All of these might contribute to peace studies

Answer: D

D. All of these might contribute to peace studies.

(D) All of these might contribute to peace studies. (A) Geography might examine the current and historical borders between two regions or nations, for instance. (B) History would contribute information on the origins of conflict and peace between peoples. Because scarcity of goods and differences in the relative wealth of nations are often factors in conflict and cooperation, (C) economics can be included in peace studies.

TEACHER CERTIFICATION STUDY GUIDE

33. Which of the following sets of terms relates to the Davisian erosion cycle?

- A. Youth, maturity, old age

- B. Atmospheric erosion, subsurface erosion, superficial erosion

- C. Fluvial, alluvial, estuarine

- D. Mississippian, Pennsylvanian, Illinoisian

Answer: A

A.   Youth, maturity, old age

The Davisian erosion cycle was developed by physical geographer William Morris Davis to describe three main stages in the life of a stream. Davis called these stages (A) Youth, maturity, and old age. In youth, a stream is forced into channels and cuts downward to a base level. In maturity, it begins to cut away at the sides of the channel and broaden. Finally, in old age, it develops into a wide flood plain. (B) Atmospheric erosion, subsurface erosion, and superficial erosion are types of soil erosion and do not describe the Davisian cycle. (C) Fluvial, alluvial, and estuarine are geological terms referring to rivers but not to erosion. (D) Mississippian and Pennsylvanian refer to geologic periods in North America. An Illinoisian is someone from Illinois

34. What is a drumlin?

- A. A narrow ridge of sand, gravel, and boulders deposited by a stream flowing on, in, or under a nonmoving glacier

- C. Accumulated earth, pebbles, and stones carried by and then deposited by a glacier

- C. The active front face of a non-stagnant glacier

- D. An elongated or oval hill formed by drift material of glaciers

Answer: D

D.   An elongated or oval hill formed by drift material of glaciers

Glacial material moving over land sometimes form long or oval hills, usually in groups, that are oriented in the direction of the ice flow. These hills, which can be of varying composition, are called drumlins.

MIDDLE LEVEL SOCIAL STUDIES

TEACHER CERTIFICATION STUDY GUIDE

35. **A coral island or series of islands which consists of a reef which surrounds a lagoon describes a(n):**

    A. Needle

    B. Key

    C. Atoll

    D. Mauna

Answer: C

C.   Atoll

An (C) atoll is a formation that occurs when a coral reef builds up around the top of a submerged volcanic peak, forming a ring or horseshoe of islands with a seawater lagoon in the center.

36. **What type of cloud usually produces rain?**

    A. Cirrus

    B. Cumulonimbus

    C. Altostratus

    D. Cirrostratus

Answer: B

B.   Cumulonimbus

(B) Cumulonimbus clouds reach high into the sky and are usually associated with instability and thundershowers. (A) Cirrus clouds are thin and wispy and are usually seen in fair weather. (C) Altostratus clouds are thin and spread out and can sometimes produce rain if they thicken. (D) Cirrostratus clouds are high, thin clouds that are nearly transparent and do not normally produce rain.

TEACHER CERTIFICATION STUDY GUIDE

37. Which of the following is NOT a type of rainfall?

    A. Convectional

    B. Cyclonic

    C. Adiabatic

    D. Frontal

Answer: C

C.   Adiabatic

(A) Convectional rain occurs when hot air rises quickly and is cooled and is usually accompanied by thunderstorms. (B) Cyclonic and (D) frontal rain occurs at the place where hot and cool air masses meet, called the "front." (C) Adiabatic is a term used in physics and is not a type of rainfall.

38. The Mediterranean type climate is characterized by:

    A. Hot, dry summers and mild, relatively wet winters

    B. Cool, relatively wet summers and cold winters

    C. Mild summers and winters, with moisture throughout the year

    D. Hot, wet summers and cool, dry winters

Answer: A

A.   Hot, dry summers and mild, relatively wet winters

Westerly winds and nearby bodies of water create stable weather patterns along the west coasts of several continents and along the coast of the Mediterranean Sea, after which this type of climate is named. Temperatures rarely fall below the freezing point and have a mean between 70 and 80 degrees F in the summer. Stable conditions make for little rain during the summer months.

39. The climate of Southern Florida is the _____ type.

    A. Humid subtropical

    B. Marine West Coast

    C. Humid continental

    D. Tropical wet-dry

Answer: A

A.   Humid subtropical

The (B) marine west coast climate is found on the western coasts of continents. Florida is on the eastern side of North America. The (C) humid continental climate is found over large land masses, such as Europe and the American Midwest, not along coasts such as where Florida is situated. The (D) tropical wet-dry climate occurs within about 15 degrees of the equator, in the tropics. Florida is sub-tropical. Florida is in a (A) humid subtropical climate, which extends along the East Coast of the United States to about Maryland, and along the gulf coast to northeastern Texas.

40. Which of the following is an island nation?

    A. Luxembourg

    B. Finland

    C. Monaco

    D. Nauru

Answer: D

D.   Nauru

(D) Nauru is located in Micronesia in the South Pacific and is the world's smallest island nation. (A) Luxembourg is a small principality in Europe, bordered by Belgium, France, and Germany. (B) Finland is a Scandinavian country on the Baltic Sea bordered by Norway, Sweden, and Russia. (C) Monaco is a small principality on the coast of the Mediterranean Sea that is bordered by France.

TEACHER CERTIFICATION STUDY GUIDE

41. Which location may be found in Canada?

    A. 27 N 93 W

    B. 41 N 93 E

    C. 50 N 111 W

    D. 18 N 120 W

Answer: C

C.   50 N 111 W

(A) 27 North latitude, 93 West longitude is located in the Gulf of Mexico. (B) 41 N 93 E is located in northwest China. (D) 18 N 120 W is in the Pacific Ocean, off the coast of Mexico. (C) 50 N 111 W is located near the town of Medicine Hat in the province of Alberta, in Canada.

42. The highest point on the North American continent is:

    A. Mt. St. Helen's

    B. Denali

    C. Mt. Everest

    D. Pike's Peak

Answer: B

B.   Denali

(B) Denali, also known as Mt. McKinley, has an elevation of 20,320 feet, and is in the Alaska Range of North America. It is the highest point on the continent. (A) Mt. St. Helen's, an active volcano located in the state of Washington, is 8,364 feet in elevation since its eruption in 1980. (D) Pike's Peak, located in Colorado, is 14,100 feet in elevation. (C) Mt. Everest, in the Himalayan Mountains between China and Tibet is the highest point on the earth at 29,035 feet but is not located in North America.

43. Concerning the present political map of Africa, which statement most closely applies?

A. The modern states reflect an effort to establish political units based on ethnic groupings

B. The international community allowed for a period of elasticity with regard to boundaries, so that a condition of relative equilibrium could develop

C. Africans were given the task of delineating the modern states, using whatever criteria they chose

D. The modern states reflect imposed boundaries, without regard to ethnic groupings or other indigenous considerations

Answer: B

B. The international community allowed for a period of elasticity with regard to boundaries, so that a condition of relative equilibrium could develop.

Many African states were originally colonized by other countries and had borders drawn up (D) without regard to ethnic groupings or other indigenous considerations. With the relatively recent independence of colonial states, border disputes have arisen, but no complete delineation has taken place along ethnic or any other grounds, as described in answers (A) and (C). The international community has been involved individually and jointly, as members of the United Nations, providing diplomacy and refugee aid in some of the recent border disputes, as in that between Eritrea and Ethiopia, but has largely taken the stance that these issues should be worked out between the nations involved.

44. Which of the following areas would NOT be a primary area of hog production?

   A. Midland England

   B. The Mekong delta of Vietnam

   C. Central Syria

   D. Northeast Iowa

Answer: C

C.   Central Syria

Pork is a common ingredient in the American, English, and Vietnamese cuisine, so one would reasonably expect to find hog production in (A) Midland England, (B) The Mekong Delta of Vietnam and (D) Northeast Iowa. The population of Syria is predominantly Islamic, and Islam prohibits the eating of pork. Therefore, one would be unlikely to find extensive hog production in (C) Central Syria.

45. Indo-European languages are native languages to each of the following EXCEPT:

   A. Germany

   B. India

   C. Italy

   D. Finland

Answer: D

D.   Finland

German, the native language of (A) Germany, Hindi, the official language of (B) India, and Italian, spoken in (C) Italy, are three of the hundreds of languages that are part of the Indo-European family, which also includes French, Greek, and Russian. Finnish, the language of (D) Finland, is part of the Uralic family of languages, which also includes Estonian. It developed independently of the Indo-European family.

TEACHER CERTIFICATION STUDY GUIDE

46. A cultural geographer is investigating the implications of <u>The Return of the Native</u> by Thomas Hardy. He or she is most likely concentrating on:

    A. The reactions of British city-dwellers to the in-migration of French professionals

    B. The activities of persons in relation to poorly drained, coarse-soiled land with low-lying vegetation

    C. The capacity of riverine lands to sustain a population of edible amphibians

    D. The propagation of new crops introduced by settlers from North America

Answer: B

B.   The activities of persons in relation to poorly drained, coarse-soiled land with low-lying vegetation

Thomas Hardy's novel <u>The Return of the Native</u> takes place in England, in a fictional region based on Hardy's home area, Dorset. Hardy describes the people and landscape of this area, which is primarily heath. A heath is a poorly drained, coarse-soiled land with low-lying vegetation, as described in answer (B). This is the most likely concentration for a cultural geographer studying Hardy's novel.

47. Which of the following is NOT considered to be an economic need:

    A. Food

    B. Transportation

    C. Shelter

    D. Clothing

Answer: B

B.   Transportation

An economic need is something that a person absolutely must have to survive. (A) Food, (C) shelter and (D) clothing are examples of these needs. While an individual may also require (B) transportation to participate in an economy, it is not considered an absolute need.

TEACHER CERTIFICATION STUDY GUIDE

48. As your income rises, you tend to spend more money on entertainment. This is an expression of the:

   A. Marginal propensity to consume

   B. Allocative efficiency

   C. Compensating differential

   D. Marginal propensity to save

Answer: A

A.   Marginal propensity to consume

The (A) marginal propensity to consume is a measurement of how much consumption changes compared to how much disposable income changes. Entertainment expenses are an example of disposable income. Dividing your change in entertainment spending by your total change in disposable income will give you your marginal propensity to consume.

49. A student buys a candy bar at lunch. The decision to buy a second candy bar relates to the concept of:

   A. Equilibrium pricing

   B. Surplus

   C. Utility

   D. Substitutability

Answer: C

C.   Utility

As used in the social science of economics, (C) utility is the measurement of happiness or satisfaction a person receives from consuming a good or service. The decision of the student to increase his satisfaction by buying a second candy bar relates to this concept because he is spending money to increase his happiness.

50. If the price of Good G increases, what is likely to happen with regard to comparable Good H?

    A. The demand for Good G will stay the same

    B. The demand for Good G will increase

    C. The demand for Good H will increase

    D. The demand for Good H will decrease

Answer: C

C. The demand for Good H will increase.

If Good G and Good H are viewed by consumers as equal in value but then the cost of Good G increases, it follows that consumers will now choose Good H at a higher rate, increasing the demand.

51. A teacher has an extra $1,000 which she wishes to invest and wants to minimize the risk. The best choice for investment, from the following, is:

    A. Money market account

    B. Treasury bills

    C. Stock in a new company

    D. Certificate of deposit

Answer: D

D. Certificate of deposit

(A) Money market funds will fluctuate in value based on international currency trading. (B) Treasury bills are issued by the federal government and carry very little risk but are available only at prices close to $10,000. The teacher does not have enough to invest. (C) Stock in a new company is very likely to change rapidly and carries a high degree of risk. A (D) Certificate of deposit is a certificate issued by a bank promising to pay a fixed amount of interest for a fixed period of time. Because most deposits are insured up to $100,000 by the federal government, there is little risk of losing money with this investment.

TEACHER CERTIFICATION STUDY GUIDE

52. In a command economy:

A. The open market determines how much of a good is produced and distributed

B. The government determines how much of a good is produced and distributed

C. Individuals produce and consume a specified good as commanded by their needs

D. The open market determines the demand for a good, and then the government produces and distributes the good

Answer: B

B. The government determines how much of a good is produced and distributed.

A command economy is where (B) the government determines how much of a good is produced and distributed, as was the case in the Soviet Union and is still the case in Cuba and North Korea. A command economy is the opposite of a market economy, where (A) the open market determines how much of a good is produced and distributed.

53. In a barter economy, which of the following would not be an economic factor?

A. Time

B. Goods

C. Money

D. Services

Answer: C

C. Money

A barter economy is one where (B) goods and (D) services are exchanged for one another and not for money. Just as in an economy with currency, (A) time is a factor in determining the value of goods and services. Since no money changes hands in a barter economy, the correct answer is (C) money.

MIDDLE LEVEL SOCIAL STUDIES 273

54. Of the following, the best example of an oligopoly in the US is:

    A. Automobile industry

    B. Electric power provision

    C. Telephone service

    D. Clothing manufacturing

Answer: A

A.   Automobile industry

An oligopoly exists when a small group of companies controls an industry. In the United States at present, there are hundreds of (B) electric power providers, (C) telephone service providers and (D) clothing manufacturers. There are currently still just three major automobile manufacturers, however, making the (A) automobile industry an oligopoly.

55. Which best describes the economic system of the United States?

A. Most decisions are the result of open markets, with little or no government modification or regulation

B. Most decisions are made by the government, but there is some input by open market forces

C. Most decisions are made by open market factors, with important regulatory functions and other market modifications the result of government activity

D. There is joint decision making by government and private forces, with final decisions resting with the government

Answer: C

C. Most decisions are made by open market factors, with important regulatory functions and other market modifications the result of government activity.

The United States does not have a planned economy, as described in answers (B) and (D) where the government makes major market decisions. Neither is the U.S. market completely free of regulation, as described in answer (A). Products are regulated for safety, and many services are regulated by certification requirements, for example. The best description of the U.S. economic system is therefore (C) Most decisions are made by open market factors, with important regulatory functions and other market modifications the result of government activity.

56. An agreement in which a company allows a business to use its name and sell its products, usually for a fee, is called a:

   A. Sole proprietorship

   B. Partnership

   C. Corporation

   D. Franchise

Answer: D

D.   Franchise

A (A) sole proprietorship is where a person operates a company with his own resources. All income from this kind of business is considered income to the proprietor. A (B) partnership is an agreement between two or more people to operate a business and divide the proceeds in a specified way. A (C) corporation is a formal business arrangement where a company is considered a separate entity for tax purposes. In a (D) franchise, individuals can purchase the rights to use a company's name, designs, logos, etc., in exchange for a fee. Examples of franchise companies are McDonald's and Krispy Kreme.

57. What is a major difference between monopolistic competition and perfect competition?

   A. Perfect competition has many consumers and suppliers, while monopolistic competition does not

   B. Perfect competition provides identical products, while monopolistic competition provides similar but not identical products

   C. Entry to perfect competition is difficult, while entry to monopolistic competition is relatively easy

   D. Monopolistic competition has many consumers and suppliers, while perfect competition does not

Answer: B

B.   Perfect competition provides identical products, while monopolistic competition provides similar but not identical products.

A perfect market is a hypothetical market used in economics to discuss the underlying effects of supply and demand. To control for differences between products, it is assumed in perfect competition that all products are identical, with no differences, and the prices for these products will rise and fall based on a small number of factors. Monopolistic competition takes place in a market where each producer can act monopolistically and raise or lower the cost of its product, or change its product to make different from similar products. This is the primary difference between these two models; (B) perfect competition provides identical products, while monopolistic competition provides similar but not identical products.

TEACHER CERTIFICATION STUDY GUIDE

58. Which concept is not embodied as a right in the First Amendment to the U.S. Constitution?

    A. Peaceable assembly

    B. Protection against unreasonable search and seizure

    C. Freedom of speech

    D. Petition for redress of grievances

Answer: B

B.   Protection against unreasonable search and seizure

The first amendment to the Constitution reads, "Congress shall make no law respecting an establishment of religion, or prohibiting the free exercise thereof; or abridging the (C) freedom of speech, or of the press; or the right of the people (A) peaceably to assemble, and to (D) petition the government for a redress of grievances." The protection against (B) unreasonable search and seizure is a constitutional right, however it is found in the fourth amendment, not the first.

59. In the Constitutional system of checks and balances, a primary "check" which accrues to the President is the power of:

   A. Executive privilege

   B. Approval of judges nominated by the Senate

   C. Veto of Congressional legislation

   D. Approval of judged nominated by the House of Representatives

Answer: C

C. Veto of Congressional legislation

The power to (C) veto congressional legislation is granted to the U.S. President in Article I of the Constitution, which states that all legislation passed by both houses of the Congress must be given to the president for approval. This is a primary check on the power of the Congress by the President. The Congress may override a presidential veto by a two-thirds majority vote of both houses, however. (A) Executive privilege refers to the privilege of the president to keep certain documents private. Answers (B) and (D) are incorrect, as Congress does not nominate judges. This is a presidential power.

60. According to the Constitution any amendment must be ratified by _____ of the states to become a part of the Constitution:

   A. Three-fourths

   B. Two-thirds

   C. Three-fifths

   D. Five-sixths

Answer: A

A. Three-fourths

Article V of the Constitution spells out how the document may be ratified. First, an amendment must be proposed by a two-thirds majority of both houses of Congress. Then it is passed to the state legislatures. If (A) three-fourths of the states pass the amendment, it is adopted as part of the constitution. The constitution currently has 27 amendments.

61. Collectively, the first ten Amendments to the Constitution are known as the:

A. Articles of Confederation

B. Mayflower Compact

C. Bill of Rights

D. Declaration of the Rights of Man

Answer: C

C. Bill of Rights

The (A) Articles of Confederation was the document under which the thirteen colonies of the American Revolution came together and was the first governing document of the United States. The (B) Mayflower Compact was an agreement signed by several of the pilgrims aboard the Mayflower before establishing their colony at Plymouth in 1620. The (D) Declaration of the Rights of Man was the French document adopted after the French Revolution in 1789. The first ten amendments of the US Constitution, spelling out the limitations of the federal government, are referred to as (C) the Bill of Rights.

62. In the United States, if a person is accused of a crime and cannot afford a lawyer:

A. The person cannot be tried

B. A court will appoint a lawyer, but the person must pay the lawyer back when able to do so

C. The person must be tried without legal representation

D. A court will appoint a lawyer for the person free of charge

Answer: D

D. A court will appoint a lawyer for the person free of charge

The sixth amendment to the Constitution grants the right to a speedy and public jury trial in a criminal prosecution, as well as the right to "the assistance of counsel for his defense." This has been interpreted as the right to receive legal assistance at no charge if a defendant cannot afford one. (D) A court will appoint a lawyer for the person free of charge, is the correct answer.

63. **Which of the following lists elements usually considered responsibilities of citizenship under the American system of government?**

    A. Serving in public office, voluntary government service, military duty

    B. Paying taxes, jury duty, upholding the Constitution

    C. Maintaining a job, giving to charity, turning in fugitives

    D. Quartering of soldiers, bearing arms, government service

Answer: B

B.   Paying taxes, jury duty, upholding the Constitution.

Only paying taxes, jury duty, and upholding the Constitution are responsibilities of citizens as a result of rights and commitments outlined in the Constitution – for example, the right of citizens to a jury trial in the Sixth and Seventh Amendments and the right of the federal government to collect taxes in Article 1, Section 8. (A) Serving in public office, voluntary government service, military duty and (C) maintaining a job, giving to charity, and turning in fugitives are all highly admirable actions undertaken by many exemplary citizens, but they are considered purely voluntary actions, even when officially recognized and compensated. The United States has none of the compulsory military or civil service requirements of many other countries. (D) The quartering of soldiers is an act, which, according to Amendment III of the Bill of Rights, requires a citizen's consent. Bearing arms is a right guaranteed under Amendment II of the Bill of Rights.

64. Consider the following passage from the Mayflower Compact: "...covenant & combine ourselves together into a Civil body politick;" This demonstrates what theory of social organization?

    A. Darwinian

    B. Naturalistic

    C. Nonconsensual

    D. Constitutional

Answer: D

D.   Constitutional

(D) Constitutional social organization requires at its heart clearly stated and mutually agreed on constitutional principles, which all involved parties promise to uphold. (B) A naturalistic theory of social organization is one freely chosen by its participants and not yet bound by a clear set of constitutional principles. A (A) Darwinian theory would reflect the "survival of the fittest" element of Darwin's theory of the evolution of natural life, as applied to the relationship of different groups within a society. (C) Nonconsensual theories compel participation in a system of social organization and thus would never be characterized by the word "covenant," which means an agreement entered into freely by both parties.

65. Why is the system of government in the United States referred to as a federal system?

    A. There are different levels of government

    B. There is one central authority in which all governmental power is vested

    C. The national government cannot operate except with the consent of the governed

    D. Elections are held at stated periodic times, rather than as called by the head of the government

Answer: A

A.   There are different levels of government

(A) The United States is composed of fifty states, each responsible for its own affairs but united under a federal government. (B) A centralized system is the opposite of a federal system. (C) That national government cannot operate except with the consent of the governed is a founding principle of American politics. It is not a political system like federalism. A centralized democracy could still be consensual but would not be federal. (D) This is a description of electoral procedure, not a political system like federalism

66. Which of the following are NOT local governments in the United States?

    A. Cities

    B. Townships

    C. School boards

    D. All of these are forms of local government

Answer: D

D.   All of these are forms of local government

A local government is a body with the authority to make policy and enforce decisions on behalf of a local community. Cities and townships are by definition local, not statewide or federal, governments. A more central authority might make school policy in other countries, but, in the United States, school boards are local authorities. [However, according to the 2002 Census, several states run certain school districts themselves, without a local school board.

67. The major expenditures of state governments in the United States go toward:

    A. Parks, education, and highways

    B. Law enforcement, libraries and highways

    C. Education, highways, and law enforcement

    D. Recreation, business regulation, and education

Answer: C

C. Education, highways, and law enforcement

Education and highways are among the largest expenditures of state governments. Law enforcement is also significant, if much smaller than these other expenditures. Parks and recreation, business regulation, and libraries are all minor items by comparison

68. **How does the government of France differ from that of the United States?**

   A. France is a direct democracy, while the United States is a representative democracy

   B. France has a unitary form of national government, while the United States has a federal form of government

   C. France is a representative democracy, while the United States is a direct democracy

   D. France does not elect a President, whole the United States elects a President

Answer: B

B.   France has a unitary form of national government, while the United States has a federal form of government.

The United States has a federal form of government, since its 50 states are responsible for their own affairs and do not have their governments appointed or supervised by a central government. France has a unitary form of national government, where the central government is responsible for regional as well as national affairs. Neither the U.S. nor France is a direct democracy, and both have an elected President.

69. In the Presidential Election of 1888, Grover Cleveland lost to Benjamin Harrison, although Cleveland received more popular votes. How is this possible?

- A. The votes of certain states (New York, Indiana) were thrown out because of voting irregularities

- B. Harrison received more electoral votes than Cleveland

- C. None of the party candidates received a majority of votes, and the House of Representatives elected Harrison according to Constitutional procedures

- D. Because of accusations of election law violations, Cleveland withdrew his name and Harrison became President

Answer: B

B. Harrison received more electoral votes than Cleveland

Presidential elections, according to the United States Constitution, are decided in the Electoral College. This college mirrors the composition of the House of Representatives. The popular vote for each presidential candidate determines which slate of electors in each state is selected. Thus, while Cleveland won enough support in certain states to win a majority of the national popular vote, he did not win enough states to carry the Electoral College. If neither candidate had won the necessary majority, the House of Representatives would have made the final decision, but this did not occur in 1888. The other two answers are not envisioned by the Constitution and did not occur.

TEACHER CERTIFICATION STUDY GUIDE

70. **How are major party candidates chosen to run for President in the United States?**

    A. Caucuses of major party officeholders meet to select a state's choice for the party, and the candidate selected by the most states becomes the nominee

    B. Potential Presidential nominees seek pledges from each state party's chair and co-chair, and the candidate with the most pledges becomes the nominee

    C. Nationwide primaries are held by each party, to select delegates to a national nominating convention

    D. Each state party decides how to select delegates to a nominating convention; these selection processes may be caucuses, primaries, or any other method chosen by the state party

Answer: D

D.   Each state party decides how to select delegates to a nominating convention; these selection processes may be caucuses, primaries, or any other method chosen by the state party.

A nominating convention selects each party nominee, and the delegates from each state are chosen as the state party sees fit. Caucuses are only one possible method. Pledges or nationwide primaries have never been a way of determining the nominee.

TEACHER CERTIFICATION STUDY GUIDE

71. A person who receives more votes than anyone else in an election is said to have a of the votes cast; a person who has over 50% of the votes in an election is said to have a of the votes cast.

    A. Plurality; majority

    B. Majority; minority

    C. Plurality; minority

    D. Majority; plurality

Answer: A

A.   Plurality; majority

A majority means more than half of the whole. A plurality means the largest portion, when no one achieves a majority. A minority of the votes would be less than half of the votes.

72. Which of the following developments is most closely associated with the Neolithic Age?

    A. Human use of fire

    B. First use of stone chipping instruments

    C. Domestication of plants

    D. Development of metallurgical alloys

Answer: C

C.   Domestication of plants

The Neolithic or "New Stone" Age, as its name implies, is characterized by the use of stone implements, but the first use of stone chipping instruments appears in the Paleolithic period. Human use of fire may go back still farther and certainly predates the Neolithic era. The Neolithic period is distinguished by the domestication of plants. The development of metallurgical alloys marks the conclusion of the Neolithic Age.

TEACHER CERTIFICATION STUDY GUIDE

73. The Tigris-Euphrates Valley was the site of which two primary ancient civilizations?

   A. Babylonian and Assyrian

   B. Sumerian and Egyptian

   C. Hyksos and Hurrian

   D. Persian and Phoenician

Answer: A

A.   Babylonian and Assyrian

(B) While the Sumerians also lived in the southern Tigris-Euphrates valley, Egyptian civilization grew up in the Nile delta (3500BC-30 BC). (C) The Hyksos were an Asiatic people who controlled the Nile Delta during the 15th and 16th Dynasties (1674BC-1548BC). The Hurrians (2500BC-1000BC) came from the Khabur River Valley in northern Mesopotamia, where they spread out to establish various small kingdoms in the region. (D) The Persians (648BC- early 19th century AD) had a succession of empires based in the area known as modern-day Iran. The Phoenicians were a seafaring people who dominated the Mediterranean during the first century BC.

74. The politics of classical Athens is best described by which of the following?

   A. Limited democracy, including both slaves and free men

   B. One man dictatorial rule

   C. Universal democracy among free owners of property

   D. Oligarchy with a few families controlling all decisions

Answer: C

C.   Universal democracy among free owners of property.

A citizen of Athens was a free man who owned property. Each had an equal vote in the governance of the city. All the other answers are thereby excluded by definition.

MIDDLE LEVEL SOCIAL STUDIES

75. The _____ were fought between the Roman Empire and Carthage.

    A. Civil Wars

    B. Punic wars

    C. Caesarian Wars

    D. Persian Wars

Answer: B

B.   Punic wars

The Punic Wars (264-146 BC) were fought between Rome and Carthage. (D) The Persian Wars were fought between Greece and Persia. (A) could refer to anything but doesn't apply to the Roman-Carthaginian conflicts. (C) is not a description of any series of conflicts.

TEACHER CERTIFICATION STUDY GUIDE

76. What Holy Roman Emperor was forced to do public penance because of his conflict with Pope Gregory VII over lay investiture of the clergy?

   A. Charlemagne

   B. Henry IV

   C. Charles V

   D. Henry VIII

Answer: B

B.   Henry IV

Henry IV (1050-1106) clashed with Pope Gregory VII by insisting on the right of a ruler to appoint members of the clergy to their offices but repented in 1077. Charlemagne & Charles V were also Holy Roman Emperors but in the 9th and 16th centuries, respectively. Henry VIII, King of England, broke with the Roman Church over his right to divorce and remarry in 1534.

77. The _____ declared monophysitism (the belief that Jesus was completely divine with no admixture of humanity) to be a heresy?

   A. Council of Nicaea

   B. Diet of Worms

   C. Council of Trent

   D. Council of Chalcedon

Answer: D

D.   Council of Chalcedon

(A) In response to the Arian heresy asserting that Christ was a created being like other created beings, the Council of Nicaea (325 AD) established the divinity of Jesus Christ by declaring him to be of the same substance as God the Father, an article of faith then enshrined in the Nicene Creed. (B) At the Diet of Worms (1521 AD), the Holy Roman Empire tried and condemned Martin Luther and his writings. (C) The Council of Trent (1545 AD-1563 AD), an ecumenical council of the Roman Catholic Church, clarified many aspects of Catholic doctrine and liturgical life in an attempt to counter the Protestant Reformation. (D) The Council of Chalcedon (451 AD) confirmed the humanity of Christ by affirming that the Virgin Mary was indeed his human mother and therefore worthy of the Greek title Theotokos ("God-bearer").

78. **The painter of the Sistine Ceiling was:**

   A. Raphael

   B. Michelangelo

   C. Leonardo da Vinci

   D. Titian

Answer: B

B.   Michelangelo

(A) Raphael (1483-1520 AD), (B) Michelangelo (1475-1564 AD), (C) Leonardo da Vinci (1452-1519 AD) and (D) Titian (1488-1576 AD) were all contemporary Italian Renaissance masters, but only Michelangelo painted the Sistine Chapel ceiling (1508-1512 AD).

79. Luther issued strong objection to all but which of the following practices of the 15th Century Roman Catholic Church?

   A. The sacrament of baptism

   B. Absolution of sins through the intermediation of a priest and through ceremony

   C. The sale of indulgences, whereby the buyer may purchase purgation of sins

   D. Imposed church control over the individual conscience

Answer: A

A.   The sacrament of baptism

Absolution of sins by priests, the sale of indulgences and imposed church control over individual consciences were all practices which Martin Luther (1483-1546) and subsequent Protestants objected to on the basis that they required the Church to act as an intermediary between God and the individual believer. The sacrament of baptism, however, continues to be practiced in some form in most Protestant denominations, as the rite of initiation into the Christian community.

TEACHER CERTIFICATION STUDY GUIDE

80. The first explorer to reach India by sailing around the southern tip of Africa was:

A. Amerigo Vespucci
B. Vasco da Gama
C. Ferdinand Magellan
D. John Cabot

Answer: B

B. Vasco da Gama

(A) Amerigo Vespucci (1454-1512) was the Italian explorer to first assert that the lands to the west of Africa and Europe were actually part of a new continent and thus the name "America" was derived from his own "Amerigo." (B) Portuguese Vasco da Gama (1469-1524) built on the discoveries of previous explorers to finally round Africa's Cape of Good Hope and open a sea route for European trade with the east and the eventual Portuguese colonization of India. (C) Portuguese explorer Ferdinand Magellan (1480-1521), working for the Spanish crown, led the first successful expedition to circumnavigate the globe (1519-1522). Magellan himself actually died before the voyage was over, but his ship and 18 crewmembers did return safely to Spain. (D) John Cabot (1450-1499) was an Italian explorer working for the English crown and is thought to have been the first European to discover North America (1497) since the Vikings.

81. Vasco Nunez de Balboa accomplished which of the following?

A. Sighting of the Pacific Ocean from lands discovered by Europeans in the 1500's
B. The conquest of the Inca civilization through treachery and deceit
C. The murder of the Aztec ruler and subsequent subjugation of the Empire
D. None of the above

Answer: A

A. Sighting of the Pacific Ocean from lands discovered by Europeans in the 1500's.

(A) Spanish explorer and conquistador Vasco Nunez de Balboa (1475-1519) was the first European known to have seen and sailed on the Pacific Ocean (1513) from newly discovered Panama. (B) The conquest of the Incas through treachery and deceit was carried out by Spanish conquistador Francisco Pizarro (1475-1541) in 1532. (C) The murder of Montezuma II, ruler of the Aztecs, and subsequent subjugation of the Empire was achieved by Spanish conquistador Hernan Cortez (1485-1547) between the years 1519 and 1521.

82. Great Britain became the center of technological and industrial development during the nineteenth century chiefly on the basis of:

A. Central location relative to the population centers of Europe

B. Colonial conquests and military victories over European powers

C. Reliance on exterior sources of financing

D. Resources of coal and production of steel

Answer: D

D.   Resources of coal and production of steel

Great Britain possessed a unique set of advantages in the 18th and 19th century, making it the perfect candidate for the technological advances of the Industrial Revolution. (A) Relative isolation from the population centers in Europe meant little to Great Britain, which benefited from its own relatively unified and large domestic market, enabling it to avoid the tariffs and inefficiencies of trading on the diverse (and complicated) continent. (B) Colonial conquests and military victories over European powers were fueled by Great Britain's industrial advances in transportation and weaponry, rather than being causes of them. (C) Reliance on exterior sources of funding – while Great Britain would enjoy an increasing influx of goods and capital from its colonies, the efficiency of its own domestic market consistently generated an impressive amount of capital for investment in the new technologies and industries of the age. (D) Great Britain's rich natural resources of coal and ore enabled steel production and, set alongside new factories in a Britain's landscape, allowed the production of goods quickly and efficiently.

83. The years 1793-94 in France, characterized by numerous trials and executions of supposed enemies of the Revolutionary Convention, were known as the:

A. Reign of Terror

B. Dark Ages

C. French Inquisition

D. Glorious Revolution

Answer: A

A. Reign of Terror

(A) The period of the French Revolution known as the Reign of Terror (1793-94) is estimated to have led to the deaths of up to 40,000 people: aristocrats, clergy, political activists, and anyone else denounced as an enemy of the Revolutionary Convention, many falsely so. (B) The Dark Ages is the term commonly used for the Early Middle Ages in Europe, from the fall of Rome in 476 to 1000. (C) The French Inquisition was the Roman Catholic Church's attempts to codify into ecclesiastical and secular law the prosecution of heretics, most notably at the time, the Albigensians, in the 13th century. (D) The Glorious Revolution (1688-1689) is the title given to the overthrow of the last Catholic British monarch, James II, in favor of his Protestant daughter Mary and her husband, the Dutch prince William of Orange.

84. In the <u>first</u> aggression of World War II outside the Orient, identify the aggressor nation and the nation which was invaded:

A. Germany; Sudetenland

B. Italy; Abyssinia

C. Germany; Poland

D. Italy; Yugoslavia

Answer: B

B.   Italy; Abyssinia

(A) The Sudetenland (part of Czechoslovakia) was ceded to Nazi Germany in 1938 by the Munich Agreement of France, Britain, Italy, and Germany. The pretense for the annexation was the mistreatment of resident Germans by the Czechs. (B) Italy's invasion and annexation of Abyssinia in 1935-36 was condemned by the League of Nations but left unchallenged until the East African Campaign of World War II in 1941. Nazi Germany invaded Poland in 1939 and would occupy it until 1945. (D) After attempts to convince the Yugoslavians to join the Axis powers, Germany and Italy invaded Yugoslavia in 1941 and established the Independent State of Croatia.

TEACHER CERTIFICATION STUDY GUIDE

85. In issuing an ultimatum for Soviet ships not to enter Cuban waters in October 1962, President John F. Kennedy, as part of his decision, used the provisions of the:

   A. Monroe Doctrine

   B. Declaration of the Rights of Man

   C. Geneva Convention

   D. Truman Doctrine

Answer: A

A.   Monroe Doctrine

(A) The Monroe Doctrine, initially formulated by Presidents James Monroe (1758-1831) and John Quincy Adams (1767-1848) and later enhanced by President Theodore Roosevelt (1858-1915), opposed European colonization or interference in the Americas, perceived any such attempts as a threat to US security, and promised U.S. neutrality in conflicts between European powers and/or their already established colonies. (B) The Declaration of the Rights of Man, widely adapted in future declarations about international human rights, was formulated in France during the French Revolution and adopted by the National Constituent Assembly in 1789 as the premise of any future French constitution. (C) The Geneva Conventions (1864, 1929, and 1949, with later additions and amendments) established humanitarian and ethical standards for conduct during times of war and has been widely accepted as international law. (D) The Truman Doctrine (1947), formulated by President Harry Truman (1884-1972), provided for the support of Greece and Turkey as a means of protecting them from Soviet influence. It thereby began the Cold War (1947-1991), a period in which the U.S. sought to contain the Soviet Union by limiting its influence in other countries.

TEACHER CERTIFICATION STUDY GUIDE

86. In 1990, Alberto Fujimori was elected president of:

   A. Japan

   B. Okinawa

   C. South Korea

   D. Peru

Answer: D

D.   Peru

(A) Japan has a constitutional monarchy, symbolically led by an emperor, and has never elected presidents. (B) Okinawa is a part of Japan and as such does not elect a president. (C) With a modern history including 35 years of Japanese occupation, it is highly unlikely that South Korea would ever elect a Japanese citizen as President. (D) Alberto Fujimori, a dual citizen of Peru and Japan, was the first Asian to lead a Latin American country.

87. Which of the following most closely characterizes the geopolitical events of the USSR in 1991-92:

   A. The USSR established greater military and economic control over the fifteen Soviet republics
   B. The Baltic States (Estonia, Latvia, and Lithuania) declared independence, while the remainder of the USSR remained intact.
   C. Fourteen of fifteen Soviet republics declared some degree of autonomy; the USSR was officially dissolved; the Supreme Soviet rescinded the Soviet Treaty of 1922
   D. All fifteen Soviet republics simultaneously declared immediate and full independence from the USSR, with no provisions for a transitional form of government

Answer: C

C.   Fourteen of fifteen Soviet republics declared some degree of autonomy; the USSR was officially dissolved; the Supreme Soviet rescinded the Soviet Treaty of 1922. The unraveling of the USSR in 1991-92 and the establishment of independent republics in its wake was a complex if relatively peaceful end to its existence. After a succession of declarations of autonomy by constituent states forced the dissolution of the central government, the Baltic States of Latvia, Lithuania, and Estonia immediately declared their independence. Other republics took longer to reconfigure their relationships to one another. There was no serious attempt by the central government to resist these changes militarily or economically.

MIDDLE LEVEL SOCIAL STUDIES

88. **Chinese civilization is generally credited with the original development of which of the following sets of technologies:**

   A. Movable type and mass production of goods

   B. Wool processing and domestication of the horse

   C. Paper and gunpowder manufacture

   D. Leather processing and modern timekeeping

Answer: C

C.   Paper and gunpowder manufacture

(A) While China's Bi Sheng (d. 1052) is credited with the earliest forms of movable type (1041-48), mass production was spearheaded by America's Henry Ford (1863-1947) in his campaign to create the first truly affordable automobile, the Model T Ford. (B) While wool has been processed in many ways in many cultures, production on a scale beyond cottage industries was not possible without the many advances made in England during the Industrial Revolution (18th century). Various theories exist about the domestication of the horse, with estimates ranging from 4600 BC to 2000 BC in Eurasia. Recent DNA evidence suggests that the horse may actually have been domesticated in different cultures at independent points. (C) The earliest mention of gunpowder appears in ninth century Chinese documents. The earliest examples of paper made of wood pulp come from China and have been dated as early as the second century BC. (D) Leather processing and timekeeping have likewise seen different developments in different places at different times.

TEACHER CERTIFICATION STUDY GUIDE

89. **Extensive exports of gold and copper; elaborate court and constitution; trade links on both the Atlantic and Indian Oceans; use of heavy stone architecture; these most closely characterize the civilization of:**

    A. Mwene Mutapa

    B. Chichen Itza

    C. Great Zimbabwe

    D. Muscat and Oman

Answer:

C.   Great Zimbabwe

The medieval kingdom of Great Zimbabwe left the largest ruins in Africa from which archeologists have been able to discern the nature of their civilization. (B) Chichen Itza is a Mayan temple complex complete with other supporting buildings which has been excavated in Yucatan, Mexico, and is thought to date from 987 AD. (D) Muscat and Oman was an empire that dominated the southern Persian Gulf and Saudi peninsula and parts of the East African coast and Iranian Plateau. Its main export, however, was slaves.

90. **Which of the following is NOT one of the Pillars of Faith of Islam?**

    A. Alms-giving (zakah)

    B. Pilgrimage (hajj)

    C. Membership in a school of law (al-madhahib)

    D. Fasting (sawm)

Answer: C

C.   Membership in a school of law (al-madhahib)

The Five Pillars of Islam are the faith profession that there is no God but Allah and Muhammad is his prophet, prayer (salah), pilgrimage to Mecca (hajj), alms-giving (zakah), and fasting during the holy month of Ramadan (sawm).

MIDDLE LEVEL SOCIAL STUDIES   303

TEACHER CERTIFICATION STUDY GUIDE

91. The native metaphysical outlook of Japan, usually characterized as a religion, is:

A. Tao

B. Shinto

C. Nichiren Shoju

D. Shaolin

Answer: B

B. Shinto

(A) Tao is the Chinese philosophical work that inspired Taoism, the religious tradition sourced in China. (B) Shinto is the system of rituals and beliefs honoring the deities and spirits believed to be native to the landscape and inhabitants of Japan. (C) Nichiren Shoju is a strand of Nichiren Buddhism, a tradition started by a Japanese Buddhist monk, Nichiren (1222-1282). (D) The Shaolin temple (originally built in 497 AD) is the Chinese Buddhist monastery considered to be the source of Zen Buddhism and its subsequent martial arts.

92. The Native Americans of the Eastern Woodlands lived on:

A. Buffalo and crops such as corn, beans, and sunflowers

B. Chiefly farming of squash, beans, and corn

C. A variety of game (deer, bear, moose) and crops (squash, pumpkins, corn)

D. Wolves, foxes, polar bears, walruses, and fish

Answer: C

C. A variety of game (deer, bear, moose) and crops (squash, pumpkins, corn)

(A) Buffalo live in the plains habitat found in Western and Midwestern North America. (B) & (C) While the Native Americans did farm the "Three Sisters" of corn, squash and beans, the woods of the East also meant that a variety of game (deer, bear, moose) were widely available for them to hunt. (D) However, wolves, foxes, walruses, polar bears, and fish are found together only within the Arctic Circle, not in eastern woodlands.

TEACHER CERTIFICATION STUDY GUIDE

93. **Apartments built out of cliff faces; shared government by adult citizens; absence of aggression toward other groups. These factors characterize the Native American group known as:**

   A. Pueblos

   B. Comanches

   C. Seminoles

   D. Sioux

Answer: A

A.   Pueblos

(B) The Comanches were a nomadic Native American group that emerged around 1700 AD in the North American Plains and were decidedly aggressive towards their neighbors. (C) The Seminoles are a native American group which originally emerged in Florida in the mid-18th century and was made up of refugees from other Native tribes and escaped slaves. (D) The Sioux were a Native American people who originally lived in the Dakotas, Nebraska and Minnesota and clashed extensively with white settlers.

94. **Columbus first reached Western Hemisphere lands in what is now:**

   A. Florida

   B. Bermuda

   C. Puerto Rico

   D. Bahamas

Answer: D

D.   Bahamas

Christopher Columbus (1451-1506) visited the Bahamas in 1492 and Puerto Rico in 1493 but never landed on either Bermuda or Florida.

95. The "Trail of Tears" relates to:

A. The removal of the Cherokees from their native lands to Oklahoma Territory

B. The revolt and subsequent migration of the Massachusetts Pilgrims under pressure from the Iroquois

C. The journey of the Nez Perce under Chief Joseph before their capture by the U.S. Army

D. The 1973 standoff between federal marshals and Native Americans at Wounded Knee, S.D.

Answer: A

A. The removal of the Cherokees from their native lands to Oklahoma Territory (1838-39).

(B) There never was a revolt and migration of the Massachusetts Pilgrims under pressure from the Iroquois. (C) The 1877 journey of the Nez Perce under Chief Joseph was a strategically impressive attempt to retreat from an oncoming U.S. Army into Canada. (D) The 1973 Wounded Knee incident was the occupation of the town of Wounded Knee, South Dakota, by the American Indian Movement to call attention to issues of Native American civil rights. Their action led to a 71-day standoff with U.S. Marshals, which was eventually resolved peacefully.

TEACHER CERTIFICATION STUDY GUIDE

97. Bartholomeu Dias, in seeking a route around the tip of Africa, was forced to turn back. Nevertheless, the cape he discovered near the southern tip of Africa became known as:

   A. Cape Horn

   B. Cabo Bojador

   C. Cape of Good Hope

   D. Cape Hatteras

Answer: C

C. Cape of Good Hope

(A) Cape Horn is located at the southern tip of Chile, and therefore South America. It was discovered by Sir Francis Drake as he sailed around the globe in 1578. (B) Cajo Bojador, on the Western coast of northern Africa, was first successfully navigated by a European, Portuguese Gil Eanes, in 1434. (D) Cape Hatteras is located on the U.S. Atlantic coast, at North Carolina.

97. The Middle Colonies of the Americas were:

   A. Maryland, Virginia, North Carolina

   B. New York, New Jersey, Pennsylvania, Delaware

   C. Rhode Island, Connecticut, New York, New Jersey

   D. Vermont and New Hampshire

Answer: B

B.   New York, New Jersey, Pennsylvania, Delaware

(A), (C) & (D). Maryland, Virginia, and North Carolina were Southern colonies, Rhode Island, Connecticut ,and New Hampshire were New England colonies and Vermont was not one of the 13 original colonies.

98. Slavery arose in the Southern Colonies partly as a perceived economical way to:

- A. Increase the owner's wealth through human beings used as a source of exchange

- B. Cultivate large plantations of cotton, tobacco, rice, indigo, and other crops

- C. Provide Africans with humanitarian aid, such as health care, Christianity, and literacy

- D. Keep ships' holds full of cargo on two out of three legs of the "triangular trade" voyage

Answer: B

B. Cultivate large plantations of cotton, tobacco, rice, indigo, and other crops.

The Southern states, with their smaller populations, were heavily dependent on slave labor as a means of being able to fulfill their role and remain competitive in the greater U.S. economy. (A) When slaves arrived in the South, the vast majority would become permanent fixtures on plantations, intended for work, not as a source of exchange. (C) While some slave owners instructed their slaves in Christianity, provided health care or some level of education, such attention was not their primary reason for owning slaves – a cheap and ready labor force was. (D) Whether or not ships' holds were full on two or three legs of the triangular journey was not the concern of Southerners as the final purchasers of slaves. Such details would have concerned the slave traders.

99. Of the following, which contributed most to penetration of western areas by colonial Americans?

   A. Development of large ships capable of sailing upstream in rivers such as the Hudson, Susquehanna, and Delaware

   B. The invention of the steamboat

   C. Improved relations with Native Americans, who invited colonial Americans to travel west to settle

   D. Improved roads, mail service, and communications

Answer: D

D.   Improved roads, mail service and communications

(A) Because the Susquehanna, Delaware, and Hudson are limited to the northeast, they would not have helped the colonists penetrate any further West. (B) Since these were the waterways that they had immediate access to, the development of the steamboat was similarly unhelpful in this regard. (C) In general, colonist-Native American relations got worse, not better as colonists moved West, so colonists were unlikely to have been invited yet further west. (D) Improved roads, mail service, and communications made traveling west easier and more attractive because they meant not being completely cut off from news and family in the east.

TEACHER CERTIFICATION STUDY GUIDE

100. A major quarrel between colonial Americans and the British concerned a series of British Acts of Parliament dealing with:

   A. Taxes

   B. Slavery

   C. Native Americans

   D. Shipbuilding

Answer: A

A.   Taxes

Acts of Parliament imposing taxes on the colonists always provoked resentment. Because the colonies had no direct representation in Parliament, they felt it unjust that that body should impose taxes on them, with so little knowledge of their very different situation in America and no real concern for the consequences of such taxes. (B) While slavery continued to exist in the colonies long after it had been completely abolished in Britain, it never was a source of serious debate between Britain and the colonies. By the time Britain outlawed slavery in its colonies in 1833, the American Revolution had already taken place and the United States were free of British control. (C) There was no series of British Acts of Parliament passed concerning Native Americans. (D) Colonial shipbuilding was an industry that received little interference from the British.

101. The first shots in what was to become the American Revolution were fired in:

   A. Florida

   B. Massachusetts

   D. New York

   D. Virginia

Answer: B

B.   Massachusetts

(A) At the time of the American Revolution, Florida, while a British possession, was not directly involved in the Revolutionary War. (B) The American Revolution began with the battles of Lexington and Concord in 1775. (C) There would be no fighting in New York until 1776 and none in Virginia until 1781.

MIDDLE LEVEL SOCIAL STUDIES   310

TEACHER CERTIFICATION STUDY GUIDE

102. The U.S. Constitution, adopted in 1789, provided for:

    A. Direct election of the President by all citizens

    B. Direct election of the President by citizens meeting a standard of wealth

    C. Indirect election of the President by electors

    D. Indirect election of the President by the U.S. Senate

Answer: C

C.   Indirect election of the President by electors

The United States Constitution has always arranged for the indirect election of the President by electors. The question, by mentioning the original date of adoption, might mislead someone to choose B, but while standards of citizenship have been changed by amendment, the President has never been directly elected. Nor does the Senate have anything to do with presidential elections. The House of Representatives, not the Senate, settles cases where neither candidate wins in the Electoral College.

103. The area of the United States was effectively doubled through purchase of the Louisiana Territory under which President?

    A. John Adams

    B. Thomas Jefferson

    C. James Madison

    D. James Monroe

Answer: B

B.   Thomas Jefferson

(B) The Louisiana Purchase, an acquisition of territory from France, in 1803 occurred under Thomas Jefferson. (A) John Adams (1735-1826) was president from 1797-1801, before the purchase, and (C) James Madison, (1751-1836) after the Purchase (1809-1817). (D) James Monroe (1758-1831) was actually a signatory on the Purchase but also did not become President until 1817.

104. What was a major source of contention between American settlers in Texas and the Mexican government in the 1830s and 1840s?

    A. The Americans wished to retain slavery, which had been outlawed in Mexico

    B. The Americans had agreed to learn Spanish and become Roman Catholic, but failed to do so

    C. The Americans retained ties to the United States, and Santa Anna feared the power of the U.S.

    D. All of the above were contentious issues between American settlers and the Mexican government

Answer: D

D. All of the above were contentious issues between American settlers and the Mexican government. The American settlers simply were not willing to assimilate into Mexican society but maintained their prior commitments to slave holding, the English language, Protestantism, and the United States government.

105. "Fifty-four Forty or Fight" refers to the desire of some nineteenth century Americans to:

   A. Explore the entire Missouri River valley to its source in the Oregon Territory

   B. Insist that Mexico cede all of Texas to the U.S. or face war

   C. Demand that American territory reaches to the border of Russian America

   D. Pay only $54,040,000 for all of the Oregon Territory

Answer: C

C. Demand that American territory reaches to the border of Russian America.

"Fifty-four Forty or Fight" refers to the latitude of the northern border of the Oregon Territory with Russian Alaska. Britain and the United States were negotiating a division of the Territory, but some Americans used this slogan to campaign for demanding all of it for the United States. (A) Has the merit of speaking of Oregon Territory, although it has nothing to do with the controversy, while (B) speaks of threatening war, although the wrong one. (D) Might be tempting only because it recalls the famous Louisiana Purchase.

106. Which President helped postpone a civil war by supporting the Compromise of 1850?

    A. Henry Clay

    B. Franklin Pierce

    C. Millard Fillmore

    D. James Buchanan

Answer: C

C.   Millard Fillmore

Millard Fillmore was the President who signed the Compromise of 1850. Henry Clay was instrumental in negotiating the compromise but was never President. Presidents Franklin Pierce and James Buchanan were later involved in the 1854 Kansas-Nebraska Act, which undid this Compromise.

107. Which American Secretary of War oversaw the purchase of present-day southern Arizona (the Gadsden Purchase) for the purpose of building a railroad to connect California to the rest of the United States?

    A. Henry Clay

    B. William Seward

    C. Franklin Pierce

    D. Jefferson Davis

Answer: D

D.   Jefferson Davis

Jefferson Davis was the Secretary of War in question. Franklin Pierce was President at the time. Neither Henry Clay nor William Seward was ever Secretary of War.

108. **A consequence of the Gold Rush of Americans to California in 1848 and 1849 was that:**

   A. California spent the minimum amount of time as a territory, and was admitted as a slave state

   B. California was denied admission on its first application, since most Americans felt that the settlers were too "uncivilized" to deserve statehood

   C. California was purchased from Mexico for the express purpose of gaining immediate statehood

   D. California did not go through the normal territorial stage but applied directly for statehood as a free state

Answer: D

D. California did not go through the normal territorial stage but applied directly for statehood as a free state.

California, suddenly undergoing a massive increase in population and wealth and desiring orderly government, found it had little recourse but to claim status as a free state and appeal directly for statehood. Congress had moved too slowly on the question of making California United States Territory. California was never a territory but only a military district. California was not denied admission to the Union but was an essential part of the Compromise of 1850. Immediate statehood was definitely not an express policy of the U.S. in acquiring California, but the Gold Rush changed attitudes quickly.

109. Of the following groups of states, which were slave states?

    A. Delaware, Maryland, Missouri

    B. California, Texas, Florida

    C. Kansas, Missouri, Kentucky

    D. Virginia, West Virginia, Indiana

Answer: A

A.   Delaware, Maryland, Missouri.

(A) Delaware, Maryland and Missouri were all slave states at the time of the Civil War. (B) Florida and Texas were slave states, while California was a free state. (C) Kansas, Missouri, and Kentucky were all originally slave territories, and Missouri and Kentucky were admitted to the Union as such. However, Kansas' petition to join the union in 1858 was blocked in order to preserve the balance between slave and free states. Kansas was admitted as a free state in 1861. (D) Indiana was a free state.

110. In the American Civil War, who was the first commander of the forces of the United States?

    A. Gen. Ulysses S. Grant

    B. Gen. Robert E. Lee

    C. Gen. Irwin McDowell

    D. Gen. George Meade

Answer: C

C.   General Irwin McDowell

(A) Gen. Ulysses S. Grant was the final commander of the Union army during the Civil War. (B) Gen. Robert E. Lee was the commander of the Confederate army. (D) Gen. George Meade was the Union commander at the Battle of Gettysburg in 1863.

TEACHER CERTIFICATION STUDY GUIDE

111. Abraham Lincoln won re-election in 1864 chiefly through:

    A. His overwhelming force of personality and appeal to all segments of the electorate

    B. His reputation as the Great Emancipator

    C. The fact that people felt sorry for him because of his difficulties

    D. His shrewd political manipulation, clever use of patronage jobs, and wide-appeal selection of cabinet members

Answer: D

D.   His shrewd political manipulation, clever use of patronage jobs, and wide-appeal selection of cabinet members

President Lincoln in his own lifetime was a hugely divisive figure, even in the North. He did not appeal to all segments of the electorate, his reputation as the Great Emancipator really developed after the war, and few felt sorry for him for his personal and political difficulties. Rather, Lincoln constantly maneuvered to maintain the advantage, using all the powers of the Presidency to win re-election despite his own unpopularity.

TEACHER CERTIFICATION STUDY GUIDE

112. How many states re-entered the Union before 1868?

State	Date of Readmission
Alabama	1868
Arkansas	1868
Florida	1868
Georgia	1870
Louisiana	1868
Mississippi	1870
North Carolina	1868
South Carolina	1868
Tennessee	1866
Texas	1870
Virginia	1870

- A. 0 states
- B. 1 state
- C. 2 states
- D. 3 states

Answer: B

B.   1 state

Only Tennessee was readmitted before 1868, as the above table indicates.

MIDDLE LEVEL SOCIAL STUDIES   318

TEACHER CERTIFICATION STUDY GUIDE

113. The Interstate Commerce Commission (ICC) was established in reaction to abuses and corruption in what industry?

   A. Textile

   B. Railroad

   C. Steel

   D. Banking

Answer: B

B.   Railroad

The ICC was established to fight abuses in the railroad industry.

TEACHER CERTIFICATION STUDY GUIDE

114. **Which of the following sets of inventors is correctly matched with the area in which they primarily worked?**

   A. Thomas Edison and George Westinghouse: transportation

   B. Cyrus McCormick and George Washington Carver: household appliances

   C. Alexander Graham Bell and Samuel F. B. Morse: communications

   D. Isaac Singer and John Gorrie: agriculture

Answer: C

C.   Alexander Graham Bell and Samuel F. B. Morse: communications

Bell, inventor of the telephone, and Morse, inventor of the telegraph and Morse code, were both working in the area of communications. While Westinghouse did invent various technologies crucial to the railroads and thus transportation, Edison did not; both are strongly linked to electrical inventions. McCormick and Carver specialized in agricultural inventions, while Singer, an inventor of the sewing machine, and Gorrie, the inventor of air conditioning and refrigeration, were best known for their household appliances.

TEACHER CERTIFICATION STUDY GUIDE

115. The Teapot Dome scandal related to:

    A. The improper taxing of tea surpluses in Boston

    B. The improper awarding of building contracts in Washington, D.C.

    C. The improper sale of policy decisions by various Harding administration officials

    D. The improper sale of oil reserves in Wyoming

Answer: D

D.   The improper sale of oil reserves in Wyoming

This scandal refers to the improper sale of federal oil reserves in Teapot Dome, Wyoming, an infamous event in the Harding Administration (1921-25). C would be tempting, especially since the Secretary of the Interior personally benefited from the sale, but no significant policy decisions were involved. No building of a dome or tea to put in the Teapot were involved in the making of this scandal.

116. Which of the following was NOT a factor in the United States' entry into World War I?

A. The closeness of the Presidential Election of 1916

B. The German threat to sink all allied ships, including merchant ships

C. The desire to preserve democracy as practiced in Britain and France as compared to the totalitarianism of Germany

D. The sinking of the Lusitania and the Sussex

Answer: A

A. The closeness of the Presidential Election of 1916

Not sure where the facts are on this one: Wilson won re-election in 1916! Since there was no presidential election of 1916, this could not have been a factor the United States' entry into the war; the last election had been in 1914. All the other answers were indeed factors.

TEACHER CERTIFICATION STUDY GUIDE

117. **What 1924 Act of Congress severely restricted immigration in the United States?**

    A. Taft-Hartley Act

    B. Smoot-Hawley Act

    C. Fordney-McCumber Act

    D. Johnson-Reed Act

Answer: D

D.   Johnson-Reed Act

(A) The Taft-Harley Act (1947) prohibited unfair labor practices by labor unions. (B) The Smoot-Hawley Act (1930) raised U.S. tariffs on imported goods to negative effect on the U.S. economy and world trade as (C) the Fordney-McCumber Act (1922) had done before it.

118. **The first territorial governor of Florida after Florida's purchase by the United States was:**

    A. Napoleon B. Broward

    B. William P. Duval

    C. Andrew Jackson

    D. Davy Crockett

Answer: C

C.   Andrew Jackson

119. President Truman suspended Gen. Douglas MacArthur from command of Allied forces in Korea because of:

A. MacArthur's inability to make any progress against North Korea

B. MacArthur's criticism of Truman, claiming that the President would not allow him to pursue aggressive tactics against the Communists

C. The harsh treatment MacArthur exhibited toward the Japanese after World War II

D. The ability of the U.S. Navy to continue the conflict without the presence of MacArthur

Answer: B

B. MacArthur's criticism of Truman, claiming that the President would not allow him to pursue aggressive tactics against the Communists

Truman suspended MacArthur because of clear insubordination: MacArthur had publicly criticized the President, his Commander in Chief, and had openly undermined his policy of negotiating a settlement with the Communists. MacArthur was a general of proven effectiveness; so, (A) cannot be correct. MacArthur was actually rather lenient to the Japanese after World War II, and he was a general, not an admiral of the Navy.

120. Which of the following most closely characterizes the Supreme Court's decision in Brown v. Board of Education?

    A. Chief Justice Warren had to cast the deciding vote in a sharply divided Court

    B. The decision was rendered along sectional lines, with northerners voting for integration and southerners voting for continued segregation

    C. The decision was 7-2, with dissenting justices not even preparing a written dissent

    D. Chief Justice Warren was able to persuade the Court to render a unanimous decision

Answer: D

D.   Chief Justice Warren was able to persuade the Court to render a unanimous decision. The Supreme Court decided 9-0 against segregated educational facilities.

121. The economic practices under President Ronald Reagan ("Reaganomics") were characterized by:

    A. Low inflation, high unemployment, high interest rates, high national debt

    B. High inflation, low unemployment, low interest rates, low national debt

    C. Low inflation, high unemployment, low interest rates, depletion of national debt

    D. High inflation, low unemployment, high interest rates, low national debt

Answer: A

A.   High inflation, low unemployment, high interest rates, high national debt.

122. The Harlem Renaissance of the 1920s refers to:

A. The migration of black Americans out of Harlem, and its resettlement by white Americans

B. A movement whereby the residents of Harlem were urged to "Return to Africa"

C. A proliferation in the arts among black Americans, centered on Harlem

D. The discovery of lost 15th century Italian paintings in a Harlem warehouse

Answer: C

C. A proliferation in the arts among black Americans, centered on Harlem.

(C) During the Harlem Renaissance (1919-1930s), America's black community expressed itself in art, literature, and music with new fervor and creativity. (A) Harlem's continues to enjoy Black Americans as the majority of its population. (B) & (D) are fictitious events.

TEACHER CERTIFICATION STUDY GUIDE

123. Which of the following is most descriptive of the conflict between the U.S. government and the Seminoles between 1818 and 1858?

    A. There was constant armed conflict between the Seminoles and the U.S. during these years

    B. Historians discern three separate phases of hostilities (1818, 1835-42, 1855-58), known collectively as the Seminole Wars

    C. On May 7, 1858, the Seminoles admitted defeat, signed a peace treaty with the U.S., and left for Oklahoma, except for fifty-one individuals

    D. The former Seminole chief Osceola helped the U.S. defeat the Seminoles and effect their removal to Oklahoma

Answer: B

B. Historians discern three separate phases of hostilities (1818, 1835-42, 1855-58), known collectively as the Seminole Wars.

(A) Intermittent conflicts between the U.S. government and the Seminole Native Americans can be classified into (B) three separate phases of hostilities. (C)

124. **Match the railroad entrepreneur with the correct area of development:**

   A. Henry Plant: Tampa and the West Coast

   B. Cornelius Vanderbilt: Jacksonville and the Northeast

   C. Henry Flagler: Orlando and the Central Highlands

   D. J.P. Morgan: Pensacola and the Northwest

Answer: A

A. Henry Plant: Tampa and the West Coast

(A) Henry Plant (1819-1899) was responsible for building railroad along the West Coast of Florida, making Tampa the end of the line. (B) Cornelius Vanderbilt (1794-1877), transportation mogul, concentrated his efforts in the Northeast of the country and was largely uninvolved in Florida. (C) Henry Flagler (1830-1913) was a Floridian involved in railways and oil production but is more closely associated with Miami than Orlando. (D) J.P. Morgan (1837-1913) was a New York-based banker.

125. **Florida's space exploration industry is centered in:**

   A. Baker County

   B. Broward County

   C. Brevard County

   D. Bradford County

Answer: C

C. Brevard County

(C) Florida's Kennedy Space complex is on Cape Canaveral in Brevard County.

XAMonline, INC. 21 Orient Ave. Melrose, MA 02176

Toll Free number 800-509-4128

TO ORDER Fax 781-662-9268 OR www.XAMonline.com

<u>CERTIFICATION EXAMINATION FOR OKLAHOMA</u>
<u>EDUCATORS - CEOE - 2007</u>

PO#   Store/School:

Address 1:

Address 2 (Ship to other):

City, State Zip

Credit card number _____-_____-_____-_____   expiration_____

EMAIL _____

PHONE   **FAX**

13# ISBN 2007	TITLE	Qty	Retail	Total
978-1-58197-781-3	CEOE OSAT Advanced Mathematics Field 11			
978-1-58197-775-2	CEOE OSAT Art Sample Test Field 02			
978-1-58197-780-6	CEOE OSAT Biological Sciences Field 10			
978-1-58197-776-9	CEOE OSAT Chemistry Field 04			
978-1-58197-778-3	CEOE OSAT Earth Science Field 08			
978-1-58197-794-3	CEOE OSAT Elementary Education Fields 50-51			
978-1-58197-795-0	CEOE OSAT Elementary Education Fields 50-51 Sample Questions			
978-1-58197-777-6	CEOE OSAT English Field 07			
978-1-58197-779-0	CEOE OSAT Family and Consumer Sciences Field 09			
978-1-58197-786-8	CEOE OSAT French Sample Test Field 20			
978-1-58197-798-1	CEOE OGET Oklahoma General Education Test 074			
978-1-58197-792-9	CEOE OSAT Library-Media Specialist Field 38			
978-1-58197-787-5	CEOE OSAT Middle Level English Field 24			
978-1-58197-789-9	CEOE OSAT Middle Level Science Field 26			
978-1-58197-790-5	CEOE OSAT Middle Level Social Studies Field 27			
978-1-58197-788-2	CEOE OSAT Middle Level-Intermediate Mathematics Field 25			
978-1-58197-791-2	CEOE OSAT Mild Moderate Disabilities Field 29			
978-1-58197-782-0	CEOE OSAT Physical Education-Health-Safety Field 12			
978-1-58197-783-7	CEOE OSAT Physics Sample Test Field 14			
978-1-58197-793-6	CEOE OSAT Principal Common Core Field 44			
978-1-58197-796-7	CEOE OPTE Oklahoma Professional Teaching Examination Fields 75-76			
978-1-58197-784-4	CEOE OSAT Reading Specialist Field 15			
978-1-58197-785-1	CEOE OSAT Spanish Field 19			
978-1-58197-797-4	CEOE OSAT U.S. & World History Field 17			
			SUBTOTAL	
FOR PRODUCT PRICES GO TO WWW.XAMONLINE.COM			Ship	$8.25
			TOTAL	